# Other Books and Series by Jeff Bowen

*Cherokee Intermarried White 1906 Volume I thru X*

*Applications for Enrollment of Creek Newborn Act of 1905*
*Volumes I thru XIV*

*Applications for Enrollment of Choctaw Newborn Act of 1905  Volumes I thru XX*

*Choctaw By Blood Enrollment Cards 1898-1914 Volumes I thru XX*

*Oglala Sioux Indians Pine Ridge Reservation 1932 Census  Book I*
*Oglala Sioux Indians Pine Ridge Reservation Birth and Death Rolls 1924-1932*
*Book II*

*Census of the Sioux and Cheyenne Indians of Pine Ridge Agency*
*1896 - 1897   Book I*
*Census of the Sioux and Cheyenne Indians of Pine Ridge Agency*
*1898 - 1899  Book II*

*Northern Cheyenne Tongue River, Montana 1904 - 1932 Census*
*1904-1916 Volume I*

*Northern Cheyenne Tongue River, Montana 1904 - 1932 Census*
*1917-1926 Volume II*

*Identified Mississippi Choctaw Enrollment Cards 1902-1909   Volumes I, II & III*

*Sac & Fox - Shawnee Estates 1885-1910 (Under Sac & Fox Agency)*
*Volumes I-V*

Visit our website at **www.nativestudy.com** to learn more about these
and other books and series by Jeff Bowen

Portrait of Tecumseh from Lossing's
*The Pictorial Field-Book of the War of 1812*
is a pencil sketch drawn by Pierre Le Dru,
a young French trader at Vincennes, circa 1808.

## Other Books and Series by Jeff Bowen

*Compilation of History of the Cherokee Indians and Early History of the Cherokees by Emmet Starr with Combined Full Name Index*
(Hardbound & Softbound)

*1901-1907 Native American Census  Seneca, Eastern Shawnee, Miami, Modoc, Ottawa, Peoria, Quapaw, and Wyandotte Indians  (Under Seneca School, Indian Territory)*

*1932 Census of The Standing Rock Sioux Reservation with Births And Deaths 1924-1932*

*Census of The Blackfeet, Montana, 1897- 1901  Expanded Edition*

*Eastern Cherokee by Blood, 1906-1910, Volumes I thru XIII*

*Choctaw of Mississippi Indian Census 1929-1932 with Births and Deaths 1924-1931    Volume I*
*Choctaw of Mississippi Indian Census 1933, 1934 & 1937, Supplemental Rolls to 1934 & 1935 with Births and Deaths 1932-1938, and Marriages 1936-1938 Volume II*

*Eastern Cherokee Census Cherokee, North Carolina 1930-1939*
*Census 1930-1931 with Births And Deaths 1924-1931 Taken By Agent L. W. Page Volume I*
*Eastern Cherokee Census Cherokee, North Carolina 1930-1939*
*Census 1932-1933 with Births And Deaths 1930-1932 Taken By Agent R. L. Spalsbury    Volume II*
*Eastern Cherokee Census Cherokee, North Carolina 1930-1939*
*Census 1934-1937 with Births and Deaths 1925-1938 and Marriages 1936 & 1938 Taken by Agents R. L. Spalsbury And Harold W. Foght Volume III*

*Seminole of Florida Indian Census, 1930-1940 with Birth and Death Records, 1930-1938*

*Texas Cherokees 1820-1839  A Document For Litigation 1921*

*Starr Roll 1894   (Cherokee Payment Rolls) Districts: Canadian, Cooweescoowee, and Delaware Volume One*
*Starr Roll 1894 (Cherokee Payment Rolls) Districts: Flint, Going Snake, and Illinois    Volume Two*
*Starr Roll 1894 (Cherokee Payment Rolls) Districts: Saline, Sequoyah, and Tahlequah; Including Orphan Roll  Volume Three*

*Cherokee Intruder Cases  Dockets of Hearings 1901-1909  Volumes I & II*

*Indian Wills, 1911-1921  Records of the Bureau of Indian Affairs*
*Books One* thru *Seven*

# Other Books and Series by Jeff Bowen

*Native American Wills & Probate Records 1911-1921*

*Turtle Mountain Reservation Chippewa Indians 1932 Census with Births & Deaths, 1924-1932*

*Chickasaw By Blood Enrollment Cards 1898-1914 Volume I thru V*

*Cherokee Descendants East An Index to the Guion Miller Applications Volume I*
*Cherokee Descendants West An Index to the Guion Miller Applications Volume II (A-M)*
*Cherokee Descendants West An Index to the Guion Miller Applications Volume III (N-Z)*

*Applications for Enrollment of Seminole Newborn Freedmen, Act of 1905*

*Eastern Cherokee Census, Cherokee, North Carolina, 1915-1922, Taken by Agent James E. Henderson*        *Volume I (1915-1916)*
                                                                *Volume II (1917-1918)*
                                                                *Volume III (1919-1920)*
                                                                *Volume IV (1921-1922)*

*Complete Delaware Roll of 1898*

*Eastern Cherokee Census, Cherokee, North Carolina, 1923-1929, Taken by Agent James E. Henderson*        *Volume I (1923-1924)*
                                                                *Volume II (1925-1926)*
                                                                *Volume III (1927-1929)*

*Applications for Enrollment of Seminole Newborn Act of 1905 Volumes I & II*

*North Carolina Eastern Cherokee Indian Census 1898-1899, 1904, 1906, 1909-1912, 1914 Revised and Expanded Edition*

*1932 Hopi and Navajo Native American Census with Birth & Death Rolls (1925-1931) Volume 1 - Hopi*
*1932 Hopi and Navajo Native American Census with Birth & Death Rolls (1930-1932) Volume 2 - Navajo*

*Western Navajo Reservation Navajo, Hopi and Paiute 1933 Census with Birth & Death Rolls 1925-1933*

*Cherokee Citizenship Commission Dockets 1880-1884 and 1887-1889 Volumes I thru V*

*Applications for Enrollment of Chickasaw Newborn Act of 1905 Volumes I thru VII*

# SAC & FOX - SHAWNEE
# ESTATES
# 1911-1919
## (UNDER SAC & FOX AGENCY)
# VOLUME VI

TRANSCRIBED BY
# JEFF BOWEN

NATIVE STUDY
**Gallipolis, Ohio**
**USA**

Originally published:
Santa Maria, California
2018




Reprinted by:

Native Study LLC
Gallipolis, OH
*www.nativestudy.com*




Library of Congress Control Number: 2022900261

ISBN: 978-1-64968-135-5

*Made in the United States of America.*

This series is dedicated to
Tanner Tackett
the Constant Gardner
and Friend
and
In memory of
Raina Mae Fulks.

# Ab·sen·tee

noun: **absentee**; plural noun: **absentees**

>    1. a person who is expected or required to be present at a place or event but is not.

(According to Webster)


# Shawnee

noun, plural Shaw-nees, (especially collectively) Shaw-nee.

>    1. a member of an Algonquian-speaking tribe formerly in the east-central U.S., now in Oklahoma.

(According to Dictionary.com)

# Shawnee Teaching

*"Tagi nsi walr mvci-lutvwi mr-pvyaci-grlahkv, xvga mytv inv gi mvci-lutvwv, gi mvci-ludr-geiv. Walv uwas-panvsi inv, wa-ciganv-hi gi gol-utvwv u kvgesakv-namv manwi-lanvwawewa yasi golutv-mvni geyrgi.*

*"Tagi bemi-lutvwi walr segalami mr-pvyaci-grlahkv, xvga mvtv inv gi bemi-lutvwv, gi bemi-ludr-geiv gelv. Wakv vhqalami inv, xvga nahfrpi Moneto ut vhqalamrli nili yasi vhqalamahgi gelv!"*

Translation:

"Do not kill or injure your neighbor, for it is not him that you injure, you injure yourself. But do good to him, therefore add to his days of happiness as you add to your own.

"Do not wrong or hate your neighbor, for it is not him that you wrong, you wrong yourself. But love him, for Moneto loves him also as He loves you!"

Thomas Wildcat Alford
*circa 1936*

v

## Special Note

You will notice throughout these volumes the author has attempted to duplicate from the original documents places on the page that were destroyed due to water damage. Whole sections of a page could be missing or torn into multiple pieces. In order to duplicate the damage you will find various shapes with a white format to try to represent the damage and the loss of the ability to completely transcribe many of the pages.

# INTRODUCTION

The history of the Shawnee is fascinating. Naturally the most famous Shawnee known would be Tecumseh, born circa. 1768, after four other siblings before him. His father was Puckeshinwa, a Shawnee war chief from Ohio. Puckeshinwa crossed the Ohio close to what is now Gallipolis with his fourteen year son Chiksika by his side. As they followed the lead of Chief Cornstalk during the fall of 1774. Tecumseh's famous father was mortally wounded during the fight they would soon encounter. The Shawnees were unexpectedly discovered by a couple of early morning turkey hunters from the settlement called Point Pleasant. These hunters ran as fast as possible back to where the Ohio and Kanawha Rivers meet and sounded the alarm that the Shawnees were coming, the fight lasted most of the day but not without loss to both sides. The Shawnees were badly outnumbered. Pucheshinwa was carried back across the Ohio or as the Shawnees called it the *Spaylaywitheepi*, with the intention to take him back to his village. He must have known his time was short as he laid there telling Chiksika to make sure he devoted his time not only to Tecumseh's but also his younger brothers training in becoming warriors. Pucheshinwa succumbed to his wounds shortly after that request and was secretly buried deep in the forest that day. Chiksika saw his father mortally wounded while defending their home. He had a reverence for his father as a great warrior. He wanted to follow his father's path and not die an average death. In his heart, it had to be on the battlefield as a warrior. Tecumseh followed his brother's every step and planned to die defending his land as his father and brother had. There was no surrendering or giving in to the Americans.

There are several descriptions out there of Tecumseh from his contemporaries, but David Edmunds found one during his research that seems to be the most commanding of any found. "Captain John B. Glegg, Brock's aide-de-camp, who was present at the meetings between Brock and Tecumseh, recorded one of the most vivid descriptions of the Shawnee. According to Glegg, in August 1812 Tecumseh still was in the prime of his life, giving the impression of a man ten years younger. Tecumseh's appearance was very prepossessing; his figure light and finely proportioned; his age I imagined to be about five and thirty [he actually was forty four]; in height, five feet nine or ten inches; his complexion, light copper; countenance, oval, with bright hazle eyes, beaming cheerfulness, energy, and decision. Three small silver crowns, or coronets were suspended from the lower cartilage of his aquiline nose; and a large silver medallion of George the Third, which I believe his ancestor had received from Lord Dorchester, when governor-general of Canada, was attached to a mixed coloured wampum string, and hung around his neck. His dress consisted of a plain, neat uniform, tanned deer-skin jacket, with long trousers of the same material, the seams of both being covered with neatly cut fringe; and he had on his feet leather moccasins, much ornamented with work made from the dyed quills of the porcupine."[1]

There were approximately 39 years that passed between Tecumseh's and his father's deaths.

It is hard to believe that the Shawnee's history being as extensive as it was during the early stages of the United States that their descendants' records were so closely guarded under the care of a vegetable bind in an leaky attic. Not only the Shawnee's but also the Sac & Fox, the Pottawatomie and the Kickapoo. There are also many other tribal affiliates to be found in this series, not to mention someone like Jim Thorpe and his family members of the Sac and Fox tribe. Not only was he a gold metal Olympian and multiple sport competitor, but at the time one of America's favorite sons. Thank goodness someone was finally conscious of the situation. The description in the next paragraph explains the neglect of these important documents as given by the Oklahoma Historical Societies Microfilm Catalog.

"In 1933 a survey of Indian tribal records in Oklahoma revealed that the files of the Shawnee and the old Sac and Fox agencies had been sadly neglected, and the lack of space for storing them properly had resulted in much loss. Charles Eggers, Superintendent of the Shawnee Agency, reported that most of the non-current records of his agency were boxed in a storehouse. The papers of the old Sac and Fox Agency were in the loft of a warehouse which was also used for storing vegetables. The roof of the building leaked and the papers were in danger of destruction from moisture. Following the passage of the Congressional Act of March 27, 1934 (H.R. 5631 Public No. 133) which placed the tribal records in the custody of the Oklahoma Historical Society."

As described above the history of the Shawnee people isn't an ordinary history but an extraordinary time in all of our ancestors' lives. Reading Allen W. Eckert's extensive studies taken from what is known as the Draper Papers, a historical record meticulously documented beginning circa 1830. Though Draper covered an approximate time between the 1740's to the 1810's, his collection covered documents and transcriptions concerning Boone, Kenton, Rogers Clark and Joseph Brant, not to mention a considerable amount of Shawnee history from the entirety of the Ohio and Mississippi Valley's. Other authors such as Colin G. Calloway and R. David Edmunds provide an in depth study of the Shawnee people as well as Tecumseh and his life leaving no rock unturned in their research.

As you read different references you find diverse opinions on Tecumseh's mother as to what tribe she came from. Eckert through Draper's work says, "This was

---

[1]  Tecumseh, R. David Edmunds Pg. 162-163, Para. 3-4

when Pucksinwah, then twenty-six, led the war party against the Cherokees that had resulted in the capture of Methotasa."[2] Indicating Tecumseh's mother might have been Cherokee. Yet, R. David Edmunds writes, "In 1768, while the Iroquois were selling Shawnee lands at the Treaty of Fort Stanwix, a Creek woman married to a Shawnee man gave birth to a son at Old Piqua, a Shawnee village on the Mad River in Western Ohio. The woman had a difficult labor before giving birth in the small lodge especially constructed for that purpose, some distance from the family's wigwam. The mother, Methoataske (Turtle Laying Its Eggs), had grown up among the Creek villages in Alabama and had met her husband when some of the Shawnee sought refuge among the Creeks during the 1750s. The father Puckeshinwa, remained with his wife's people until about 1760, when the family left Alabama and migrated to Ohio."[3]

You also will find different opinions on how they dressed back then or wore their hair. In Edmunds' book *Tecumseh*, his brother the Prophet Tenskwatawa states, "Warriors should again shave their heads and wear the scalp locks worn by their ancestors." And yet in Thomas Wildcat Alford's *Civilization*, he says, "We boys wore our hair short, very much as the girls of today wear their hair bobbed. This is the way Shawnee men always have worn their hair. Never did they braid it, as some other tribes do."

Alford's book *Civilization* out of the many resources read was likely one of the most informative and enjoyable references in the study. Thomas Wildcat Alford was born in 1860 and belonged to the Absentee Shawnee tribe. He states that he was a descendant of Tecumseh. He spoke about when his family slept under the stars each night and that he never had an English name until his father had him go to school at a Quaker mission. Mr. Alford also talks about two things with real clarity. Alford educates us about clans in the sixth chapter, expounding upon the active history of the Shawnees and the different responsibilities of each as well as divisions among the clans that created tribal changes. These dissensions were nothing new. Anyone that has read extensively about the Shawnee will realize that Alford understood his people and their history. When he wrote about tribal clashes or divisions during the early days, he managed to translate on paper their strength and character. He showed for generations they literally believed they were given an ability to make themselves self-reliant when it came to survival. They traveled far and wide following their own path while installing their own way of life that made them powerful adversaries whether it be against the British, the French or the Americans moving west. Other tribes found them to be awful enemies or potent allies. Then he compares their tribal government

---

[2] A Sorrow in Our Heart, Allen W. Eckert Pg. 22, Para. 3
[3] Tecumseh, R. David Edmunds, Pg. 17 Para. 1

and the clan leaders to being quite similar to the U.S. Presidency and the different government entities. Alford also brings up business committees for the tribe.

He starts with a concise description of the clans, "Originally there were five clans composing the Shawnee tribe, including the two principle clans, Tha-we-gi-la and Cha-lah-kaw-tha, from one of which came the national or principal chief. The remaining three, the Pec-ku-we, the Kis-pu-go, and the May-ku-jay, each had its own chief who was subordinate to the principal chief in national matters, but independent in matters pertaining to the duties of his clan. Each clan had a certain duty to perform for the whole tribe. For instance the Pec-ku-we clan, or its chief, had charge of the maintenance of order and looked after the celebration of things pertaining to religion or faith; the Kis-pu-go clan had charge of matters pertaining to war and the preparation and training of warriors; the May-ku-jay clan had charge of things relating to health and medicine and food for the whole tribe. But the two powerful clans, the Tha-we-gi-la and the Cha-lah-kaw-tha, had charge of political affairs and all matters that affected the tribe as a whole. Indeed, the tribal government may be likened to the government of the United States, in which each state (clan), with it governor (chief), is sovereign in local matters, but subordinate to the president of the United States (principal chief) in national matters. The difference is that the president of the United States must be elected, and may be changed with each election, while the principal chief came to his office by heritage and held it for life, or during good behavior.

At the time of which I write the Shawnee tribe had been divided for many years, and only the Tha-we-gi-la, the Pec-ku-we, and the Kis-pu-go clans were represented in the Absentee Shawnee band. These three clans always had been closely related, while the Cha-lah-kaw-tha and the May-ku-jay had always stood together, and were represented in the group that I have mentioned as living in Kansas at the time of the Civil War."[4]

As referenced earlier Thomas Wildcat Alford brought up their present Indian agent, Thomas, on September 13, 1893, wanting him to present a list of prominent men in their tribe to hold positions on a business committee. This presented a whole new world for the tribe with new pressures through white change so to speak. The government was instilling in their world the destruction of their heritage in tribal customs and culture all to control Indian land through allotment. When he was being told to help form this committee, he was actually being told, what we are doing is we are wiping out your way of life forever. The Congress of the United States was presenting the abolition of all tribal governments so the land could be manipulated through the Curtis Act of 1898. They said, we are splitting the land up. They were allotting so many acres to each tribal member. How much they got depended on

---

[4] Civilization, Alford; Pg. 44, Para. 1-2

whether they planned to farm or raise cattle. If they were building herds they were given double the land for grazing. Alford said, "It was on the thirteenth day of September, 1893 that Agent Thomas informed the Shawnees that he had been directed by the Commissioner of Indian Affairs to submit for approval the names of seven of the most prominent men of the tribe who would constitute a Business Committee to supersede the chiefs and councilors of the old tribal government. The Business Committee was to represent the Absentee Shawnees as a tribe in all dealings with the United States and to act in an advisory capacity to the individual members of the tribe. They were to certify to the identity of grantors of sales of land and to act for the tribe in other matters.[5]

During the study it was noticed that the Curtis Act being enacted on June 28, 1898 and Alford's mentioning its initiation during 1893 became a point of interest or at least premature. It was found that Congress had actually started working in this area of seizure approximately five years prior to the agent's notification, "In 1893 Congress began a special allotment process for the Five Tribes, enacting a number of laws that affect the governmental powers of the tribes. Some of these laws, like the 1889 and 1890 Acts, extended certain Arkansas laws over Indian Territory and expanded federal court jurisdiction; they are relevant today only insofar as they may indirectly affect tribal judicial powers."[6]

Their mention of these laws only being relevant today, though actually not spoken, plead plausible deniability while coinciding with the Indian Reorganization Act of 1934. The government was on a mission. Land and control. The allotment had to take place. They were wanting statehood. They were wanting the Native people to be under one umbrella with everyone else. Tribes were nations. Just like a foreign nation, they were their own government. Originally our constitution was modeled after the Iroquois model, had to start somewhere? So what we did was split up the land among the people that already owned it. Then we took what was left, approximately 90 million acres and sold it at a profit. Who got the money? Only the politicians at the time know? But years after taking the chiefs and councils away there was likely mass chaos like a town hall today. So the government likely was wanting out of the tribal control business. At least enough that they could just control it without being in the bullseye so to speak. Congress and the state had already achieved its goals. So this act was written with the statement that it was a model to make all think we do this for you. "The IRA was intended to provide a mechanism for the tribe as a governmental unit to interact with and adapt to a modern society, rather than to force the assimilation of individual Indians.

---

[5] Civilization, Alford; Pg. 161, Para. 2

[6] Federal Indian Law, Cohen; Pg. 781, Para. 3

The IRA was also an attempt to improve the economic situation of Indians. The Act was intended to stop the alienation of tribal land needed to support Indians, and to provide for acquisition of additional acreage for tribes. Tribes were encouraged to organize along the lines of modern business corporations; a system of financial credit was included to reach this economic objective."[7]   Interestingly enough Cohen and Alford both mention this same organizational technique, only one as law and another as a tribal member.

It is disconcerting just in reading a reference from Senator Charles Curtis as he mentioned in his biography that by the time Congress finished rewriting the bill he had submitted he hardly recognized it. "Officially titled the "Act for the Protection of the People of Indian Territory", the Act is named for Charles Curtis, congressman from Kansas and its author. He was of mixed Native American and European descent: on his mother's side -Kansa, Osage, Potawatomi, and French; and on his father's - three ethnic lines of British Isles ancestry. Curtis was raised in part on the Kaw Reservation of his maternal grandparents, but also lived with his paternal grandparents and attended Topeka High School. He read law, became an attorney, and later was elected to the United States House of Representatives and Senate. He served as Vice-President under Herbert Hoover. In the usual fashion, by the time the bill HR 8581 had gone through five revisions in committees in both the House of Representatives and the Senate, there was little left of Curtis' original draft. In his hand-written autobiography, Curtis noted having been unhappy with the final version of the Curtis Act. He believed that the Five Civilized Tribes needed to make changes. He thought that the way ahead for Native Americans was through education and use of both their and the majority cultures, but he also had hoped to give more support to Native American transitions."[8]

The records within this series concern The Absentee Shawnee as well as many other people with different tribal affiliations. Also within these pages are closely related tribes that were under the same agency (The Sac & Fox Agency, Oklahoma) for many years like the Sac & Fox, the Pottawatomie and the Kickapoo. There are likely state recognized Shawnee tribes in the United States, but, "The Absentee Shawnee Tribe of Indians of Oklahoma (or Absentee Shawnee) is one of three federally recognized tribes of Shawnee people. Historically residing in the Eastern United States, the original Shawnee lived in the areas that are now Ohio, Indiana, Illinois, Kentucky, Tennessee, Pennsylvania, and other neighboring states. It is documented that they occupied and traveled through lands from Canada to Florida, from the Mississippi River to the eastern continental coast. In contemporary times, the Absentee Shawnee Tribe headquarters in Shawnee, Oklahoma; its tribal jurisdiction

---

[7] Federal Indian Law, Cohen; Pg. 147 Para. 1-2
[8] Curtis Act of 1898, Wikipedia

area includes land properties in Oklahoma in both Cleveland County and Pottawatomie County." [Today] "There are approximately 3,050 enrolled Absentee Shawnee tribal members, 2,315 of whom live in Oklahoma. Tribal membership follows blood quantum criteria, with applicants requiring a minimum of one eighth (1/8) documented Absentee-Shawnee blood to be placed on its membership rolls, as set forth by the tribal constitution. Though it is not a formal division, there is a social separation within its current tribal membership between the traditionalist Big Jim Band, which kept cultural traditions and ceremonies and has its primary populace in the Little Axe, Norman area, and the assimilationist White Turkey Band, which adopted European ways of the European majority, with many families based in the Shawnee area. Regardless of historical viewpoints, the bands cooperate for the future of the tribe."[9]

When this study was first pursued an old Xerox copy of a catalog that sat on the shelf for twenty five years was the first place searched for a viable source. It was titled, "Catalog of Microfilm Holdings in the Archives & Manuscripts Div. Oklahoma Historical Society 1976-1989". As mentioned in the description from this catalog's Introduction for the Sac and Fox Indian Agencies, it states, "In 1901 the Sac and Fox Agency was divided. The Sac and Fox Agency itself remained at the old site near Stroud with jurisdiction over the Sac and Fox and the Iowa. The Shawnee, Potawatomi and Kickapoo Agency (sometimes simply called the Shawnee Agency) was established about two miles south of Shawnee, Oklahoma. The agencies continued their separate existence until 1919 when they were merged becoming the Shawnee Agency.

Of course today in 2018, everything is digital and on the computer. You have to be thankful for having an old catalog and books on a shelf. There is nothing like the feel of holding a book in your hand. You can pick it up when you want and let your eyes travel to anywhere or any time in history. It has solid print that nobody can manipulate or change. It's just yours to wrap yourself up in without any glowing distractions as Native Americans call them, "Talking Leaves".

Jeff Bowen
Gallipolis, Ohio
*NativeStudy.com*

---

[9] Absentee-Shawnee Tribe of Indians Wikipedia

NOTICE OF HEARING TO DETERMINE HEIRS

# DEPARTMENT OF THE INTERIOR
### UNITED STATES INDIAN SERVICE.

Sac & Fox Indian School,
Stroud, Okla., Feb. 25, 191 4

M  Thomas P. Myers, Stroud, Okla.,
Guardian-Ad-Litem for William H.
Jefferson, minor;
Isaac Struble, Cushing, Okla.,
Logan Kakaque, Meeker, Okla.,
Alexander Connolly, Stroud, Okla.,

Notice is hereby given that on the     28th    day of       March          ,
191 4, at  Sac and Fox Indian Agency, Okla.      , I will take testimony to be
submitted to the Secretary of the Interior for the purpose of determining the heirs
of     Irene Harris      , deceased.

All persons having an interest in the estate of the decedent are hereby notified
to be present at the hearing and furnish such evidence as they desire.

Respectfully,

Horace J. Johnson
Superintendent.

**\*\*\*\*\*\*\*\*\***

APPOINTMENT OF GUARDIAN-AD-LITEM.

Sac and Fox Indian Agency,
Stroud, Okla., Feb. 25, 1914.

Thomas P. Meyers,
Sac and Fox Indian Agency,
Stroud, Oklahoma.

Sir:-

In the matter of determining the heirs of Irene Harris, it appearing that there is a
certain minor, to wit:

William H. Jefferson

who is interested in the estate, you are hereby appointed in accordance with the
regulations of the Indian Office as Guardian-ad-litem for the said minor heir, and you

1

will see to it that the interest of the said minor heir in the said estate is at all times protected until you are discharged from such obligation.

___Horace J Johnson___<br>
Supt. & S. D. A.

---

# DEPARTMENT OF THE INTERIOR
### UNITED STATES INDIAN SERVICE.

SHAWNEE INDIAN AGENCY,

Shawnee, Oklahoma.
April 3, 1911.

Mr. G. L. Williams,

    Superintendent,

        Nadeau, KANSAS.

Dear Sir:

Referring to your remittance of $130.59 for Mrs. Sophia Johnson, would say that as Mrs. Johnson understands this this[sic] is her lease money on the Peter the Great estate and she believes that there is still some money due her from the sale of this land.

If this is correct Mrs. Johnson would like to have this money sent to her as promptly as possible and we would also appreciate it if you would secure authority to pay the total amount direct to Mrs. Johnson.

Very respectfully,

E.L. Seymour

Dic.ELS                                    Clerk in Charge.

This represents all of Mrs. Johnsons share in the Peter the Great estate, both rents and sale of land.

Respt

G.L. Williams

Supt.

---

NOTICE OF HEARING TO DETERMINE HEIRS

---

# DEPARTMENT OF THE INTERIOR

## UNITED STATES INDIAN SERVICE.

Sac & Fox Indian School,
Stroud, Okla., Feb. 25, 191 4

M  John Brown, Hocker, Okla.,
Thomas Brown, Hocker, Okla.              Isaac Struble, Cushing, Okla.,
Thomas P. Myers, Stroud, Okla.           Alexander Connolly, Stroud, Okla.
Guardian-Ad-Litem for Harry
Brown and Mary E Brown, minors;
Logan Kakaque, Meeker, Okla.,

Notice is hereby given that on the      28th.   day of      March      .
191 4, at  Sac and Fox Indian Agency, Okla.       , I will take testimony to be
submitted to the Secretary of the Interior for the purpose of determining the heirs
of      Josephine Brown       , deceased.

All persons having an interest in the estate of the decedent are hereby notified
to be present at the hearing and furnish such evidence as they desire.

Respectfully,

Horace J. Johnson
Superintendent.

\*\*\*\*\*\*\*\*\*\*

APPOINTMENT OF GUARDIAN-AD-LITEM.

Sac & Fox Indian Agency,
Stroud, Okla., Feb. 25, 1914.

Thomas P. Meyers,
Sac & Fox Indian Agency,
Stroud, Okla.

Sir:-

In the matter of determining the heirs of Josephine Brown, it appearing that there
are certain minors, to-wit:

Harry Brown and Mary E. Brown

who are interested in the estate, you are hereby appointed in accordance with the regulations of the Indian Office as Guardian-ad-litem for the said minor heirs, and you will see to it that the interest of the said minor heirs in the said estate are at all times protected until you are discharged from such obligation.

   Horace J Johnson   
Supt. & S. D. A.

**NOTICE OF HEARING TO DETERMINE HEIRS**

# DEPARTMENT OF THE INTERIOR
### UNITED STATES INDIAN SERVICE.

Sac & Fox Indian Agency,
Stroud, Okla., Feb. 27, 191 4

M   George Littlebear, Okema[sic], Okla.,
Thomas P. Myers, Stroud, Okla.
Guardian-Ad-Litem for Florien
Littlebear, minor;
Isaac Struble, Cushing, Okla.,
Logan Kakaque, Meeker, Okla.,
Alexander Connolly, Stroud, Okla.,

Notice is hereby given that on the    30th. day of    March    . 191 4, at  Sac and Fox Indian Agency, Okla.    , I will take testimony to be submitted to the Secretary of the Interior for the purpose of determining the heirs of    Carrie Jefferson    , deceased.

All persons having an interest in the estate of the decedent are hereby notified to be present at the hearing and furnish such evidence as they desire.

Respectfully,

Horace J. Johnson
Superintendent.

\*\*\*\*\*\*\*\*\*\*
APPOINTMENT OF GUARDIAN-AD-LITEM.

Sac & Fox Indian Agency,
Stroud, Okla., Feb. 27, 1914.

Thomas P. Meyers,
Sac & Fox Indian Agency,
Stroud, Okla.

4

Sir:-

In the matter of determining the heirs of Carrie Jefferson, it appearing that there is a certain minor, to-wit:

Florien Littlebear

who is interested in the estate, you are hereby appointed in accordance with the Regulations of the Indian Office as Guardian-Ad-Litem for the said minor heir, and you will see to it that the interest of the said minor heir in the said estate are at all times protected until you are discharged from such obligation.

Horace J Johnson
Supt. & S. D. A.

---

**NOTICE OF HEARING TO DETERMINE HEIRS**

---

# DEPARTMENT OF THE INTERIOR

### UNITED STATES INDIAN SERVICE.

Sac & Fox Indian School,
Stroud, Okla., Feb. 27, 191 4

M   Anna McKosato, Prague, Okla.,
Thomas P. Myers, Stroud, Okla.
Guardian-Ad-Litem for Grover
Wakole, minor;
Logan Kakaque, Meeker, Okla.,
Isaac Struble, Cushing, Okla.,
Alexander Connolly, Stroud, Okla.,

Notice is hereby given that on the      30th.   day of      March        .
191 4, at   Sac and Fox Indian Agency, Okla.      , I will take testimony to be submitted to the Secretary of the Interior for the purpose of determining the heirs of      Rufus Wakole      , deceased.

All persons having an interest in the estate of the decedent are hereby notified to be present at the hearing and furnish such evidence as they desire.

Respectfully,

Horace J. Johnson
Superintendent.

**********

5

APPOINTMENT OF GUARDIAN-AD-LITEM.

Sac & Fox Indian Agency,
Stroud, Okla., Feb. 27, 1914.

Thomas P. Meyers,
    Sac & Fox Indian Agency,
        Stroud, Okla.
Sir:-

In the matter of determining the heirs of Rufus Wakole, it appearing that there is a certain minor, to-wit:

Grover Wakole

who is interested in the estate, you are hereby appointed in accordance with the Regulations of the Indian Office as Guardian-Ad-Litem for the said minor heir, and you will see to it that the interest of the said minor heir in the said estate are at all times protected until you are discharged from such obligation.

Horace J Johnson
Supt. & S. D. A.

---

**NOTICE OF HEARING TO DETERMINE HEIRS**

# DEPARTMENT OF THE INTERIOR

## UNITED STATES INDIAN SERVICE.

Sac & Fox Indian School,
Stroud, Okla., Feb. 28, 191 4

M   Grace Lee, Meeker, Okla.,
    Thomas P. Myers, Stroud, Okla.
    Guardian-Ad-Litem for Annie
    Buffalohorn, minor;
    Isaac Struble, Cushing, Okla.,
    Logan Kakaque, Meeker, Okla.,
    Alexander Connolly, Stroud, Okla.,

Notice is hereby given that on the   31st.   day of       March           .
191 4, at   Sac and Fox Indian Agency, Okla.        , I will take testimony to be submitted to the Secretary of the Interior for the purpose of determining the heirs of      Clara Buffalohorn       , deceased.

6

All persons having an interest in the estate of the decedent are hereby notified to be present at the hearing and furnish such evidence as they desire.

Respectfully,

Horace J. Johnson

Superintendent.

**********

## APPOINTMENT OF GUARDIAN-AD-LITEM.

Sac & Fox Indian Agency,
Stroud, Okla., Feb. 28, 1914.

Thomas P. Meyers,
    Sac & Fox Indian Agency,
        Stroud, Okla.
Sir:-

In the matter of determining the heirs of Clara Buffalohorn, it appearing that there is a certain minor, to-wit:

Mamie Buffalohorn

who is interested in the estate, you are hereby appointed in accordance with the Regulations of the Indian Office as Guardian-Ad-Litem for the said minor heir, and you will see to it that the interest of the said minor heir in the said estate are at all times protected until you are discharged from such obligation.

___Horace J Johnson___
Supt. & S. D. A.

---

**NOTICE OF HEARING TO DETERMINE HEIRS**

---

# DEPARTMENT OF THE INTERIOR

### UNITED STATES INDIAN SERVICE.

Sac & Fox Indian School,
Stroud, Okla., Feb. 28, 191 4

M   Edward Rice, Meeker, Okla.,
    Thomas P. Myers, Stroud, Okla.
    Guardian-Ad-Litem for Susie Rice,
    Carrie Rice, & Lucien Rice, minors;
    Isaac Struble, Cushing, Okla.,

7

Logan Kakaque, Meeker, Okla.,
Alexander Connolly, Stroud, Okla.,

Notice is hereby given that on the     31st.   day of       March          .
191 4, at  Sac and Fox Indian Agency, Okla.      , I will take testimony to be
submitted to the Secretary of the Interior for the purpose of determining the heirs
of      Edith Rice, nee Appletree      , deceased.

All persons having an interest in the estate of the decedent are hereby notified
to be present at the hearing and furnish such evidence as they desire.

Respectfully,

Horace J. Johnson

Superintendent.

\*\*\*\*\*\*\*\*\*\*

APPOINTMENT OF GUARDIAN-AD-LITEM.

Sac & Fox Indian Agency,
Stroud, Okla., Feb. 28, 1914.

Thomas P. Meyers,
Sac & Fox Indian Agency,
Stroud, Okla.

Sir:-

In the matter of determining the heirs of Edith Rice, nee Appletree, it appearing
that there are certain minors, to-wit:

Susie Rice, Carrie Rice, and Lucien Rice,

who are interested in the estate, you are hereby appointed in accordance with the
regulations of the Indian Office as Guardian-Ad-Litem for the said minor heirs, and
you will see to it that the interests of the said minor heirs in the said estate are at all
times protected until you are discharged from such obligation.

Horace J Johnson
Supt. & S. D. A.

8

NOTICE OF HEARING TO DETERMINE HEIRS

## DEPARTMENT OF THE INTERIOR

### UNITED STATES INDIAN SERVICE.

Chief McKosato, Prague, Okla.,
David [Illegible], Meeker, Okla.,
Sarah [Illegible, Meeker, Okla.,
M  Elbert [Illegible], Meeker, Okla.,
Charley [Illegible], Meeker, Okla.,
Samuel L. Brown, Avery, Okla.,
Julia Black, Avery, Okla.,
Edith Butler, Avery, Okla.,
Madeline Carter, Meeker, Okla.
Richard Duncan, Meeker, Okla.,

Sac & Fox Indian School,
Stroud, Okla., Feb. 28, 191 4

Thomas P. Myers, Stroud, Okla.
Guardian-Ad-Litem for Amos Black
Jr., Bertha Black, Ellen Mason
and Hattie Mason, minors;
Logan Kakaque, Meeker, Okla.,
Isaac Struble, Cushing, Okla.,
Alexander Connolly, Stroud, Okla.,

Notice is hereby given that on the    27th .   day of    March    .
191 4, at  Sac and Fox Indian Agency, Okla.    , I will take testimony to be
submitted to the Secretary of the Interior for the purpose of determining the heirs
of    Samuel W. Peel    , deceased.

All persons having an interest in the estate of the decedent are hereby notified
to be present at the hearing and furnish such evidence as they desire.

Respectfully,

Horace J. Johnson
Superintendent.

\*\*\*\*\*\*\*\*\*\*

APPOINTMENT OF GUARDIAN-AD-LITEM.

Sac & Fox Indian Agency,
Stroud, Okla., Feb. 25, 1914.

Thomas P. Meyers,
Sac & Fox Indian Agency,
Stroud, Okla.
Sir:-

In the matter of determining the heirs of Samuel W. Peel, it appearing that there
are certain minors, to-wit:

Amos Black, Jr., Bertha Black,
Ellen Mason & Hattie Mason,

9

who are interested in the estate, you are hereby appointed in accordance with the regulations of the Indian Office as Guardian-Ad-Litem for the said minor heirs, and you will see to it that the interests of the said minor heirs in the said estate are at all times protected until you are discharged from such obligation.

Horace J Johnson
Supt. & S. D. A.

---

Law-
    Heirship      **DEPARTMENT OF THE INTERIOR,**
       L L            **OFFICE OF INDIAN AFFAIRS,**
                          **WASHINGTON,**
                              FEB 28 1914

My dear Mr. Buntin:

The Examiner of Inheritance, Mr. Warner L. Wilmeth, will leave Washington on March 1, and will be due to arrive at Shawnee, Oklahoma, by the Rock Island R. R, at 12:20 a. m., March 3. If you can have a conveyance meet him at Shawnee sometime within the forenoon of March 3, the courtesy will be duly appreciated.

Yours truly,

EB Meritt
Assistant Commissioner.

Mr. John A. Buntin,
      Supt. Shawnee School.

2-FWS-27

---

## DEPARTMENT OF THE INTERIOR

Hearing in the          **UNITED STATES INDIAN SERVICE.**
estate of                     Sac & Fox Indian School,
Rachel Davis.                   Stroud, Okla., Mar. 2, 1914.

Claud Chandler,
      U. S. Farmer,
            Shawnee, Okla.,
Sir:-

Four copies of a notice of a hearing to determine the heirs of Rachel Davis, deceased, to be held at this Agency on April 3, 1914, are enclosed herewith.

Kindly deliver a copy of this notice to each of the following persons:

George Oliver Morton,
Logan Kakaque,
and                                   Alexander Connolly,

and post the other in a conspicuous place in your district.

                         Very respectfully,
                              Horace J Johnson
WMH.                         Supt. & S. D. A.

Enclos:
    Four copies of notice of hearing.

---

Lease returned
with dates
corrected.

                         Shawnee Oklahoma.
                              Oct, 3. 1914.

Horace J. Johnson, Supt.
    Sac and Fox Indian School.
        Stroud, Okla.

Sir:-

    Attached herewith you will find lease on the allotment of Bertha Pattequaw, made between William Pattequaw sole heir of deceased allottee and [Illegible] Scheidt. which was returned to me for some corrections in the dates of same, with the desired corrections made thereon.

                         Very respectfully,
                              U.S. Farmer.

---

NOTICE OF HEARING TO DETERMINE HEIRS

# DEPARTMENT OF THE INTERIOR

## UNITED STATES INDIAN SERVICE.

Sac & Fox Indian School,
Stroud, Okla., Mar. 2, 1914.

Frank Keokuk, Pawhuska, Okla.,

M Jesse James, Avery, Okla.,          Peyton Keokuk, Ripley, Okla.,
Mary Hurr, Avery, Okla.,          Fannie K. Foote, Stroud, Okla.,
Thomas P. Myers, Stroud, Okla.,          Orlando Johnson, Avery, Okla.,
Guardian-Ad-Litem for Sadie          Isaac Struble, Cushing, Okla.,
Rhodes, minor;          Logan Kakaque, Meeker, Okla.
Robert Davis, Avery, Okla.,          Alexander Connolly, Stroud, Okla.,
Mary A. Keokuk, Prague, Okla.,
John Merle Keokuk, Stroud, Okla.,

Notice is hereby given that on the    3rd    day of    April    .
1914, at    Sac and Fox Indian Agency, Okla.    , I will take testimony to
be submitted to the Secretary of the Interior for the purpose of determining the
heirs of    Bessie Davis    , deceased.

All persons having an interest in the estate of the decedent are hereby notified
to be present at the hearing and furnish such evidence as they desire.

Respectfully,

Horace J. Johnson
Superintendent.

\*\*\*\*\*\*\*\*\*\*

APPOINTMENT OF GUARDIAN-AD-LITEM.

Sac & Fox Indian School,
Stroud, Okla., Mar. 2, 1914.

Thomas P. Meyers,
Sac & Fox Indian Agency,
Stroud, Okla.

Sir:-

In the matter of determining the heirs of Bessie Davis, it appearing that there is a
certain minor, to-wit:

Sadie Rhodes

who is interested in the estate, you are hereby appointed in accordance with the
Regulations of the Indian Office as Guardian-Ad-Litem for the said minor heir, and

12

you will see to it that the interest of the said minor heir in the said estate are at all times protected until you are discharged from such obligation.

Horace J Johnson
Supt. & S. D. A.

---

**NOTICE OF HEARING TO DETERMINE HEIRS**

## DEPARTMENT OF THE INTERIOR

### UNITED STATES INDIAN SERVICE.

Sac & Fox Indian School,
Stroud, Okla., Mar. 2, 1914.

M William Davenport, Toledo, Iowa.
John Wityascoo, Toledo, Iowa.
Ke-we-ne-mo-che, Toledo, Iowa.
No-no-cho, Toledo, Iowa.
Thomas P. Myers, Stroud, Okla.,
Guardian-Ad-Litem for Ke-sha-sah,
Mo-na-che-qua, Josephine Ward, &
Cha-co-sa-ta, minors.

Isaac Struble, Cushing, Okla.,
Logan Kakaque, Meeker, Okla.,
Alexander Connolly, Stroud, Okla.,

Notice is hereby given that on the   1st   day of   April   . 1914, at   Sac & Fox Indian Agency, Okla.   , I will take testimony to be submitted to the Secretary of the Interior for the purpose of determining the heirs of   John McKuk   , deceased.

All persons having an interest in the estate of the decedent are hereby notified to be present at the hearing and furnish such evidence as they desire.

Respectfully,

Horace J. Johnson
Superintendent.

\*\*\*\*\*\*\*\*\*\*

APPOINTMENT OF GUARDIAN-AD-LITEM.

Sac & Fox Indian School,
Stroud, Okla., Mar. 2, 1914.

Thomas P. Meyers,
     Sac & Fox Indian Agency,
          Stroud, Okla.
Sir:-

13

In the matter of determining the heirs of John McKuk, it appearing that there is a certain minor, to-wit:

Ke-sha-sah, Mo-na-che-qua, Josephine Ward, & Cha-co-sa-ta,

who are interested in the estate, you are hereby appointed in accordance with the Regulations of the Indian Office as Guardian-Ad-Litem for the said minor heirs in the said estate, and you will see to it that the interests of the said minor heirs in the said estate are at all times protected until you are discharged from such obligation.

Horace J Johnson
Supt. & S. D. A.

---

NOTICE OF HEARING TO DETERMINE HEIRS

# DEPARTMENT OF THE INTERIOR

UNITED STATES INDIAN SERVICE.

Sac & Fox Indian School,
Stroud, Okla., Mar 2, 191 4

M  Silas Grass, Cushing, Okla.,
Thomas P. Myers, Stroud, Okla.,
Guardian-Ad-Litem for Florence
Conger, minor;
Isaac Struble, Cushing, Okla.,
Logan Kakaque, Meeker, Okla.,
Alexander Connolly, Stroud, Okla.,

Notice is hereby given that on the    2nd   day of        April            . 191 4, at  Sac & Fox Indian Agency, Okla.        , I will take testimony to be submitted to the Secretary of the Interior for the purpose of determining the heirs of     George Grass      , deceased.

All persons having an interest in the estate of the decedent are hereby notified to be present at the hearing and furnish such evidence as they desire.

Respectfully,

Horace J. Johnson
Superintendent.

\*\*\*\*\*\*\*\*\*\*

APPOINTMENT OF GUARDIAN-AD-LITEM.

Sac and Fox Indian Agency,
Stroud, Okla., Mar. 2, 1914.

Thomas P. Meyers,
    Sac & Fox Indian Agency,
    Stroud, Oklahoma.

Sir:-

In the matter of determining the heirs of George Grass, it appearing that there is a certain minor, to wit:

Florence Conger

who is interested in the estate, you are hereby appointed in accordance with the regulations of the Indian Office as Guardian-ad-litem for the said minor heir, and you will see to it that the interest of the said minor heir in the said estate is at all times protected until you are discharged from such obligation.

<u>   Horace J Johnson   </u>
Supt. & S. D. A.

---

**NOTICE OF HEARING TO DETERMINE HEIRS**

# DEPARTMENT OF THE INTERIOR

## UNITED STATES INDIAN SERVICE.

Sac & Fox Indian School,
Stroud, Okla., Mar 2, 191 4

M  Emma Goodman, Tulsa, Okla.,
    Thomas P. Myers, Stroud, Okla.,
    Guardian-Ad-Litem for Helen Jones;
    Isaac Struble, Cushing, Okla.,
    Logan Kakaque, Meeker, Okla.,
    Alexander Connolly, Stroud, Okla.,

Notice is hereby given that on the    1st.   day of    April    . 191 4, at  Sac & Fox Indian Agency, Okla.    , I will take testimony to be submitted to the Secretary of the Interior for the purpose of determining the heirs of    Henry C. Jones, Jr.,    , deceased.

All persons having an interest in the estate of the decedent are hereby notified to be present at the hearing and furnish such evidence as they desire.

Respectfully,

Horace J. Johnson

Superintendent.

**********

APPOINTMENT OF GUARDIAN-AD-LITEM.

Sac and Fox Indian Agency,
Stroud, Okla., Mar. 2, 1914.

Thomas P. Meyers,
Sac & Fox Indian Agency,
Stroud, Oklahoma.

Sir:-

In the matter of determining the heirs of Henry C. Jones Jr., it appearing that there is a certain minor, to wit:

Helen Jones

who is interested in the estate, you are hereby appointed in accordance with the regulations of the Indian Office as Guardian-ad-litem for the said minor heir in the said estate, and you will see to it that the interest of the said minor heir in the said estate is at all times protected until you are discharged from such obligation.

___Horace J Johnson___
Supt. & S. D. A.

---

Cushing  Okla
Mar 4 1914

RECEIVED
MAR 8 1914
SAC & FOX AGENCY
OKLAHOMA

Mr Horace J Johnson

Dear Sir

Inclosed find some Heir ship notices that was miss sent to me

Very Respt
Arza B Collins

---

16

RECEIVED
MAR 12 1914
SAC Distribution NCY,
of estate OMA.
for deposit,

MAR 9 1914

SAC & FOX SAN
RECEI

TOLEDO -

Sac and Fox Indian School,
Stroud, Okla., March 6, 1914.

R. L. Russell, Supt.,
  Sac and Fox Sanatorium,
          Toledo, Iowa.

Sir:-

I hand you herewith check No. 3653 drawn upon the First National
Bank of Chandler, Okla., in your favor, in the sum of $12.78 to be deposited
to the credit of Winfield Scott, who is shown by the records of this office to
be a son of William Scott.

I shall be pleased to have you sign the receipt on the duplicate of this
letter and return it to this office.

                    Very respectfully,
                    Horace J Johnson
AM                  Supt. & S. D. A.
Enc. check & duplicate letter.

        Received the above mentioned check and have deposited same as
indicated this __10__ day of __March__ 1914.

                    ____RL Russell____
                    Supt. & S. D. A.

Refer in reply to the following:
  Law-Heirship
    L L   **DEPARTMENT OF THE INTERIOR**        RECEI
            OFFICE OF INDIAN AFFAIRS             MAR 9
                WASHINGTON
                        MAR -6 1914          SAC & FOX A
                                               OKLAHO

Mr. H. J. Johnson,

    Supt. Sac & Fox School, Oklahoma.

Sir:

It is desired that special efforts be made to bring up to date the heirship work under your jurisdiction. If you are in need of additional stenographic assistance to bring about the desired results, submit immediately your request, with complete justification

Respectfully,

EB Meritt

---

1-19838

Finance-Bookpg
24050-1914
  R E S

Typewriter.

The Remington Typewriter Co.,                    MAR 14 1914

   1340 New York Avenue,

      Washington, D. C.

Gentlemen:

You are requested to deliver to the superintendent of the Shawnee Indian School, Oklahoma, for use of the Examiner of Inheritance in taking evidence to determine heirs of deceased allottees, one No. 3, 10.6-inch carriage, Monarch typewriter, at a cost of $70.00, delivered f.o.b. Shawnee, Oklahoma.

Payment therefor will be made from "Determining Heirs of Deceased Indian Allottees, 1914."

Please prepare voucher in triplicated on the inclosed blank forms, but sign only the one marked "Original". mail the original and both memorandum copies to the Superintendent of the Shawnee School, who will receipt for the typewriter on its arrival in good condition and will then forward the completer voucher to this Office for settlement. No invoice or statement in any other form is necessary or desirable.

Respectfully,

**(Signed)  C. F Hauke**

3-PML-13

Acting Commissioner

Carbon to Shawnee.

---

Distribution
of estate
for deposit.

Sac and Fox Indian School,
Stroud, Okla., Mar. 18, 1914,

First National Bank of Chandler,
Chandler, Oklahoma.

Gentlemen:-

Enclosed herewith you will find check No. 660 drawn upon the First National Bank of Stroud, Oklahoma in your favor for $5.82 which I shall be pleased to have you credit to Indian Account as follows:

| Acct. No. | Name | Amount. | Distribution |
|---|---|---|---|
| 564 | Elbert Mack | $5.82 | of estate. |

Please sign the receipt on the duplicate of this letter and return it to this office.

A return penalty envelope is enclosed for this purpose.

Very respectfully,
Horace J Johnson
Supt. & S. D. A.

AM
Enc. check, envelope &
duplicate letter.

Received the above noted check and have credited same to Indian Account as indicated this __20__ day of __Mch__, 1914.

_____Roy Dawson_____

TRIPLICATE

Sac and Fox Indian School,
Stroud, Okla., Mar. 18, 1914.

The United States Dr.

David Tohee Jr.,

Otoe, Oklahoma.

To 1/2 day, services as witness at an heirship hearing
 at $2 per day,............................. $1.00
" mileage fees, 40 miles at 10¢  per mile,................. 4.00
 Total,.............. $5.00

 I certify on honor that the foregoing claim is correct and just and
that no part of same has been paid.

Witnesses:                                        __David Tohee Jr____

____CG Morris_____
 _____Otoe, Okla_____
____HZ Mitchell_____
 _____Otoe, Okla____

 Paid by check No. 385, dated March 18, 1914, for $5.00 drawn on the
the Treasurer of the United States.

**********

TRIPLICATE

Sac and Fox Indian School,
Stroud, Okla., Mar. 18, 1914.

The United States Dr.

To William Fawfaw,
 Otoe, Oklahoma.

To 1/2 days, services as witness at an heirship hearing
 at $2 per day,............................. $1.00

 I certify on honor that the foregoing claim is correct and just and
that no part of same has been paid.

Witnesses:                                        ___William Fawfaw_____

____CG Morris_____
 _____Otoe, Okla_____
____HZ Mitchell_____
 _____Otoe, Okla____

Paid by check No. 388, dated March 18, 1914, for $1.00 drawn on the the Treasurer of the United States.

**********

Witness and
interpreter
fees.

Sac and Fox Indian School,
Stroud, Okla., May 5, 1914.

Mr. R. P. Stanion,
      Supt. Indian School,
            Otoe, Oklahoma.

Dear Sir,-

Please find inclosed herewith checks Nos. 385 for $5 and 388 for $1, the same to be delivered to David Tohee, Jr., and William Fawfaw, respectively, after they have signed the accompanying claims for fees due for services connected with heirship hearings held on the Iowa reservation under this jurisdiction.

Thanking you in advance for this trouble and requesting that the claims be returned to this office when signed, I am,

Very respectfully,


TPM                                                    Supt. & S. D. A.
Inc. as noted.
CC of letter to Tohee.

**********

Witness
and in-
terpreter
fees.

Sac and Fox Indian School,
Stroud, Okla., May 5, 1914.

Mr. David Tohee, Jr.,
      Red Rock, Okla.


Dear Friend,-

In connection with the services of yourself and William Fawfaw as witnesses at heirship hearings held on the Iowa reservation under this jurisdiction I am this day forwarding to Mr. Stanion, Supt. Otoe, checks for delivery to both of you in settlement for said services.   Accompanying the checks are claims requiring your signatures.

Requesting that you give this matter prompt attention and that you also notify William Fawfaw, I am,

Sincerely yours,

TPM                                                             Supt. & S. D. A.
Copy to Mr. Stanion.

**********

| 11 | Alex Connolly $2^{00}$ $2^{00}$ $2^{00}$ $2^{00}$ $2^{00}$ $2^{00}$ | $12^{00}$ |
|----|------------------------------------------------------------------------|-----------|
| 12 | Sarah Bear $2^{00}$ $2^{00}$ $1^{00}$ $3^{15}$ | $8^{15}$ |
| 13 | Jane Shaw $2^{00}$ $3^{30}$ | $5^{30}$ |
| 14 | Bettie Groinhorn $2^{00}$ | $2^{00}$ |
| 15 | Isaac Strubble $2^{00}$ $1^{00}$ $1^{00}$ | $4^{00}$ |
| 16 | William G. Foster $1^{00}$ $1^{00}$ | $2^{00}$ |
| 17 | John Brown $2^{00}$ | $2^{00}$ |
| 18 | Sarah Ellis $2^{00}$ | $2^{00}$ |
| 19 | Edward McClellan $2^{00}$ | $2^{00}$ |
| 20 | George Appletree $2^{00}$ $2^{35}$ | $4^{35}$ |
| 21 | Rosa Appletree $2^{00}$ $2^{35}$ | $4^{35}$ |
| 22 | Liza Martin $2^{00}$ $3^{05}$ | $5^{05}$ |
| 1 | Jacob Dole $1^{00}$ $1^{00}$ $20$ | $2^{20}$ |
| 2 | David Tohee $1^{00}$ $2^{00}$ $35$ | $3^{35}$ |
| 3 | John Moses $1^{00}$ $4^{00}$ | $5^{00}$ |
| 4 | Joseph Springer $1^{00}$ $1^{00}$ | $2^{00}$ |
| 5 | Dave Tohee Jr. (Little) $1^{00}$ $4^{00}$ | $5^{00}$ |
| 6 | Annie Perry Tohee $1^{00}$ | $1^{00}$ |
| 7 | Frank Kent $1^{00}$ $1^{00}$ $2^{00}$ $25$ $25$ | $4^{50}$ |
| 8 | William Fawfaw $1^{00}$ | $1^{00}$ |
| 9 | Charley Tohee $1^{00}$ | $1^{00}$ |
| 10 | Robert Small $2^{00}$ $35$ | $2^{35}$ |

**********

# Sac & Fox – Shawnee Estates
## 1911-1919   Volume VI

SCHEDULE OF FEES DUE INTERPRETER &
DISINTERESTED WITNESSES IN HEIRSHIP
CASES.
SAC AND FOX, OKLAHOMA, ALLOTTEES.

| CASE NO. | DECEDENT. | HEARING HELD | WITNESSES & INTERPRETER | WITNESS & INTERPRETER FEES. | MILEAGE FEES. | TOTAL. |
|---|---|---|---|---|---|---|
| 10 | Thomas Long | July 21, 1913 at | Alex Connolly | 2.00 | | 2.00 |
| 11 | Agnes Long | Sac & Fox Agcy. | (interpreter) | | | |
| | | | | | | |
| 93 | Benjamin Butler | Sept. 8, 1913 at | Alex Connolly, Int. | 2.00 | | |
| 94 | James Bear | Sac & Fox Agcy. | and witness. | | | |
| | | | Sarah Bear | 2.00 | | 4.00 |
| | | | | | | |
| 95 | John Nahashe | Oct. 1, 1913 at | Alex Connolly, Int. | 2.00 | | |
| 96 | Susan Nahashe | Sac & Fox Agcy. | Sarah Bear | 2.00 | 3.15 | |
| | | | Jane Shaw | 2.00 | 3.30 | 12.45 |
| | | | | | | |
| 97 | Cora Bass | Sept. 9, 1913 at | Alex Connolly, Int. | 2.00 | | |
| | | Sac & Fox Agcy. | and witness. | | | |
| | | | Bettie Groinhorn | 2.00 | | |
| | | | Isaac Strubble | 2.00 | | 6.00 |
| | | | | | | |
| 98 | Grace Mason | Sept. 10, 1913 at | William G. Foster, | 1.00 | | |
| | | Sac & Fox Agcy. | Int. and witness. | | | |
| | | | Isaac Strubble | 1.00 | | 2.00 |
| | | | (Allowed 1/2 day in | | | |
| | | | Morton cases.) | | | |
| | | | | | | |
| 100 | Clifford H. Morton | Sept. 10, 1913 at | William G. Foster, Interpreter. | 1.00 | | |
| 101 | Oliver P. Morton | Sac & Fox Agcy. | Isaac Strubble | 1.00 | | |
| 102 | Mellisa Morton | | Sarah Bear | 1.00 | | 3.00 |
| | | | | | | |
| 103 | Maw-mel-lo-haw | Sept. 11, 1913 at | Alex Connolly, Int. | 2.00 | | |
| | | Sac & Fox Agcy. | and witness. | | | |
| | | | John Brown | 2.00 | | 4.00 |
| | | | | | | |
| 107 | Unice Paddock, | Dec. 2, 1913 at | Alex Connolly, Int. | 2.00 | | |
| | nee Hawk | Sac & Fox Agcy. | and witness. | | | |
| | | | Sarah Ellis | 2.00 | | |
| | | | Edward McClellan | 2.00 | | 6.00 |
| | | | | | | |
| 113 | Lidia Walker | Oct. 27, 1913 at | George Appletree, | 2.00 | 2.35 | |
| | | Sac & Fox Agcy. | Interpreter. | | | |
| | | | Rosa Appletree | 2.00 | 2.36 | |
| | | | Liza Martin | 2.00 | 3.05 | 13.75 |
| | | | | $39.00 | $14.20 | $53.20 |

I certify on honor that the above schedule shows the amount due witnesses and interpreters in various heirship hearings, as shown in schedule, held under this jurisdiction, in accordance with the Regulations made to carry out an Act of Congress approved June 25, 1910.

I further certify that where we were able to secure all the necessary data to satisfy the requirements from two disinterested witnesses, only these two are included in the schedule, but where complete and satisfactory evidence could not be obtained from two persons other witnesses as necessary were called and their names have been included. I further certify that the charges shown in this schedule represent only the charges incurred on account of disinterested witnesses for the Government and that in addition to this schedule there are fees of various persons for giving testimony including the heirs themselves, settlement of which will be made from the estate.

Horace J Johnson
Supt. & S. D. A.
Sac & Fox Indian School, Oklahoma.
December 30,    191 3

WMH.

**********

SCHEDULE OF FEES DUE INTERPRETER &
DISINTERESTED WITNESSES IN HEIRSHIP
CASES.
IOWA, OKLAHOMA, ALLOTTEES.

| CASE NO. | DECEDENT. | HEARING HELD | WITNESSES & INTERPRETER | WITNESS & INTERPRE-TER FEES. | MILEAGE FEES. | TOTAL. |
|---|---|---|---|---|---|---|
| 91 | Joe Vetters | July 14, 1913 at Iowa Mission, Perkins, Okla. | Jacob Dole, Int. David Tohee John Moses Joseph Springer | 1.00 1.00 1.00 1.00 | .20 4.00 | 8.20 |
| 92 | Lee Patrick Tohee | July 14, 1913 at Iowa Mission, Perkins, Okla. | Jacob Dole, Int. (Little) Dave Tohee Jr. Annie Perry Tohee | 1.00 1.00 1.00 | 4.00 | 7.00 |
| 104 105 | Townsend Sha-th-cher | Sept. 16, 1913 at Iowa Mission, Perkins, Okla. | Joseph Springer, Int. and witness. Frank Kent William Fawfaw | 1.00 1.00 1.00 | | 3.00 |
| 106 | Maggie Burgess, nee Mohee | Sept 16, 1913 at Iowa Mission, Perkins, Okla. | Frank Kent Charley Tohee | 1.00 1.00 | .25 | 2.25 |
| 19 111 112 | Benjamin Hollow-ell. Nannie Hollowell Irene Hollowell | Oct. 30, 1913 at Iowa Mission, Perkins, Okla. | Robert Small, Int. Frank Kent David Tohee | 2.00 2.00 2.00 | .35 .25 .35 | 6.95 |
| | | | | $18.00 | $9.40 | $27.40 |

I certify on honor that the above schedule shows the amount due witnesses and interpreters in various heirship hearings, as shown in schedule, held under this jurisdiction, in accordance with the Regulations made to carry out an Act of Congress approved June 25, 1910.

I further certify that where we were able to secure all the necessary data to satisfy the requirements from two disinterested witnesses, only these two are included in the schedule, but where complete and satisfactory evidence could not be obtained from two persons other witnesses as necessary were called and their names have been included.

I further certify that the charges shown in this schedule represent only the charges incurred on account of disinterested witnesses for the Government and that in addition to this schedule

24

there are fees of various persons for giving testimony including the heirs themselves, settlement of which will be made from the estate.

Horace J Johnson
Supt. & S. D. A.
Sac & Fox Indian School, Okla. Dec. 30 19 13

### RECAPITULATION.

Paid interpreter and disinterested witnesses connected with hearings held to determine heirs of

Iowa Allottees, . . . . . . . . . . . . . . . . . . . . . . . . . . . . $27.40
Sac and Fox Allottees, . . . . . . . . . . . . . . . . . . . . . . . 53.20
Total, . . . . . . . . . . . . . . . . . . . . . . $80.60

Paid from the fund, "Determining Heirs of Deceased Indian Allottees, 1914."

REFER IN REPLY TO THE FOLLOWING:

Law-Heirship
19720-14
21106-14
F W S

Detail, Examiner
of Inheritance.

**DEPARTMENT OF THE INTERIOR,**
**OFFICE OF INDIAN AFFAIRS,**
**WASHINGTON,**
MAR 18 1914

ADDRESS ONLY THE
COMMISSIONER OF INDIAN AFFAIRS

RECEIVED
MAR 21 A M.
SAC & FOX AGENCY,
OKLAHOMA

Mr. H. J. Johnson,

Supt., Sac & Fox School, Oklahoma.

Sir:-

Receipt is acknowledged of your letter of February 23, 1914, with reference to the determination of heirs to estates under your jurisdiction, in which you state that in your judgement the assignment of Examiner of Inheritance Edwin A. Upton, to the Indians under your jurisdiction, will not be necessary.

You are advised that the Office has already taken cognizance of this situation as given in your letter and the Mr. Upton's orders to proceed to the Sac & Fox School, Oklahoma, have been cancelled.

Respectfully,

EB Meritt
Assistant Commissioner.

3-AS-14

**********

25

REFER IN REPLY TO THE FOLLOWING:                                            ADDRESS ONLY THE
L-H                                                                                     COMMISSIONER OF INDIAN AFFAIRS

## DEPARTMENT OF THE INTERIOR,

### OFFICE OF INDIAN AFFAIRS,
### WASHINGTON,

FEB 16 1914

Mr. Horace J. Johnson,

Supt. Sac and Fox School.

My dear Mr. Johnson:

Mr. Edwin A. Upton has been appointed an Examiner of Inheritance to conduct and report on hearings among the Indians of the Sac and Fox Reservation.

Mr. Upton is now under instructions in this Office and possibly by the latter part of the month will be in a position to proceed to the Sac and Fox Reservation.

In order that the work may be expedited as much as possible you are requested to publish notice of hearing in a sufficient number of cases to enable Mr. Upton to immediately proceed with the work to which he is assigned as soon as he arrives.  Such courtesies as you may extend to him in his work will be duly appreciated.

Very truly yours,

Assistant          EB Meritt
Commissioner.

**********

L-H

Sac and Fox Indian School,
Stroud, Okla., Feb. 23, 1914.

Commissioner of Indian Affairs,
Washington, D.C.

Sir:

I have the honor to acknowledge receipt of the above noted communication, dated Feb. 16, 1914 concerning the appointment of Mr. Edwin A Upton as an Examiner of Inheritance and to state that I have set a number of cases for Hearing March 20, 1914 and have given the required notice.

Unless to carry out some Regulation it does not seem that such an appointment here is necessary as at the present rate of progress we shall be able to clean up all cases ourselves during the present calendar year unless some unforeseen thing develops. Since December 1, 1913 we have submitted 14 cases for the consideration of the Office. We have 3 more cases that we shall submit during the present week. This will make a total of 17 cases in three months, or nearly six cases per month. While there are about 75 cases left for handling, only about 50 of them have any funds to their credit. At the rate of six cases per month and I see no reason why we shall not be able to get in at least that many we can clean up in about eight months. Until during the past three months we have not been able to do as much with this work as we would like to have done on account of the Oil and Gas work we had to handle. There has been a lull in this work and one of our clerks is able to give quite a considerable of his time to the work of determining heirship cases. He has been doing this during the past three months with the result above mentioned. I do not wish to be understood as saying that he has given all or nearly all of his time to this work for this is not the case. Had he done this, other work of the office would have suffered.

Again, in practically all the cases that are left there seems to be no necessity for haste in having the heirs declared except to have the incident closed, for the reason that the prospective heirs already have sufficient funds for all practical purposes except those that subserve the people who are desirous of getting their hands upon the funds of the Indian as rapidly as possible.

There are a few of the prospective heirs who do not come in the above class and it is these that we are intending to provide for first, except in a couple of cases where it seems it is going to be impossible to get sufficient testimony upon which to base a report which will not be open to objection on the part of the Office for the reason that we have not furnished sufficient information to eliminate possible heirs.

Very Respectfully,

Very Respectfully,[sic]

Sac and Fox Indian School,
Stroud, Okla., Feb. 21, 1914.

TO WHOM IT MAY CONCERN:-

Alice Faw Faw has authority to purchase the following:

| One team mules | One wagon |
| One set harness | Feed |

---

Stroud, Okla., Feb. 23, 1914.

Indian Office,
　　Washington, D. C.

Office letter sixteenth.  Examiner of inheritances appears unnecessary here.  Letter follows.

GNC                                    (S) Johnson,
Phoned   4:47   p.m.                    Supt.

---

Education-
　Employees.
16169-1914.
　H V B

MAR 6 1914

The Commissioner

　　of Indian Affairs.

Sir:

OFFICE OF INDIAN AFFAIRS
RECEIVED
MAR 6 1914
24611

　　　　Departmental authority, dated February 17, 1914, establishing a position of stenographer and typewriter at $900 a year, with actual necessary traveling expenses, exclusive of subsistence, at the Sac and Fox Agency, Oklahoma, payable from "Determining Heirs of Deceased Indian Allottees, 1914", effective March 1, 1914, is hereby canceled.

　　　　In lieu thereof authority is granted for the establishment of a similar position at $900 a year, with actual necessary traveling expenses, exclusive of subsistence, at the Seger Agency, Oklahoma, payable from the same appropriation, effective April 1, 1914.

Respectfully,
*Signed*
Lewis C. Laylin
Assistant Secretary.

2-AAC-27

Official copy for Superintendent          Sac & Fox, Okla.

John [Illegible]
Chief Education Division.

---

Shawnee  Oklahoma.

March 20th, 1914.

Elbert Mack.

Meeker  Oklahoma.

Sir:-

You are hereby notified that a hearing will be held at the Sac and Fox Indian Office on March 27th, 1914. to determine the heirs of Samuel W. Peel deceased. and you are notified to be present on that date, at the place mentioned above.

Claud Chandler _ _ _ _ _ _.
U.S. Farmer.

I Elbert Mack hereby acknowledge receipt of the above notice this the _20_ _. day of March 1914.

_ _ _ Elbert Mack _ _ _ _ _ _

---

**DEPARTMENT OF THE INTERIOR**
OFFICE OF INDIAN AFFAIRS
WASHINGTON

OFFICE OF INDIAN AFFAIRS
RECEIVED
MAR 17 1914
28965

A

*Authority is hereby granted for you to expend, during the fiscal year 1914 , the sum of $ 100. from the appropriation*

| | | DO NOT WRITE IN THIS SPACE | |
|---|---|---|---|
| (1) Determination of Heirs of Deceased Indian Allottees, | $ | $ | |
| (2) | 1914, $100.00 | $ | |
| (3) | $ | $ | |
| (4) | $ | $ | |

*for the following:*

| OBJECT. | UNIT PRICE. | AMOUNT. |
|---|---|---|

This sheet to be detached and retained by Disbursing Officer.

<u>Agency</u>

For witness expenses, and expenses of
interpreters in determining heirs of
deceased Indian allottees – Hearing cases *****

| | TOTAL. | 100|00 |

TO:

Sup't. & Spcl. Disbg. Agent.
(Title or name.)

Shawnee Indian Training School
(School.)

Shawnee, Oklahoma.
(Post Office.)

MAR 24 1914

COPY.—To be filed by the disbursing officer with proper voucher in his copy of memorandum account.

*(Signed) C. F. Hauke*

MEMORANDUM.

VOUCHER FOR MISCELLANEOUS EXPENSES, SUCH AS RENT OF BUILDINGS, TELEPHONE
SERVICE, GAS, ELECTRIC LIGHT, AND WATER SUPPLY. ETC.

**THE UNITED STATES,**                    April 8th-1914  *19*14

*To*          Wah-Pe-Pah          , *Dr.*
(Give post-office address.)   McLoud, Oklahoma

| DATE 1914 | ENTER BELOW THE SUBJECT MATTER OF THE CLAIM, SHOWING OF WHAT IT CONSISTS. | AMOUNT. |
|---|---|---|
| Apr. 8 | For Service as Witness in Hearing for determination of heirs of Wah-Cut-Tah-Peah-She, Deceased Allottee, #164, one day----------------------------------------------------- | 2|00 |

30

| | | |
|---|---|---|
| | | |

TOTAL.............................. $ 200

THE ABOVE IS A TRUE COPY OF ORIGINAL VOUCHER, EXCEPT AS TO CERTIFICATES.
PAID IN CASH, UNLESS OTHERWISE NOTED AT THE BOTTOM HEREOF.

Services procured under authority dated _____ March 24 (28965) ___, 1914, attached to original or to voucher No. ____6____ to account for __4th_____ Quarter, 1914, and in accordance with sections _____ and _____ of the methods stated on original.
Letter)    (Number)

Dated __April 8_____, 1914

Paid by Check No. ___2189___, dated _____ April 8_____, 1914, for $2.00_____,
on _____ U.S. Treasurer _____, to order of claimant.

**********

MEMORANDUM.

CASH

*Voucher No.* 8____, 4th_____ *Quarter, 19*14

FOR

MISCELLANEOUS EXPENSES.

IN FAVOR OR

_____ WAH-PE-PAH _____

*For $* 2.00_____

*Paid by* _____ John A. BUNTIN _____

Supt. and Special Disb. Agt.
(Official title.)

Shawnee Indian Training School
(Agency or School.)

Any disbursing or other officer of the United States or other person who shall knowingly present, or cause to be presented, any voucher, account, or claim to any officer of the United States for approval or payment, or for the purpose of securing a credit in any account with the United States, relating to any matter pertaining to the Indian Service, which shall contain any material misrepresentation of fact in regard to the amount due or paid, the name or character of the article furnished or received, or of the service rendered, or to the date of purchase, delivery, or performance of service, or in any other particular, shall not be entitled to payment or credit for any part of said voucher, account, or claim; and if any such credit shall be given or received, or payment made, the United States may recharge the same to the officer or person receiving the credit or payment and recover the amount from either or both, in the same manner as other debts due the United States are collected; PROVIDED, That where an account contains more than one voucher, this section shall apply only to such vouchers as contain the mis'representation; AND PROVIDED FURTHER, That the officers and persons by and between whom the business is transacted shall be presumed to know the facts in relation to the matter set forth in the voucher, account, or claim; AND PROVIDED FURTHER, That the foregoing shall be in addition to the penalties now prescribed by law, and in no way to affect proceedings under existing law for like offenses. That, where practicable, this section shall be printed on the blank forms of vouchers provided for general use. (Act March 1, 1833 § 8, 22 Stat., 451; Ace July 4, 1884, § 8; Cir. 113 Ind. O.)

MEMORANDUM.

## CASH

*Voucher No.* 9___, ___4th___ *Quarter, 19* 14

FOR

**MISCELLANEOUS EXPENSES.**

IN FAVOR OR

MUCH-E-NE-NE

*For $* 2.00

*Paid by* ___John A. BUNTIN___

(Official title.)

(Agency or School.)

Any disbursing or other officer of the United States or other person who shall knowingly present, or cause to be presented, any voucher, account, or claim to any officer of the United States for approval or payment, or for the purpose of securing a credit in any account with the United States, relating to any matter pertaining to the Indian Service, which shall contain any material misrepresentation of fact in regard to the amount due or paid, the name or character of the article furnished or received, or of the service rendered, or to the date of purchase, delivery, or performance of service, or in any other particular, shall not be entitled to payment or credit for any part of said voucher, account, or claim; and if any such credit shall be given or received, or payment made, the United States may recharge the same to the officer or person receiving the credit or payment and recover the amount from either or both, in the same manner as other debts due the United States are collected; PROVIDED, That where an account contains more than one voucher the foregoing shall apply only to such vouchers as contain the misrepresentation; AND PROVIDED FURTHER, That the officers and persons by and between whom the business is transacted shall be presumed to know the facts in relation to the matter set forth in the voucher, account, or claim; AND PROVIDED FURTHER, That the foregoing shall be in addition to the penalties now prescribed by law, and in no way to affect proceedings under existing law for like offenses. That, where practicable, this section shall be printed on the blank forms of vouchers provided for general use. (Act March 1, 1883 § 8, 22 Stat., 451; Ace July 4, 1884, § 8; Cir. 113 Ind. O.)

\*\*\*\*\*\*\*\*\*\*

MEMORANDUM.

VOUCHER FOR MISCELLANEOUS EXPENSES, SUCH AS RENT OF BUILDINGS, TELEPHONE
SERVICE, GAS, ELECTRIC LIGHT, AND WATER SUPPLY. ETC.

**THE UNITED STATES,**          April 8th    *19* 14

*To*        Joe Murdock        *, Dr.*

(Give post-office address.)   McLoud, Oklahoma

| DATE 1914 | ENTER BELOW THE SUBJECT MATTER OF THE CLAIM, SHOWING OF WHAT IT CONSISTS. | AMOUNT. |
|---|---|---|
| Apr. 8 | For Service as Interpreter in taking testimony in Hearing for determination of Heirs of Wah-Cut-Tah-Peah-She, Deceased Allottee, #164, one day------------------------------ | 250 |

32

TOTAL........................... $ 250

THE ABOVE IS A TRUE COPY OF ORIGINAL VOUCHER, EXCEPT AS TO CERTIFICATES.
PAID IN CASH, UNLESS OTHERWISE NOTED AT THE BOTTOM HEREOF.

Services procured under authority dated ___March 24. (28965)___, 1914, attached to original or to voucher No. ___8___ to account for ___4th___ Quarter, 1914, and in accordance with sections _____ and _____ of the methods stated on original.

(Letter)   (Number)

Dated __April 8th. 1914__, 19

Paid by Check No. __2191__, dated __April 8. 1914__, 19, for $ __2.50__

on _____U.S. Treasurer_____, to order of claimant.

**********

MEMORANDUM.

## CASH

*Voucher No.* 10 , 4th *Quarter, 19*14

FOR

**MISCELLANEOUS  EXPENSES.**

IN FAVOR OR

__JOE MURDOCK__

*For $* 2.50

*Paid by* __John A. BUNTIN__

(Official title.)

(Agency or School.)

Any disbursing or other officer of the United States or other person who shall knowingly present, or cause to be presented, any voucher, account, or claim to any officer of the United States for approval or payment, or for the purpose of securing a credit in any account with the United States, relating to any matter pertaining to the Indian Service, which shall contain any material misrepresentation of fact in regard to the amount due or paid, the name or character of the article furnished or received, or of the service rendered, or to the date of purchase, delivery, or performance of service, or in any other particular, shall not be entitled to payment or credit for any part of said voucher, account, or claim; and if any such credit shall be given or received, or payment made, the United States may recharge the same to the officer or person receiving the credit or payment and recover the amount from either or both, in the same manner as other debts due the United States are collected; PROVIDED, That where an account contains more than one voucher the foregoing shall apply only to such vouchers as contain the misrepresentation; AND PROVIDED FURTHER, That the officers and persons by and between whom the business is transacted shall be presumed to know the facts in relation to the matter set forth in the voucher, account, or claim; AND PROVIDED FURTHER, That the foregoing shall be in addition to the penalties now prescribed by law, and in no way to affect proceedings under existing law for like offenses. That, where practicable, this section shall be printed on the blank forms of vouchers provided for general use. (Act March 1, 1883 § 8, 22 Stat., 451; Ace July 4, 1884, § 8; Cir. 113 Ind. O.)

Transfer of
Bank Acct.

RECEIVED
MAR 30 A.M.
SAC & FOX AGENCY,
OKLAHOMA.

Sac and Fox Indian School,
Stroud, Okla., Mar. 25, 1914.

The Bristow National Bank,
    Bristow, Oklahoma.

Gentlemen,-

    For credit to the account of the Heirs of Jerome Wolf, Account No. 2005, please find inclosed herewith check No. 3670 drawn on the First National Bank, Chandler, Okla., in your favor for $199.01.

    Kindly sign the certificate in the accompanying copy of this letter and return same to this office.

            Very respectfully,

TPM                                         Supt. & S. D. A.
Inc. Check No. 3670
    Copy of letter.

    I hereby certify that I have this __28th__ day of March, 1914, received the amount as stated above and credited same to the Indian account as indicated.

        The Bristow National Bank, Bristow, Okla.

        By ____R Steinhout____, Cashier.

---

**DEPARTMENT OF THE INTERIOR**
OFFICE OF INDIAN AFFAIRS
WASHINGTON

OFFICE OF INDIAN AFFAIRS
RECEIVED
MAR 18 1914
29656

A

    Authority is hereby granted for you to expend, during the fiscal year 1914 , the sum of $ _30.00_ from the appropriation

| | | | DO NOT WRITE IN THIS SPACE |
|---|---|---|---|
| (1) Determination of Heirs of Deceased Indian Allottees, | $ | | $ |
| (2) | 1914, | $ 30.00 | $ |
| (3) | | $ | $ |
| (4) | | $ | $ |

for the following:

34

| OBJECT. | | UNIT PRICE. | AMOUNT. |
|---|---|---|---|
| *This sheet to be detached and retained by Disbursing Officer.* Agency<br><br>For paying registry fees on notices sent to witnesses where it is necessary to serve notice on them by registered mail ** | | | 30 00 |
| | | TOTAL. | 30 00 |

TO:

Sup't. & Spcl. Disbg. Agent.
(Title or name.)

Shawnee Indian Training School
(School.)

Shawnee, Oklahoma.
(Post Office.)

APR -6 1914

COPY.—To be filed by the disbursing officer with proper voucher in his copy of memorandum account.

*(Signed)* C. F. Hauke

REFER IN REPLY TO THE FOLLOWING:

Ed-Industries
19061-14
50597-14
C H S

ADDRESS ONLY THE
COMMISSIONER OF INDIAN AFFAIRS

**DEPARTMENT OF THE INTERIOR**
OFFICE OF INDIAN AFFAIRS,
WASHINGTON,
APR -6 1914

R E C E I V E D
APR 9 A.M.
SAC & FOX AGENCY,
OKLAHOMA.

Mr. Horace J. Johnson,

Supt., Sac and Fox School, Okla.

Sir:

The Office has received your letter of February 16, 1914, stating that owing to the failure on your part to properly designate Indian bank accounts in requesting authority to sign and approve checks in settlement of witness fees incurred in holding heirship hearings, you request that your action in drawing the checks on the authorities as now granted be approved.

Since this will avoid the necessity of re-writing the request, and of possible exceptions to the accounts on which checks were drawn before the error was noted, the following accounts, properly designated, are hereby approved:

| Acct. No. | Name of Depositor. | Date authority approved. | Name as given in request. |
|-----------|--------------------|--------------------------|---------------------------|
| 266 | Heirs of Harvey Madison, | Feb. 6, 1914 | Harvey Madison |
| 288 | Heirs of Mary Plumb, | Feb. 6, 1914 | Mary Plumb |
| 293 | Heirs of Maggie Burgess, | Feb. 6, 1914 | Maggie Burgess |
| 294 | Heirs of Dosh Kakaque, | Feb. 6, 1914 | Dosh Kakaque |
| 296 | Heirs of Maw-mel-lo-haw | Feb. 6, 1914 | Maw-mel-lo-haw |
| 298 | Heirs of Susie Grant, | Feb. 6, 1914, | Susie Grant |
| 300 | Heirs of Benjamin Franklin | Feb. 6, 1914, | Benjamin Franklin |
| 804 | Heirs of Irene Hallowell | Feb. 6, 1914, | Irene Hallowell |
| 805 | Heirs of Nannie Hallowell | Feb. 6, 1914, | Nannie Hallowell |
| 806 | Heirs of Lizzie Whitecloud | Feb. 6, 1914, | Lizzie Whitecloud |
| 807 | Heirs of Edgar Mack, | Feb. 6, 1914, | Edgar Mack |
| 809 | Heirs of Jerome Wolf, | Feb. 6, 1914, | Jerome Wolf |
| 822 | Heirs of Robert Hunter | Feb. 6, 1914 | Robert Hunter |
| 823 | Heirs of Francis Harris | Feb. 6, 1914 | Francis Harris |
| 829 | Heirs of Waw-ko-pah-she-toe | Feb. 6, 1914 | Waw-ko-pah-she-toe |
| 833 | Heirs of Hog-gra-ah-chey | Feb. 6, 1914 | Hog-gra-ah-chey |
| 835 | Heirs of Mary Hodge | Feb. 6, 1914 | Mary Hodge |
| 836 | Heirs of Joe Vetter | Feb. 6, 1914 | Joe Vetter |
| 844 | Heirs of Jennie Bigwalker | Feb. 6, 1914 | Jennie Bigwalker |
| 846 | Heirs of James Bear | Feb. 6, 1914 | James Bear |
| 853 | Heirs of Walter Mathews, | Feb. 6, 1914 | Walter Mathews |
| 854 | Heirs of Lena Seaborn, nee McCoonse, | Feb. 6, 1914 | Lena Seaborn, nee McCoonse |
| 858 | Heirs of Townsend | Feb. 6, 1914 | Townsend |
| 859 | Heirs of Sha-th-cher | Feb. 6, 1914 | Sha-th-cher |
| 860 | Heirs of Benjamin Hallowell | Feb. 6, 1914 | Benjamin Hallowell |
| 861 | Heirs of William Ingalls, | Feb. 6, 1914 | William Ingalls |
| 624 | Heirs of John Grant | Feb. 6, 1914 | John Grant |
| 629 | Heirs of Hiram Gibbs | Feb. 6, 1914 | Hiram Gibbs |
| 631 | Heirs of Kirwin Murray | Feb. 6, 1914 | Kirwin Murray |
| 634 | Heirs of Thomas Long, | Feb. 6, 1914 | Thomas Long |
| 635 | Heirs of Agnes Long | Feb. 6, 1914 | Agnes Long |
| 637 | Heirs of Henry Shaquequot | Feb. 6, 1914 | Henry Shaquequot |

| 638 | Heirs of May Murray | Feb. 6, 1914 | May Murray |
| 639 | Heirs of Abby Redrock | Feb. 6, 1914 | Abby Redrock |
| 643 | Heirs of Hiram Thorp | Feb. 6, 1914 | Hiram Thorp |
| 664 | Heirs of Jefferson Whitecloud | Feb. 6, 1914 | Jefferson Whitecloud |
| 1018 | Heirs of Julia Hodge | Feb. 6, 1914 | Julia Hodge |
| 269 | Heirs of Walter Kakaque | Jan. 17, 1914 | Walter Kakaque |
| 294 | Heirs of Dosh Kakaque | Jan. 17, 1914 | Dosh Kakaque |
| 833 | Heirs of Hog-gra-ah-chey | Jan. 17, 1914 | Hog-gra-ah-chey |
| 848 | Heirs of Augre | Jan. 28, 1914 | Augre |
| 853 | Heirs of Walter Mathews | Jan. 17, 1914 | Walter Mathews |

The above expenditures are approved, provided they are in harmony with the Regulations as to the amounts for which they were drawn.

Respectfully,

3-ANB-27

EB Meritt
Assistant Commissioner
**********

Ed-Industries
19061-14
C H S

Sac and Fox Indian School,
Stroud, Okla., March 15, 1914.

Commissioner of Indian Affairs,
Washington, D. C.

Sir:-

Referring to the above noted communication, I have the honor to state that the defect in the requests made by me for authority to approve checks which I have desired cured is merelt[sic] a technical one.  It is one of which no account would be taken in ordinary affairs, but the examiners of accounts in your Office some times take advantage of these technical defects especially where they occur in large numbers of cases in a single set of accounts and write long letters of exceptions which require considerable time and patience to answer.  The requests submitted from this office are made to sign and approve checks of the several depositors, only the name of the depositor being given, while the deposits are carried on our books as heirs of such depositor.  For example, in the request to sign and and[sic] approve checks on bank account No. 266, the depositor is given as "Harvey Madison" while the depositor is shown on our books as "Heirs of Harvey Madison".  The defects in other requests are of a similar nature.

It is requested that I be authorized to sign and approve checks on authorities as already given without the necessity of securing amended authorites[sic] in each case, so that if exceptions are taken to the checks as drawn, the exception can be readily answered.

Very respectfully,

Supt. & S. D. A.

HJJ/AM

**********

REFER IN REPLY TO THE FOLLOWING:
Ed-Industries
19061-14
C H S

ADDRESS ONLY THE
COMMISSIONER OF INDIAN AFFAIRS

**DEPARTMENT OF THE INTERIOR,** RECEIVED
OFFICE OF INDIAN AFFAIRS,      MAR 9
WASHINGTON,        SAC & FOX AGENCY,
MAR -6 1914    OKLAHOMA.

Mr. H. J. Johnson,

Supt. Sac & Fox School, Okla.

Sir:

The Office has your letter of February 16, 1914, requesting approval of your action in drawing checks on authorities as now granted in order to obviate the necessity of re-writing the requests and of possible exceptions to your accounts.

You assign as your reason for this request that your office failed to properly designate the Indian bank accounts when submitting these authorities to sign and approve checks in settlement of witness fees incurred in holding heirship hearings.

You append a list of the accounts properly designated together with the date of the approval of the authority and the name as given in the request.  All of these have been carefully examined and it is found that each bank account number has been affixed to its appropriate request.  If this information is not sufficient and satisfactory please indicate what is further desired in order to straighten out the difficulty.

Respectfully,

EB Meritt
Assistant Commissioner.

3-HMB-3

\*\*\*\*\*\*\*\*\*\*

Authority.

Sac & Fox Indian School,
Stroud, Okla., Jan. 8, 1914.

Commissioner of Indian Affairs,
Washington, D. C.,

Sir:-

I have the honor to enclose herewith forty requests for authority to sign and approve checks on various accounts, in the amounts stated therein, to settle witness fees and mileage due interested parties who testified at the hearings to determine the heirs of the different Sac and Fox and Iowa allottees, also those disinterested parties who were brought by the interested parties.

In some cases two or three hearings were held during one day and the same persons testified at all the hearings. The witness fees and mileage of these persons have been equally divided among the estates in which they testified.

Under dates of June 25 and December 30, 1913, I requested authority to settle indebtednesses amounting to $209.30 and $80.60 respectively, to pay witness fees and mileage of disinterested parties summonsed by the Government in various hearings held to determine the heirs of Sac and Fox and Iowa allottees, in accordance with the Regulations made to carry out an Act of Congress approved June 25, 1910, and as shown in schedules, which schedules were submitted with the requests for authority. The request of June 25th. was approved August 22, 1913, but the request of December 30th. has not as yet been approved.

These requests cover fees and mileage of all witnesses who testified in all cases during the period between July 1, 1912 and December 21, 1913 inclusive, for determining heirs of deceased allottees where there are any funds in the estate with which to make settlement of these fees, excepting that of Lidia Walker, Sac and Fox allottee No. 189. There are not sufficent[sic] funds to the credit of the estate to make settlement in this case and as the record of proceedings to determine her heirs has not been submitted to your Office I thought it just as well to hold off the settling of the fees and mileage in this case until such time as there are sufficent funds to the credit of the estate or until the record of proceedings to determine the heirs is forwarded to your Office. The requests now being submitted cover cases where determinations of heirs have been had and where they have not been had.

I should not have submitted requests in those cases where determinations have not been had only for the reason that I thought it advisable to clean up everything at one time. In most cases where the determination of heirs has been definitely settled the estates have been divided amongst the heirs and there is now to the credit of the estate only a sufficent[sic] sum to pay the witness fees and mileage.

None of the witnesses for whom requests authorizing payment are being submitted herewith so far as I know have been paid by outside persons for appearing to give testimony and none of them have been paid by the Government or through this office from funds belonging to the several estates in which they testified for doing this.

I shall be obliged if these requests for authority can be given early consideration.

Very respectfully,

Horace J Johnson

WMH.                                     Supt. & S. D. A.

Enclos:
40 requests for Authority.

**********

Authorities
for Bank Account
Disbursements.

Sac and Fox Indian School,<br>Stroud, Okla., Feb. 16, 1914.

Commissioner of Indian Affairs,
       Washington, D. C.

Sir,-

Owing to the failure on the part of this office to properly designate Indian bank accounts in requesting authority to sign and approve checks in settlement of witness fees incurred in holding heirship hearings, I have the honor to request that my action in drawing the checks on the authorities as now granted be approved. This will avoid the necessity of rewriting the requests and of possible exceptions to the accounts on which checks were drawn before the error was noted.

Below is a list of the accounts properly designated, together with the date of the approval of the authority and the name as given in the request:

| Acct. No. | Name of Depositor. | Date authority approved. | Name as given in request. |
|-----------|--------------------|--------------------------|---------------------------|
| 266 | Heirs of Harvey Madison, | Feb. 6, 1914 | Harvey Madison |
| 288 | Heirs of Mary Plumb, | Feb. 6, 1914 | Mary Plumb |
| 293 | Heirs of Maggie Burgess, | Feb. 6, 1914 | Maggie Burgess |
| 294 | Heirs of Dosh Kakaque, | Feb. 6, 1914 | Dosh Kakaque |
| 296 | Heirs of Maw-mel-lo-haw | Feb. 6, 1914 | Maw-mel-lo-haw |
| 298 | Heirs of Susie Grant, | Feb. 6, 1914, | Susie Grant |
| 300 | Heirs of Benjamin Franklin | Feb. 6, 1914, | Benjamin Franklin |
| 804 | Heirs of Irene Hallowell | Feb. 6, 1914, | Irene Hallowell |
| 805 | Heirs of Nannie Hallowell | Feb. 6, 1914, | Nannie Hallowell |
| 806 | Heirs of Lizzie Whitecloud | Feb. 6, 1914, | Lizzie Whitecloud |
| 807 | Heirs of Edgar Mack, | Feb. 6, 1914, | Edgar Mack |
| 809 | Heirs of Jerome Wolf, | Feb. 6, 1914, | Jerome Wolf |
| 822 | Heirs of Robert Hunter | Feb. 6, 1914 | Robert Hunter |
| 823 | Heirs of Francis Harris | Feb. 6, 1914 | Francis Harris |
| 829 | Heirs of Waw-ko-pah-she-toe | Feb. 6, 1914 | Waw-ko-pah-she-toe |
| 833 | Heirs of Hog-gra-ah-chey | Feb. 6, 1914 | Hog-gra-ah-chey |
| 835 | Heirs of Mary Hodge | Feb. 6, 1914 | Mary Hodge |
| 836 | Heirs of Joe Vetter | Feb. 6, 1914 | Joe Vetter |
| 844 | Heirs of Jennie Bigwalker | Feb. 6, 1914 | Jennie Bigwalker |
| 846 | Heirs of James Bear | Feb. 6, 1914 | James Bear |
| 853 | Heirs of Walter Mathews, | Feb. 6, 1914 | Walter Mathews |
| 854 | Heirs of Lena Seaborn, nee McCoonse, | Feb. 6, 1914 | Lena Seaborn, nee McCoonse |
| 858 | Heirs of Townsend | Feb. 6, 1914 | Townsend |
| 859 | Heirs of Sha-th-cher | Feb. 6, 1914 | Sha-th-cher |
| 860 | Heirs of Benjamin Hallowell | Feb. 6, 1914 | Benjamin Hallowell |
| 861 | Heirs of William Ingalls, | Feb. 6, 1914 | William Ingalls |
| 624 | Heirs of John Grant | Feb. 6, 1914 | John Grant |
| 629 | Heirs of Hiram Gibbs | Feb. 6, 1914 | Hiram Gibbs |
| 631 | Heirs of Kirwin Murray | Feb. 6, 1914 | Kirwin Murray |
| 634 | Heirs of Thomas Long, | Feb. 6, 1914 | Thomas Long |
| 635 | Heirs of Agnes Long | Feb. 6, 1914 | Agnes Long |
| 637 | Heirs of Henry Shaquequot | Feb. 6, 1914 | Henry Shaquequot |
| 638 | Heirs of May Murray | Feb. 6, 1914 | May Murray |
| 639 | Heirs of Abby Redrock | Feb. 6, 1914 | Abby Redrock |
| 643 | Heirs of Hiram Thorp | Feb. 6, 1914 | Hiram Thorp |
| 664 | Heirs of Jefferson Whitecloud | Feb. 6, 1914 | Jefferson Whitecloud |
| 1018 | Heirs of Julia Hodge | Feb. 6, 1914 | Julia Hodge |
| 269 | Heirs of Walter Kakaque | Jan. 17, 1914 | Walter Kakaque |

| 294 | Heirs of Dosh Kakaque | Jan. 17, 1914 | Dosh Kakaque |
| 833 | Heirs of Hog-gra-ah-chey | Jan. 17, 1914 | Hog-gra-ah-chey |
| 848 | Heirs of Augre | Jan. 28, 1914 | Augre |
| 853 | Heirs of Walter Mathews | Jan. 17, 1914 | Walter Mathews |

Requesting that this be made special and I advised of the action of the Office at an early date, I am,

Very respectfully,

TPM                                            Supt. & S. D. A.


**********


[Note: The following was on the left of each receipt, in order to save space it was omitted:]  "**INFORMATION.**  To obtain a receipt showing delivery, indorse the *article, across its face,* "Receipt desired." A check mark ( / ) or ( √ ) in the space after the words "Receipt desired," the letter " A " in the space after the words " Delivery restricted to addressee in person," or the letter " O " after the words " Delivery restricted to addressee or other, " indicates that a return receipt is desired, or that delivery is restricted as stated. The absence of a check mark or of the letters " A " and " O " indicates that no return receipt is desired and that delivery is not restricted."

[Copy of an original receipt]

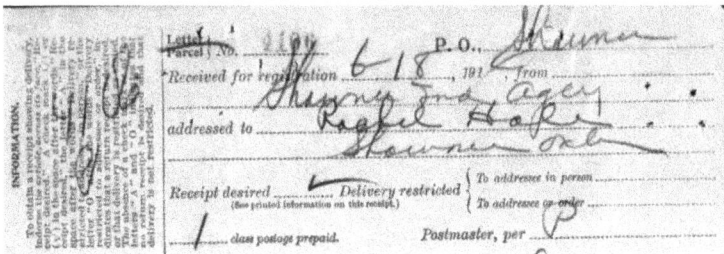


**********


Letter ⎫
Parcel ⎰ *No.* 3336                    **P. O.,**                Shawnee  Ok
*Received for registration*      4/10        *191* 4   *from*
                          Shawnee Indian Agency

*addressed to*                   Oscar [Illegible]
                             Carlisle  Pa

                                    ⎧ To addressee in person
*Receipt desired*  √ *Delivery restricted* ⎨ To addressee or order
                                    ⎩

        *class postage prepaid.*        *Postmaster, per*      [Initials Illegible]


42

**********

Letter }
Parcel } No. 3337                    P. O.,              Shawnee  Okla

*Received for registration*      4/10        191 4  *from*
                        Shawnee Indian Agency

*addressed to*              Joseph Moose
                        Sacred Heart Okla

                                    ⌠To addressee in person
*Receipt desired*    ✓Delivery restricted  ⌡To addressee or order

1   *class postage prepaid.*        *Postmaster, per*        [Initials Illegible]

**********

Letter }
Parcel } No. 3338                    P. O.,              Shawnee Okla

*Received for registration*      4/10        191 4  *from*
                   Shawnee Indian Agency

*addressed to*          Joseph Moose
                        Sacred Heart Okla

                                    ⌠To addressee in person
*Receipt desired*    ✓Delivery restricted  ⌡To addressee or order

1   *class postage prepaid.*        *Postmaster, per*        [Initials Illegible]

**********

Letter }
Parcel } No. 3458                    P. O.,              Shawnee Okla

*Received for registration*      4/16        191 4  *from*        Shawnee
                   Ind [Illegible]

*addressed to*              Mrs. Josephine Roberts
                        Tecumseh Okla

                                    ⌠To addressee in person
*Receipt desired*    ✓Delivery restricted  ⌡To addressee or order

1   *class postage prepaid.*        *Postmaster, per*        JBL

**********

43

Letter ⎱ No. **3663**
~~Parcel~~ ⎰

P. O.,                Shawnee Okla

Received for registration        5/5        191 4   from                Shawnee

Indian Agency

addressed to                Frank Pas-ka-wee

Miami Okla

Receipt desired        ✓Delivery restricted   ⎰To addressee in person
                                              ⎱To addressee or order

1    class postage prepaid.        Postmaster, per        JBL

\*\*\*\*\*\*\*\*\*\*

Letter ⎱ No. **3664**
~~Parcel~~ ⎰

P. O.,                Shawnee  Okla

Received for registration        5/5        191 4   from                Shawnee

Indian Agency

addressed to                Mrs Sallie Moxley

Miami Okla

Receipt desired        ✓Delivery restricted   ⎰To addressee in person
                                              ⎱To addressee or order

1    class postage prepaid.        Postmaster, per        [Name Illegible]

\*\*\*\*\*\*\*\*\*\*

Letter ⎱ No. **3665**
~~Parcel~~ ⎰

P. O.,                Shawnee Ok

Received for registration        5/5        191 4   from                Shawnee

Indian Agency

addressed to                Susie Walker

Hammon

Receipt desired        ✓Delivery restricted   ⎰To addressee in person
                                              ⎱To addressee or order

1    class postage prepaid.        Postmaster, per        JBL

\*\*\*\*\*\*\*\*\*\*

44

Sac & Fox – Shawnee Estates
1911-1919   Volume VI

Letter
Parcel } No. **3666**                          P. O.,              Shawnee Okla
*Received for registration*     5/5        191 4   *from*         Shawnee
                         Indian Agency

*addressed to*          Sherman Walker
                         Hammon Okla

                                    ⌠To addressee in person
*Receipt desired*  ✓*Delivery restricted* ⌡To addressee or order

  1   *class postage prepaid.*        *Postmaster, per*       JBL

**********

Letter
Parcel } No. **3700**                          P. O.,              Shawnee, Okla.
*Received for registration*     5/7        191 4   *from*         Shawnee
                         Ind Agy

*addressed to*       Minot Jackson
                         Powhattan Kans

                                    ⌠To addressee in person
*Receipt desired*  ✓*Delivery restricted* ⌡To addressee or order

  1   *class postage prepaid.*        *Postmaster, per*       JBL

**********

Letter
Parcel } No. **3701**                          P. O.,              Shawnee, Okla.
*Received for registration*     5/7        191 4   *from*         Shawnee
                         Ind Agy

*addressed to*    Stephen Ne-gahn-quit
                         Trousdale Okla

                                    ⌠To addressee in person
*Receipt desired*     *Delivery restricted* ⌡To addressee or order

  1   *class postage prepaid.*        *Postmaster, per*       JBL

**********

45

Sac & Fox – Shawnee Estates
1911-1919   Volume VI

Letter ⎫
Parcel ⎰ No. **3702**                          P. O.,          Shawnee, Okla

*Received for registration*   5/7      191 4   *from*        Shawnee
                                    Ind Agy

*addressed to*       Joe Moose
                                    Sacred Heart Okla

                                    ⎧ *To addressee in person*
*Receipt desired*   ✓*Delivery restricted*  ⎨ *To addressee or order*

   1   *class postage prepaid.*      *Postmaster, per*          JBL

**********

Letter ⎫
~~Parcel~~ ⎰ No. **3697**                        P. O.,          Shawnee, Okla

*Received for registration*   5/7      191 4   *from*        Shawnee
                                    Ind Agy

*addressed to*       Louise Sacto
                                    Mayetta Kans

                                    ⎧ *To addressee in person*
*Receipt desired*   ✓*Delivery restricted*  ⎨ *To addressee or order*

   1   *class postage prepaid.*      *Postmaster, per*          JBL

**********

Letter ⎫
~~Parcel~~ ⎰ No. **3698**                        P. O.,          Shawnee, Okla

*Received for registration*   5/7      191 4   *from*        Shawnee
                                    Ind Agy

*addressed to*       Me-nah-nee Quackee
                                    Mayetta Kans

                                    ⎧ *To addressee in person*
*Receipt desired*   ✓*Delivery restricted*  ⎨ *To addressee or order*

   1   *class postage prepaid.*      *Postmaster, per*          JBL

**********

46

Letter ⎱
~~Parcel~~ ⎰ *No.* **3699**                    *P. O.,*        Shawnee, Okla

*Received for registration*        5/7          191 4    *from*            Shawnee

Ind Agy

*addressed to*          Jimmie  Jackson

Powhattan Kans

*Receipt desired*   ✓ *Delivery restricted*   ⎰ *To addressee in person*
⎱ *To addressee or order*

1   *class postage prepaid.*          *Postmaster, per*          JBL

**********

Letter ⎱
~~Parcel~~ ⎰ *No.* **4126**                    *P. O.,*          Shawnee  Okla

*Received for registration*        6/19         191 4    *from*

Shawnee Indian Agency

*addressed to*          Mary Sacto Studyvin

R #2    Miami  Okla

*Receipt desired*        *Delivery restricted*   ⎰ *To addressee in person*
⎱ *To addressee or order*

1   *class postage prepaid.*          *Postmaster, per*          WJN

**********

Letter ⎱
~~Parcel~~ ⎰ *No.* **4152**                    *P. O.,*          Shawnee Ok

*Received for registration*        6/20         191 4    *from*

Shawnee Ind Agency

*addressed to*          O-ke-mah

Bacerac

*Receipt desired*   ✓ *Delivery restricted*   ⎰ *To addressee in person*
⎱ *To addressee or order*

1   *class postage prepaid.*          *Postmaster, per*          [Initials Illegible]

**********

Letter ⎱
~~Parcel~~ ⎰ No. **4153**            P. O.,          Shawnee Ok

*Received for registration*    6/20    191 4   *from*
            Shawnee Indian Agency

*addressed to*                R. Mitchner
                        St Marys Kan

*Receipt desired*   ✓*Delivery restricted*   ⎰To addressee in person
                                            ⎱To addressee or order

 1    *class postage prepaid.*      *Postmaster, per*      [Initials Illegible]

\*\*\*\*\*\*\*\*\*\*

Letter ⎱
~~Parcel~~ ⎰ No. **4154**            P. O.,          Shawnee Okla

*Received for registration*    6/20    191 4   *from*
            Shawnee Indian Agency

*addressed to*      John Grotz
                        Wanette Okla

*Receipt desired*   ✓*Delivery restricted*   ⎰To addressee in person
                                            ⎱To addressee or order

 1    *class postage prepaid.*      *Postmaster, per*      [Initials Illegible]

\*\*\*\*\*\*\*\*\*\*

Letter ⎱
~~Parcel~~ ⎰ No. **4155**            P. O.,          Shawnee Okla

*Received for registration*    6/20    191 4   *from*
            Shawnee Indian Agency

*addressed to*      Martin Shocman
                        Wanette Okla

*Receipt desired*   ✓*Delivery restricted*   ⎰To addressee in person
                                            ⎱To addressee or order

 1    *class postage prepaid.*      *Postmaster, per*      [Initials Illegible]

\*\*\*\*\*\*\*\*\*\*

Letter ⎱
~~Parcel~~ ⎰ *No.* **4156**          **P. O.,**          Shawnee Okl

*Received for registration*   6/20      *191* 4   *from*

Shawnee Indian Agency

*addressed to*                Francis Dimler

St Marys Kans

⎧ *To addressee in person*

*Receipt desired*   √*Delivery restricted*  ⎩*To addressee or order*

1   *class postage prepaid.*        *Postmaster, per*        [Initials Illegible]

**********

Letter ⎱
~~Parcel~~ ⎰ *No.* **4157**          **P. O.,**          Shawnee Okla

*Received for registration*   6/20      *191* 4   *from*

Shawnee Indian Agency

*addressed to*                Mike Dimler

St Mary  Kan

⎧ *To addressee in person*

*Receipt desired*   √*Delivery restricted*  ⎩*To addressee or order*

1   *class postage prepaid.*        *Postmaster, per*        [Initials Illegible]

**********

Letter ⎱
~~Parcel~~ ⎰ *No.* **4144**          **P. O.,**          Shawnee Ok

*Received for registration*   6.20      *191* 4   *from*

Shawnee Indian Agency

*addressed to*        Jennie Ah uh lu

Shawnee Okla

⎧ *To addressee in person*

*Receipt desired*   √*Delivery restricted*  ⎩*To addressee or order*

1   *class postage prepaid.*        *Postmaster, per*        [Initials Illegible]

**********

49

Letter ⎱ No. **4145**
~~Parcel~~ ⎰

P. O.,          Shawnee Ok

*Received for registration*   6/20      191 4   *from*

Shawnee Indian Agency

*addressed to*                Belitha Hood

Shawnee Okla

                                          ⎰ To addressee in person
*Receipt desired*   ✓ *Delivery restricted* ⎱ To addressee or order

1    *class postage prepaid.*       *Postmaster, per*      [Initials Illegible]

**********

Letter ⎱ No. **4146**
~~Parcel~~ ⎰

P. O.,          Shawnee Okla

*Received for registration*   6/20      191 4   *from*

Shawnee Indian Agency

*addressed to*          Nancy Hood

Shawnee Okla

                                          ⎰ To addressee in person
*Receipt desired*   ✓ *Delivery restricted* ⎱ To addressee or order

1    *class postage prepaid.*       *Postmaster, per*      [Initials Illegible]

**********

Letter ⎱ No. **4147**
~~Parcel~~ ⎰

P. O.,          Shawnee Okla

*Received for registration*   6/20      191 4   *from*

Shawnee Indian Agency

*addressed to*          Webster Tyner

Shawnee Okla

                                          ⎰ To addressee in person
*Receipt desired*   ✓ *Delivery restricted* ⎱ To addressee or order

1    *class postage prepaid.*       *Postmaster, per*      [Initials Illegible]

**********

**Letter / Parcel** *No.* **4092**     P. O.,     Shawnee
*Received for registration*   6-18   191 4   *from*
Shawnee Ind. Agcy

*addressed to*   Ellen Bourassa Wiley
Maud Okla

*Receipt desired*  ✓*Delivery restricted*   {To addressee in person
{To addressee or order

1   *class postage prepaid.*     *Postmaster, per*     P

**********

**Letter / Parcel** *No.* **4093**     P. O.,     Shawnee
*Received for registration*   6-18   191 4   *from*
Shawnee Ind. Agcy

*addressed to*   Webster Alford
Lawrence Ks

*Receipt desired*  ✓*Delivery restricted*   {To addressee in person
{To addressee or order

1   *class postage prepaid.*     *Postmaster, per*     P

**********

**Letter / Parcel** *No.* **4094**     P. O.,     Shawnee
*Received for registration*   6/18   191 4   *from*
Shawnee Ind Agcy

*addressed to*   Mary Wam-me-go
Mayetta Kan

*Receipt desired*  ✓*Delivery restricted*   {To addressee in person
{To addressee or order

1   *class postage prepaid.*     *Postmaster, per*     P

**********

Letter ⎱
Parcel ⎰ No. **4095**   P. O.,   Shawnee

Received for registration   6-18   191 4   from
Shawnee Ind. Agcny

addressed to   Kah-dot Pe-mo
Mayetta Ks

Receipt desired   ✓ Delivery restricted   ⎰ To addressee in person
⎱ To addressee or order

1   class postage prepaid.   Postmaster, per   P

\*\*\*\*\*\*\*\*\*\*

Letter ⎱
Parcel ⎰ No. **4096**   P. O.,   Shawnee

Received for registration   6-18   191 4   from
Shawnee Indian Agcy

addressed to   Stephen Negahnquit
Trousdale Ok

Receipt desired   ✓ Delivery restricted   ⎰ To addressee in person
⎱ To addressee or order

1   class postage prepaid.   Postmaster, per   P

\*\*\*\*\*\*\*\*\*\*

Letter ⎱
Parcel ⎰ No. **4097**   P. O.,   Shawnee

Received for registration   6-18   191 4   from
Shawnee Indian Agcy

addressed to   James Blandin
Mayetta Ks

Receipt desired   ✓ Delivery restricted   ⎰ To addressee in person
⎱ To addressee or order

1   class postage prepaid.   Postmaster, per   P

\*\*\*\*\*\*\*\*\*\*

Letter ⎫
~~Parcel~~ ⎬ No. **4098**          P. O.,                Shawnee

*Received for registration*   6-18    191 4   *from*
                    Shawnee Ind Agcy

*addressed to*          F. A. Bourbonnais
                    Mayetta Ks

*Receipt desired*   ✓*Delivery restricted*  ⎰ To addressee in person
                                            ⎱ To addressee or order

  1  *class postage prepaid.*      *Postmaster, per*          P

**********

Letter ⎫
~~Parcel~~ ⎬ No. **4099**          P. O.,                Shawnee

*Received for registration*   6-18    191 4   *from*
                    Shawnee Ind Agcy

*addressed to*          Me-nah-nee
                    Holton  Ks

*Receipt desired*   ✓*Delivery restricted*  ⎰ To addressee in person
                                            ⎱ To addressee or order

  1  *class postage prepaid.*      *Postmaster, per*          P

**********

Letter ⎫
~~Parcel~~ ⎬ No. **4100**          P. O.,                Shawnee

*Received for registration*   6-18    191 4   *from*
                    Shawnee Ind Agcy

*addressed to*          Stephen Negahnquit
                    Trousdale Ok

*Receipt desired*      *Delivery restricted*  ⎰ To addressee in person
                                              ⎱ To addressee or order

  1  *class postage prepaid.*      *Postmaster, per*          P

**********

Letter
Parcel } No. **4101**                         P. O.,                    Shawnee

*Received for registration*    6-18      191 4   *from*

Shawnee Ind Agcy

*addressed to*                          Mary Armstrong

Trousdale

$\begin{cases} \text{\textit{To addressee in person}} \\ \text{\textit{To addressee or order}} \end{cases}$

*Receipt desired*    ✓ *Delivery restricted*

1    *class postage prepaid.*        *Postmaster, per*         P

**********

Letter
Parcel } No. **4102**                         P. O.,                    Shawnee

*Received for registration*    6-18      191 4   *from*

Shawnee Ind Agcy

*addressed to*              Gracie Dewitt

Noble Okla

$\begin{cases} \text{\textit{To addressee in person}} \\ \text{\textit{To addressee or order}} \end{cases}$

*Receipt desired*    ✓ *Delivery restricted*

1    *class postage prepaid.*        *Postmaster, per*         P

**********

Letter
Parcel } No. **4103**                         P. O.,                    Shawnee

*Received for registration*    6-18      191 4   *from*

Shawnee Ind Agcy

*addressed to*          John Bennett

Norman Okla

$\begin{cases} \text{\textit{To addressee in person}} \\ \text{\textit{To addressee or order}} \end{cases}$

*Receipt desired*    ✓ *Delivery restricted*

1    *class postage prepaid.*        *Postmaster, per*         P

**********

Letter
Parcel } No. **4104**          P. O.,          Shawnee

*Received for registration*    6-18      191 4   *from*

Shawnee Ind. Agcy

*addressed to*          G. C. Woodrow

Norman Okla

*Receipt desired*   ✓ *Delivery restricted*   { To addressee in person
                                            { To addressee or order

1   *class postage prepaid.*          *Postmaster, per*          P

\*\*\*\*\*\*\*\*\*\*

Letter
Parcel } No. **4105**          P. O.,          Shawnee

*Received for registration*    6-18      191 4   *from*

Shawnee Ind Agcy

*addressed to*          Robert Bennett

Norman  Okla

*Receipt desired*   *Delivery restricted*   { To addressee in person
                                           { To addressee or order

1   *class postage prepaid.*          *Postmaster, per*          P

\*\*\*\*\*\*\*\*\*\*

Letter
Parcel } No. **4127**          P. O.,          Shawnee

*Received for registration*    6/19      191 4   *from*

Shawnee Indian School

*addressed to*    John Pe-an

Miami Okla

*Receipt desired*   ✓ *Delivery restricted*   { To addressee in person
                                             { To addressee or order

1   *class postage prepaid.*          *Postmaster, per*          [Initials Illegible]

\*\*\*\*\*\*\*\*\*\*

Letter ⎫
Parcel ⎬ No. **4128**                      P. O.,          Shawnee Ok
Received for registration      6/19        191 4   from
Shawnee Indian Agency

addressed to              Stephen Negahnquit
Trousdale  Okla

Receipt desired   ✓Delivery restricted  ⎰To addressee in person
⎱To addressee or order

1   class postage prepaid.      Postmaster, per      [Initials Illegible]

**********

Letter ⎫
Parcel ⎬ No. **4129**                      P. O.,          Shawnee Ok
Received for registration      6/19        191 4   from
Shawnee Indian Agency

addressed to              Agnation Sacto
Miami  Okla

Receipt desired   ✓Delivery restricted  ⎰To addressee in person
⎱To addressee or order

1   class postage prepaid.      Postmaster, per      [Initials Illegible]

**********

Letter ⎫
Parcel ⎬ No. **4130**                      P. O.,          Shawnee Ok
Received for registration      6/19        191 4   from
Shawnee Indian Agency

addressed to              Joe Sacto
Miami Okla

Receipt desired   ✓Delivery restricted  ⎰To addressee in person
⎱To addressee or order

1   class postage prepaid.      Postmaster, per      [Initials Illegible]

**********

Letter ⎱
~~Parcel~~ ⎰ *No.* **4131**　　　　　**P. O.,**　　　Shawnee Ok

*Received for registration* 　6/19　　*191* 4　*from*

Shawnee Indian Agency

*addressed to*　　　　Louise Sacto Bent

Darlington NC

　　　　　　　　　　　⎰ *To addressee in person*
*Receipt desired* 　✓*Delivery restricted* ⎱*To addressee or order*

1　*class postage prepaid.*　　　*Postmaster, per*　　[Initials Illegible]

**********

Letter ⎱
~~Parcel~~ ⎰ *No.* **4132**　　　　　**P. O.,**　　　Shawnee Ok

*Received for registration* 　6/19　　*191* 4　*from*

Shawnee Indian Agency

*addressed to*　　　J V Blandin

Mayetta Kans

　　　　　　　　　　　⎰ *To addressee in person*
*Receipt desired* 　✓*Delivery restricted* ⎱*To addressee or order*

1　*class postage prepaid.*　　　*Postmaster, per*　　[Initials Illegible]

**********

Letter ⎱
~~Parcel~~ ⎰ *No.* **4133**　　　　　**P. O.,**　　　Shawnee Ok

*Received for registration* 　6/19　　*191* 4　*from*

Shawnee Indian Agency

*addressed to*　　　Joe Moose

Sacred Heart Okla

　　　　　　　　　　　⎰ *To addressee in person*
*Receipt desired* 　✓*Delivery restricted* ⎱*To addressee or order*

1　*class postage prepaid.*　　　*Postmaster, per*　　[Initials Illegible]

**********

Letter ⎱ No. **4106**
Parcel ⎰

P. O.,                Shawnee

Received for registration        6-18        191 4   from

Shawnee Ind Agcy

addressed to              Rachel Hale

Shawnee Okla

Receipt desired    ✓Delivery restricted   ⎰To addressee in person
                                            ⎱To addressee or order

1    class postage prepaid.        Postmaster, per        P

\*\*\*\*\*\*\*\*\*\*

Letter ⎱ No. **4107**
Parcel ⎰

P. O.,                Shawnee

Received for registration        6-18        191 4   from

Shawnee Ind Agcy

addressed to              J V Blandin

Mayetta Ks

Receipt desired    ✓Delivery restricted   ⎰To addressee in person
                                            ⎱To addressee or order

1    class postage prepaid.        Postmaster, per        P

\*\*\*\*\*\*\*\*\*\*

Letter ⎱ No. **4108**
Parcel ⎰

P. O.,                Shawnee

Received for registration        6-18        191 4   from

Shawnee Ind Agcy

addressed to              Nancy Hood

Shawnee Okla

Receipt desired    ✓Delivery restricted   ⎰To addressee in person
                                            ⎱To addressee or order

1    class postage prepaid.        Postmaster, per        P

\*\*\*\*\*\*\*\*\*\*

Letter ⎫
~~Parcel~~ ⎬ No. **4109**          **P. O.,**          Shawnee
*Received for registration*   6-18      191 4   *from*
                Shawnee Ind. Agcy

*addressed to*          Jennie Charley
                Shawnee Okla

                                    ⎧ To addressee in person
*Receipt desired*   ✓ *Delivery restricted* ⎨ To addressee or order

1   *class postage prepaid.*          *Postmaster, per*          P

**********

Letter ⎫
~~Parcel~~ ⎬ No. **4110**          **P. O.,**          Shawnee
*Received for registration*   6-18      191 4   *from*
                Shawnee Ind Agcy

*addressed to*          Annie Sampson
                Shawnee Okla

                                    ⎧ To addressee in person
*Receipt desired*      *Delivery restricted* ⎨ To addressee or order

1   *class postage prepaid.*          *Postmaster, per*          P

**********

Letter ⎫
~~Parcel~~ ⎬ No. **4111**          **P. O.,**          Shawnee
*Received for registration*   6-18      191 4   *from*
                Shawnee Ind. Agcy

*addressed to*          Nancy Wilson
                Shawnee Okla

                                    ⎧ To addressee in person
*Receipt desired*   ✓ *Delivery restricted* ⎨ To addressee or order

1   *class postage prepaid.*          *Postmaster, per*          P

**********

59

Letter ⎱
~~Parcel~~ ⎰ *No.* **4171**                                          P. O.,                    Shawnee

*Received for registration*      6/22          191 4    *from*

                    Shawnee Indian Agcy

*addressed to*                      Joseph Op-tos-ke

                          Sacred Heart Okla

                                                      ⎧ *To addressee in person*
*Receipt desired*      √ *Delivery restricted*  ⎨ *To addressee or order*

    1    *class postage prepaid.*              *Postmaster, per*              [Initials Illegible]

**********

Letter ⎱
~~Parcel~~ ⎰ *No.* **4172**                                          P. O.,                    Shawnee Ok

*Received for registration*      6/22          191 4    *from*

                    Shawnee Indian Agency

*addressed to*                      Joseph Op-tos-ke

                          Sacred Heart Ok

                                                      ⎧ *To addressee in person*
*Receipt desired*      √ *Delivery restricted*  ⎨ *To addressee or order*

    1    *class postage prepaid.*              *Postmaster, per*              [Initials Illegible]

**********

Letter ⎱
~~Parcel~~ ⎰ *No.* **3567**                                          P. O.,                    Shawnee, Okla

*Received for registration*      4-28          191 4    *from*

                    Shawnee Indian Agency

*addressed to*                      James Burnett

                          Sacred Heart Okla

                                                      ⎧ *To addressee in person*
*Receipt desired*        *Delivery restricted*  ⎨ *To addressee or order*

    1    *class postage prepaid.*              *Postmaster, per*              P

**********

**Letter**
~~Parcel~~ } *No.* **3568**　　　　　　　　**P. O.,**　　Shawnee, Okla.

*Received for registration*　4-28　　191 4　*from*
　　　　Shawnee Indian Agency

*addressed to*　　　　Nack-nach-tuck
　　　　　　　　Sacred Heart Okla

　　　　　　　　　　　{ *To addressee in person*
*Receipt desired*　　*Delivery restricted* { *To addressee or order*

　1　*class postage prepaid.*　　*Postmaster, per*　　　P

**********

**Letter**
~~Parcel~~ } *No.* **3569**　　　　　　　　**P. O.,**　　Shawnee, Okla.

*Received for registration*　4-28　　191 4　*from*
　　　　Shawnee Indian Agency

*addressed to*　　　Peter Curley
　　　　　　　　Sacred Heart Okla

　　　　　　　　　　　{ *To addressee in person*
*Receipt desired*　　*Delivery restricted* { *To addressee or order*

　1　*class postage prepaid.*　　*Postmaster, per*　　　P

**********

**Letter**
~~Parcel~~ } *No.* **3570**　　　　　　　　**P. O.,**　　Shawnee, Okla.

*Received for registration*　4-28　　191 4　*from*
　　　　Shawnee Indian Agency

*addressed to*　　　Ellen Rhodd
　　　　　　　　Konawa Okla

　　　　　　　　　　　{ *To addressee in person*
*Receipt desired*　　*Delivery restricted* { *To addressee or order*

　1　*class postage prepaid.*　　*Postmaster, per*　　　P

**********

Letter ⎱ No. **3571**
Parcel ⎰

P. O., Shawnee, Okla

*Received for registration*   4-28   *191* 4   *from*

Shawnee Indian Agency

*addressed to*   Fannie Mayberry or Canalis

Pawhuska  Okla

*Receipt desired*   *Delivery restricted* ⎰ To addressee in person
⎱ To addressee or order

1   *class postage prepaid.*   *Postmaster, per*   P

\*\*\*\*\*\*\*\*\*\*

Letter ⎱ No. **3572**
Parcel ⎰

P. O., Shawnee, Okla.

*Received for registration*   4-28   *191* 4   *from*

Shawnee Indian Agency

*addressed to*   Joel Delonais

Pawhuska  Okla

*Receipt desired*   *Delivery restricted* ⎰ To addressee in person
⎱ To addressee or order

1   *class postage prepaid.*   *Postmaster, per*   P

\*\*\*\*\*\*\*\*\*\*

Letter ⎱ No. **3573**
Parcel ⎰

P. O., Shawnee, Okla

*Received for registration*   4-28   *191* 4   *from*

Shawnee Indian Agency

*addressed to*   Adam Pappan

Newkirk  Okla

*Receipt desired*   *Delivery restricted* ⎰ To addressee in person
⎱ To addressee or order

1   *class postage prepaid.*   *Postmaster, per*   P

\*\*\*\*\*\*\*\*\*\*

Letter ⎱
~~Parcel~~ ⎰ No. **3574**                        P. O.,          Shawnee, Okla.

*Received for registration*      4-28        191 4   *from*
                    Shawnee Indian Agency

*addressed to*              Andrew Curley
                              Kaw Okla

⎧ To addressee in person
*Receipt desired*      *Delivery restricted* ⎨ To addressee or order

   1    *class postage prepaid.*            *Postmaster, per*            P

\*\*\*\*\*\*\*\*\*\*

Letter ⎱
~~Parcel~~ ⎰ No. **3575**                        P. O.,        Shawnee, Okla.

*Received for registration*      4-28        191 4   *from*
                    Shawnee Indian Agency

*addressed to*              Antoine Burnett
                              Pawhuska  Okla

⎧ To addressee in person
*Receipt desired*      *Delivery restricted* ⎨ To addressee or order

   1    *class postage prepaid.*            *Postmaster, per*            P

\*\*\*\*\*\*\*\*\*\*

Letter ⎱
~~Parcel~~ ⎰ No. **3576**                        P. O.,        Shawnee, Okla.

*Received for registration*      4-28        191 4   *from*
                    Shawnee Indian Agency

*addressed to*              Carl Ogee
                              Pocatello Ida

⎧ To addressee in person
*Receipt desired*      *Delivery restricted* ⎨ To addressee or order

   1    *class postage prepaid.*            *Postmaster, per*            P

\*\*\*\*\*\*\*\*\*\*

Letter ⎫
Parcel ⎰ No. 3560          P. O.,          Shawnee, Okla.

*Received for registration*     4-28     191 4   *from*

Shawnee Indian Agency

*addressed to*              Steve  Ne-gahn-quit

Trousdale Okla

*Receipt desired*     *Delivery restricted* ⎰ To addressee in person
                                           ⎱ To addressee or order

1   *class postage prepaid.*     *Postmaster, per*          P

**********

Letter ⎫
Parcel ⎰ No. 3561          P. O.,          Shawnee, Okla.

*Received for registration*     4-28     191 4   *from*

Shawnee Indian Agency

*addressed to*              James Acton

Trousdale Okla

*Receipt desired*     *Delivery restricted* ⎰ To addressee in person
                                           ⎱ To addressee or order

1   *class postage prepaid.*     *Postmaster, per*          P

**********

Letter ⎫
Parcel ⎰ No. 3562          P. O.,          Shawnee, Okla.

*Received for registration*     4-28     191 4   *from*

Shawnee Indian Agency

*addressed to*              Steve Negahnquit

Trousdale Okla

*Receipt desired*     *Delivery restricted* ⎰ To addressee in person
                                           ⎱ To addressee or order

1   *class postage prepaid.*     *Postmaster, per*          P

**********

Letter
~~Parcel~~ } *No.* 3563                          **P. O.,**            Shawnee, Okla.

*Received for registration*      4-28      191 4   *from*          Shawnee
                        ~~Joseph Rhodd~~                  Indian Agency

*addressed to*                          Joseph Rhodd
                            Sacred Heart Okla

                                          ⌠ *To addressee in person*
*Receipt desired*      *Delivery restricted* ⌡ *To addressee or order*

1   *class postage prepaid.*              *Postmaster, per*              P

**********

Letter
~~Parcel~~ } *No.* 3564                          **P. O.,**            Shawnee, Okla.

*Received for registration*      4-28      191 4   *from*
                  Shawnee Indian Agency

*addressed to*                          Joseph Moose
                            Sacred Heart   Okla

                                          ⌠ *To addressee in person*
*Receipt desired*      *Delivery restricted* ⌡ *To addressee or order*

1   *class postage prepaid.*              *Postmaster, per*              P

**********

Letter
~~Parcel~~ } *No.* 3565                          **P. O.,**            Shawnee, Okla.

*Received for registration*      4-28      191 4   *from*
                  Shawnee Indian Agency

*addressed to*                          Mary Acton
                            Sacred Heart Okla

                                          ⌠ *To addressee in person*
*Receipt desired*      *Delivery restricted* ⌡ *To addressee or order*

1   *class postage prepaid.*              *Postmaster, per*              P

**********

Letter ⎱
Parcel ⎰ No. **3566**          P. O.,          Shawnee, Okla

Received for registration          4-28          191 4   from

Shawnee Indian Agency

addressed to                    John B Bruno

Sacred Heart  Okla

⎧ To addressee in person

Receipt desired          Delivery restricted  ⎨ To addressee or order

1    class postage prepaid.          Postmaster, per          P

**********

Letter ⎱
Parcel ⎰ No. **3350**          P. O.,          Shawnee Okla

Received for registration          4-11          191 4   from

Shawnee Indian Agency

addressed to                    W. M. Moutaw

Lexington  Okla

⎧ To addressee in person

Receipt desired          Delivery restricted  ⎨ To addressee or order

1    class postage prepaid.          Postmaster, per          [Initials Illegible]

**********

Letter ⎱
Parcel ⎰ No. **3351**          P. O.,          Shawnee Okla

Received for registration          4-11          191 4   from

Shawnee Indian Agency

addressed to                    W^m H Clark

Cleveland Okla

⎧ To addressee in person

Receipt desired          Delivery restricted  ⎨ To addressee or order

1    class postage prepaid.          Postmaster, per          [Initials Illegible]

**********

**Letter**
~~Parcel~~ ∫ *No.* 3352                      **P. O.,**          Shawnee Okla
*Received for registration*   4-11     *191* 4   *from*
                     Shawnee Indian Agency

*addressed to*                    L. B. Higbee
                              Lexington  Okla

                              ⌠*To addressee in person*
*Receipt desired*      *Delivery restricted* ⌡*To addressee or order*

1   *class postage prepaid.*        *Postmaster, per*      [Initials Illegible]

**********

**Letter**
~~Parcel~~ ∫ *No.* 3353                      **P. O.,**          Shawnee Okla
*Received for registration*   4-11     *191* 4   *from*
                     Shawnee Indian Agency

*addressed to*          Laura Bertrand Patrick
                              Roswell  N. Mex

                              ⌠*To addressee in person*
*Receipt desired*      *Delivery restricted* ⌡*To addressee or order*

1   *class postage prepaid.*        *Postmaster, per*      [Initials Illegible]

**********

**Letter**
~~Parcel~~ ∫ *No.* 3354                      **P. O.,**          Shawnee Okla
*Received for registration*   4-11     *191* 4   *from*
                     Shawnee Indian Agency

*addressed to*              Lucy Cruse
                              Roswell N. Mex

                              ⌠*To addressee in person*
*Receipt desired*      *Delivery restricted* ⌡*To addressee or order*

1   *class postage prepaid.*        *Postmaster, per*      [Initials Illegible]

**********

Letter ⎱
~~Parcel~~ ⎰ No. **3355**    **P. O.,**    Shawnee Okla

*Received for registration*    3[sic]-11    191 4    *from*

Shawnee Indian Agency

*addressed to*    Geo E Carpenter

Lexington Okl

*Receipt desired*    *Delivery restricted*    ⎰ To addressee in person
⎱ To addressee or order

1    *class postage prepaid.*    *Postmaster, per*    [Initials Illegible]

**********

Letter ⎱
~~Parcel~~ ⎰ No. **3356**    **P. O.,**    Shawnee Okla

*Received for registration*    4-11    191 4    *from*

Shawnee Indian Agency

*addressed to*    Peter WASHINGTON

Shawnee Okl

*Receipt desired*    *Delivery restricted*    ⎰ To addressee in person
⎱ To addressee or order

1    *class postage prepaid.*    *Postmaster, per*    [Initials Illegible]

**********

Letter ⎱
~~Parcel~~ ⎰ No. **3385**    **P. O.,**    Shawnee Okla

*Received for registration*    4-15    191 4    *from*

Shawnee Indian Agency

*addressed to*    Mrs Emily Holloway

Wanette  Okla

*Receipt desired*    *Delivery restricted*    ⎰ To addressee in person
⎱ To addressee or order

1    *class postage prepaid.*    *Postmaster, per*    P

**********

Letter ⎱
Parcel ⎰ No. 3386                       P. O.,                Shawnee, Okla.

Received for registration     4-15        191 4   from
                 Shawnee Indian Agency

addressed to                    Ben Beaubien
                              Wanette Okla
                                  ⎧ To addressee in person
Receipt desired        Delivery restricted  ⎩ To addressee or order

1   class postage prepaid.              Postmaster, per           P

**********

Letter ⎱
Parcel ⎰ No. 3387                       P. O.,                Shawnee, Okla.

Received for registration     4-15        191 4   from
                 Shawnee Indian Agency

addressed to                  Eliza Beaubien
                              Wanette  Okla
                                  ⎧ To addressee in person
Receipt desired        Delivery restricted  ⎩ To addressee or order

1   class postage prepaid.              Postmaster, per           P

**********

Letter ⎱
Parcel ⎰ No. 3388                       P. O.,                Shawnee, Okla.

Received for registration     4-15        191 4   from
                 Shawnee Indian Agency

addressed to                  John B. Beaubien
                              M^cComb  Okla
                                  ⎧ To addressee in person
Receipt desired        Delivery restricted  ⎩ To addressee or order

1   class postage prepaid.              Postmaster, per           P

**********

Letter ⎱
Parcel ⎰ *No.* **3389**　　　　　　　　　P. O.,　　　Shawnee, Okla.

*Received for registration*　　4-15　　191 4　*from*
　　　　　　　　Shawnee Indian Agency

*addressed to*　　　　　Mrs W C Boyer
　　　　　　　　　Purcell  Okla

　　　　　　　　　　　　⎧*To addressee in person*
*Receipt desired*　　*Delivery restricted* ⎩*To addressee or order*

　1　*class postage prepaid.*　　*Postmaster, per*　　　P

**********

Letter ⎱
Parcel ⎰ *No.* **3390**　　　　　　　　　P. O.,　　　Shawnee, Okla.

*Received for registration*　　4-14　　191 4　*from*
　　　　　　　　Shawnee Indian Agency

*addressed to*　　　　　Henrietta A Clark
　　　　　　　　　Los Angeles Calif

　　　　　　　　　　　　⎧*To addressee in person*
*Receipt desired*　　*Delivery restricted* ⎩*To addressee or order*

　1　*class postage prepaid.*　　*Postmaster, per*　　　P

**********

Letter ⎱
Parcel ⎰ *No.* **3391**　　　　　　　Shawnee, Okla.　P. O.,

*Received for registration*　　4-15　　191 4　*from*
　　　　　　　　Shawnee Indian Agency

*addressed to*　　　　　George Butler
　　　　　　　　　Stroud  Okla

　　　　　　　　　　　　⎧*To addressee in person*
*Receipt desired*　　*Delivery restricted* ⎩*To addressee or order*

　1　*class postage prepaid.*　　*Postmaster, per*　　　P

**********

Letter ⎤
Parcel ⎰ No. **3392**          P. O.,          Shawnee, Okla.
Received for registration     4-15     191 4   from
Shawnee Indian Agency

addressed to          Edward Fox
Carlisle Penn

⎧ To addressee in person
Receipt desired     Delivery restricted ⎩ To addressee or order

1   class postage prepaid.          Postmaster, per          P

**********

Letter ⎤
Parcel ⎰ No. **3393**          P. O.,          Shawnee, Okla.
Received for registration     4-14     191 4   from
Shawnee Indian Agency

addressed to          W H True
St Marys Kans

⎧ To addressee in person
Receipt desired     Delivery restricted ⎩ To addressee or order

1   class postage prepaid.          Postmaster, per          P

**********

Letter ⎤
Parcel ⎰ No. **3394**          P. O.,          Shawnee, Okla.
Received for registration     4-15     191 4   from
Shawnee Indian Agency

addressed to          Edward Butler
Stroud Okla

⎧ To addressee in person
Receipt desired     Delivery restricted ⎩ To addressee or order

1   class postage prepaid.          Postmaster, per          P

**********

Letter ⎱ No. **3395**
~~Parcel~~ ⎰

P. O.,                          Shawnee, Okla.

*Received for registration*     4-15     191 4   *from*

Shawnee Indian Agency

*addressed to*                 Riley Hood

Shawnee Okla

*Receipt desired*     *Delivery restricted* ⎰ *To addressee in person*
⎱ *To addressee or order*

1   *class postage prepaid.*     *Postmaster, per*          P

**********

Letter ⎱ No. **3396**
~~Parcel~~ ⎰

P. O.,                          Shawnee, Okla.

*Received for registration*     4-15     191 4   *from*

Shawnee Indian Agency

*addressed to*                 Belithia Hood

Shawnee

*Receipt desired*     *Delivery restricted* ⎰ *To addressee in person*
⎱ *To addressee or order*

1   *class postage prepaid.*     *Postmaster, per*          P

**********

Letter ⎱ No. **3397**
~~Parcel~~ ⎰

P. O.,

*Received for registration*     4-15     191 4   *from*

Shawnee Indian Agency

*addressed to*                 Jim Bobb Jr

Waynona[sic] Okla

*Receipt desired*     *Delivery restricted* ⎰ *To addressee in person*
⎱ *To addressee or order*

1   *class postage prepaid.*     *Postmaster, per*          P

**********

Letter }
Parcel } No. 3398                          P. O.,                    Shawnee, Okla.
Received for registration      4-15        191 4    from
                    Shawnee Indian Agency

addressed to                   Hah-mah-com-se
                                Ft. Cobb  Ok
                                    ⌠To addressee in person
Receipt desired      Delivery restricted  ⌡To addressee or order

1   class postage prepaid.          Postmaster, per              P


**********

Letter }
Parcel } No. 3434                          P. O.,                  Shawnee, Okla.
Received for registration      4-16        191 4    from
                    Shawnee Indian Agency

addressed to                   Mrs Julia Bourassa
                                Tecumseh Kans
                                    ⌠To addressee in person
Receipt desired      Delivery restricted  ⌡To addressee or order

1   class postage prepaid.          Postmaster, per              P


**********

Letter }
Parcel } No. 3435                          P. O.,              Shawnee, Okla.
Received for registration      4-16        191 4    from
                    Shawnee Indian Agency

addressed to                   A Bourassa
                                Tecumseh Okla
                                    ⌠To addressee in person
Receipt desired      Delivery restricted  ⌡To addressee or order

1   class postage prepaid.          Postmaster, per              P


**********


73

**Letter**
~~Parcel~~ ⌠ No. 3436                    P. O.,                    Shawnee, Okla.

*Received for registration*     4-16     191 4   *from*
Shawnee Indian Agency

*addressed to*                    Priscilla T Bayliss
Ossawottomie[sic] Kans

⌠To addressee in person
*Receipt desired*     *Delivery restricted* ⌊To addressee or order

1   *class postage prepaid.*          *Postmaster, per*          P

\*\*\*\*\*\*\*\*\*\*

**Letter**
~~Parcel~~ ⌠ No. 3437                    P. O.,                    Shawnee, Okla.

*Received for registration*     4-16     191 4   *from*
Shawnee Indian Agency

*addressed to*                    Mrs Jennie Best
Sedalia        Mo

⌠To addressee in person
*Receipt desired*     *Delivery restricted* ⌊To addressee or order

1   *class postage prepaid.*          *Postmaster, per*          P

\*\*\*\*\*\*\*\*\*\*

**Letter**
~~Parcel~~ ⌠ No. 3438                    P. O.,                    Shawnee, Okla.

*Received for registration*     4-16     191 4   *from*
Shawnee Indian Agency

*addressed to*                    Frank A Bourbonnais
Delia  Kans

⌠To addressee in person
*Receipt desired*     *Delivery restricted* ⌊To addressee or order

1   *class postage prepaid.*          *Postmaster, per*          P

\*\*\*\*\*\*\*\*\*\*

Letter }
Parcel } *No.* **3439**                     *P. O.,*        Shawnee, Okla.

*Received for registration*        4-16        *191* 4   *from*

Shawnee Indian Agency

*addressed to*                     Idlewild R Hutton

St Louis Mo

                                  { *To addressee in person*
*Receipt desired*        *Delivery restricted*  { *To addressee or order*

1    *class postage prepaid.*          *Postmaster, per*          P

**********

Letter }
Parcel } *No.* **3440**                     *P. O.,*        Shawnee, Okla.

*Received for registration*        4-16        *191* 4   *from*

Shawnee Indian Agency

*addressed to*                     John Pawdosh

Sacred Heart Okla

                                  { *To addressee in person*
*Receipt desired*        *Delivery restricted*  { *To addressee or order*

1    *class postage prepaid.*          *Postmaster, per*          P

**********

Letter }
Parcel } *No.* **3427**                     *P. O.,*        Shawnee, Okla.

*Received for registration*        4-16        *191* 4   *from*

Shawnee Indian Agency

*addressed to*                     Quaty Tyner

Skiatook  Okla

                                  { *To addressee in person*
*Receipt desired*        *Delivery restricted*  { *To addressee or order*

1    *class postage prepaid.*          *Postmaster, per*          P

**********

Letter
~~Parcel~~ } *No.* 3428                    **P. O.,**        Shawnee, Okla.

*Received for registration*    4-16    191 4    *from*

Shawnee Indian Agency

*addressed to*                          Billie WASHINGTON

Skiatook Okla

                             ⎰ *To addressee in person*

*Receipt desired*    *Delivery restricted* ⎱ *To addressee or order*

   1    *class postage prepaid.*        *Postmaster, per*        P

\*\*\*\*\*\*\*\*\*\*

Letter
~~Parcel~~ } *No.* 3429                    **P. O.,**        Shawnee, Okla.

*Received for registration*    4-16    191 4    *from*

Shawnee Indian Agency

*addressed to*                          John Bourassa

Mekusukey[sic]  Okla

                             ⎰ *To addressee in person*

*Receipt desired*    *Delivery restricted* ⎱ *To addressee or order*

   1    *class postage prepaid.*        *Postmaster, per*        P

\*\*\*\*\*\*\*\*\*\*

Letter
~~Parcel~~ } *No.* 3430                    **P. O.,**        Shawnee, Okla.

*Received for registration*    4-16    191 4    *from*

Shawnee Indian Agency

*addressed to*                          Maggie Bourassa

Mekusukey  Okla

                             ⎰ *To addressee in person*

*Receipt desired*    *Delivery restricted* ⎱ *To addressee or order*

   1    *class postage prepaid.*        *Postmaster, per*        P

\*\*\*\*\*\*\*\*\*\*

Letter ⎤
Parcel ⎦ *No.* **3431**                          **P. O.,**        Shawnee, Okla.

*Received for registration*        4-16        191 4   *from*

Shawnee Indian Agency

*addressed to*                        S H Vinson

Mekusukey  Okla

⎧ *To addressee in person*
*Receipt desired*        *Delivery restricted* ⎩ *To addressee or order*

1   *class postage prepaid.*                *Postmaster, per*              P

**********

Letter ⎤
Parcel ⎦ *No.* **3432**                          **P. O.,**        Shawnee, Okla.

*Received for registration*        4-16        191 4   *from*

Shawnee Indian Agency

*addressed to*                        Anna Tucker

Sperry  Okla

⎧ *To addressee in person*
*Receipt desired*        *Delivery restricted* ⎩ *To addressee or order*

1   *class postage prepaid.*                *Postmaster, per*              P

**********

Letter ⎤
Parcel ⎦ *No.* **3433**                          **P. O.,**        Shawnee, Okla.

*Received for registration*        4-16        191 4   *from*

Shawnee Indian Agency

*addressed to*                        Sam Charley

Tulsa Okla

⎧ *To addressee in person*
*Receipt desired*        *Delivery restricted* ⎩ *To addressee or order*

1   *class postage prepaid.*                *Postmaster, per*              P

**********

Letter ⎫
~~Parcel~~ ⎬ No. **3420**          P. O.,                    Shawnee, Okla.

Received for registration      4-16      191 4   from

Shawnee Indian Agency

addressed to                  Cyrus W Bayliss

Maud Okla

⎧ To addressee in person

Receipt desired     Delivery restricted  ⎨ To addressee or order

1   class postage prepaid.       Postmaster, per        P

**********

Letter ⎫
~~Parcel~~ ⎬ No. **3421**          P. O.,                    Shawnee, Okla.

Received for registration      4-16      191 4   from

Shawnee Indian Agency

addressed to          ~~Maud Okla~~        Henry Cummings

Maud  Okla

⎧ To addressee in person

Receipt desired     Delivery restricted  ⎨ To addressee or order

1   class postage prepaid.       Postmaster, per        P

**********

Letter ⎫
~~Parcel~~ ⎬ No. **3422**          P. O.,                    Shawnee, Okla.

Received for registration      4-16      191 4   from

Shawnee Indian Agency

addressed to                  Laura I Nadeau

Maud Okla

⎧ To addressee in person

Receipt desired     Delivery restricted  ⎨ To addressee or order

1   class postage prepaid.       Postmaster, per        P

**********

Letter ⎱
Parcel ⎰ No. **3423**                    P. O.,            Shawnee, Okla.

Received for registration      4-16      191 4   from

Shawnee Indian Agency

addressed to                    Andrew Cummings

Maud Okla

                              ⎰ To addressee in person
Receipt desired      Delivery restricted  ⎱ To addressee or order

1   class postage prepaid.          Postmaster, per            P

**********

Letter ⎱
Parcel ⎰ No. **3424**                    P. O.,            Shawnee, Okla.

Received for registration      4-16      191 4   from

Shawnee Indian Agency

addressed to                    Hiram Thorpe

Stroud  Okla

                              ⎰ To addressee in person
Receipt desired      Delivery restricted  ⎱ To addressee or order

1   class postage prepaid.          Postmaster, per            P

**********

Letter ⎱
Parcel ⎰ No. **3425**                    P. O.,            Shawnee, Okla.

Received for registration      4-16      191 4   from

Shawnee Indian Agency

addressed to                    Daniel O'Bright

Oklahoma   Okla

                              ⎰ To addressee in person
Receipt desired      Delivery restricted  ⎱ To addressee or order

1   class postage prepaid.          Postmaster, per            P

**********

Letter ⎱
~~Parcel~~ ⎰ No. **3426**    P. O.,    Shawnee, Okla.

*Received for registration*    4-16    191 4    *from*

Shawnee Indian Agency

*addressed to*    Elie Squirrel

Skiatook Okla

⎰ To addressee in person
*Receipt desired*    *Delivery restricted* ⎱ To addressee or order

1    *class postage prepaid.*    *Postmaster, per*    P

**********

Letter ⎱
~~Parcel~~ ⎰ No. **3399**    P. O.,    Shawnee, Okla.

*Received for registration*    4-15    191 4    *from*

Shawnee Indian Agency

*addressed to*    Arch Armstrong

St Marys Kans

⎰ To addressee in person
*Receipt desired*    *Delivery restricted* ⎱ To addressee or order

1    *class postage prepaid.*    *Postmaster, per*    P

**********

Letter ⎱
~~Parcel~~ ⎰ No. **3400**    P. O.,    Shawnee, Okla.

*Received for registration*    4-15    191 4    *from*

Shawnee Indian Agency

*addressed to*    W H Collister

27th & Jackson    Kansas City, Mo

⎰ To addressee in person
*Receipt desired*    *Delivery restricted* ⎱ To addressee or order

1    *class postage prepaid.*    *Postmaster, per*    P

**********

Sac & Fox – Shawnee Estates
1911-1919   Volume VI

**Letter**
~~Parcel~~ } *No.* **3304**                P. O.,            Shawnee  Okla
*Received for registration*        4/8        191 4   *from*
                    Shawnee Indian Agency

*addressed to*                    Ph[?]le[?]  Cu[?]illan
                             Cushing  Okla

*Receipt desired*  ✓ *Delivery restricted* { *To addressee in person*
                                            { *To addressee or order*

   1   *class postage prepaid.*        *Postmaster, per*      [Initials Illegible]

**********

**Letter**
~~Parcel~~ } *No.* **3305**                P. O.,            Shawnee  Okla
*Received for registration*        4/8        191 4   *from*
                    Shawnee Indian Agency

*addressed to*              Frank Sh[??]as
                             Cushing  Okla

*Receipt desired*  ✓ *Delivery restricted* { *To addressee in person*
                                            { *To addressee or order*

   1   *class postage prepaid.*        *Postmaster, per*      [Initials Illegible]

**********

**Letter**
~~Parcel~~ } *No.* **3287**                P. O.,            Shawnee  Okla
*Received for registration*        4/7        191 4   *from*
                    Shawnee Indian Agency

*addressed to*              Daley Daggle
                             Wanette Okla

*Receipt desired*  ✓ *Delivery restricted* { *To addressee in person*
                                            { *To addressee or order*

   1   *class postage prepaid.*        *Postmaster, per*      [Initials Illegible]

**********

Letter ⎫
Parcel ⎰ *No.* 3288    **P. O.,**    Shawnee  Okla

*Received for registration*    4/7    *191* 4    *from*

Shawnee Indian Agency

*addressed to*    Della Slavin

Lexington  Okla

⎧ *To addressee in person*
*Receipt desired*    ╱*Delivery restricted*  ⎨ *To addressee or order*

1    *class postage prepaid.*    *Postmaster, per*    [Initials Illegible]

**\*\*\*\*\*\*\*\*\*\***

Letter ⎫
Parcel ⎰ *No.* 3289    **P. O.,**    Shawnee  Okla

*Received for registration*    4/7    *191* 4    *from*

Shawnee Indian Agency

*addressed to*    Dr Mallow    [or Mullow]

Lexington  Okla

⎧ *To addressee in person*
*Receipt desired*    ╱*Delivery restricted*  ⎨ *To addressee or order*

1    *class postage prepaid.*    *Postmaster, per*    [Initials Illegible]

**\*\*\*\*\*\*\*\*\*\***

Letter ⎫
Parcel ⎰ *No.* 3413    **P. O.,**    Shawnee, Okla.

*Received for registration*    4-16    *191* 4    *from*

Shawnee Indian Agency

*addressed to*    Steve Ne-gahn-quit

Trousdale  Okla

⎧ *To addressee in person*
*Receipt desired*    *Delivery restricted*  ⎨ *To addressee or order*

1    *class postage prepaid.*    *Postmaster, per*    P

**\*\*\*\*\*\*\*\*\*\***

**Letter**
~~Parcel~~ ⎱ *No.* **3414**            **P. O.,**            Shawnee, Okla.

*Received for registration*        4-16        191 4   *from*

Shawnee Indian Agency

*addressed to*                   James Warrior

Tecumseh  Okla

⎰ *To addressee in person*
*Receipt desired*        *Delivery restricted* ⎱ *To addressee or order*

  1   *class postage prepaid.*            *Postmaster, per*       P

**********

**Letter**
~~Parcel~~ ⎱ *No.* **3415**            **P. O.,**            Shawnee, Okla.

*Received for registration*        4-16        191 4   *from*

Shawnee Indian Agency

*addressed to*                   Ruth Warrior

Tecumseh  Okla

⎰ *To addressee in person*
*Receipt desired*        *Delivery restricted* ⎱ *To addressee or order*

  1   *class postage prepaid.*            *Postmaster, per*       P

**********

**Letter**
~~Parcel~~ ⎱ *No.* **3416**            **P. O.,**            Shawnee, Okla.

*Received for registration*        4-16        191 4   *from*

Shawnee Indian Agency

*addressed to*                   Joseph Moose

Sacred Heart  Okla

⎰ *To addressee in person*
*Receipt desired*        *Delivery restricted* ⎱ *To addressee or order*

  1   *class postage prepaid.*            *Postmaster, per*       P

**********

Letter ⎱
Parcel ⎰ *No.* 3417                    **P. O.,**              Shawnee, Okla.
*Received for registration*    4-16    *191* 4   *from*
                    Shawnee Indian Agency

*addressed to*                    Adeline Rhodd
                          Sacred Heart   Okla

                              ⎰To addressee in person
*Receipt desired*    *Delivery restricted* ⎱To addressee or order

    1    *class postage prepaid.*      *Postmaster, per*        P

**********

Letter ⎱
Parcel ⎰ *No.* 3418                    **P. O.,**              Shawnee, Okla.
*Received for registration*    4-16    *191* 4   *from*
                    Shawnee Indian Agency

*addressed to*                    Frank Thorpe
                          Sacred Heart  Okla

                              ⎰To addressee in person
*Receipt desired*    *Delivery restricted* ⎱To addressee or order

    1    *class postage prepaid.*      *Postmaster, per*        P

**********

Letter ⎱
Parcel ⎰ *No.* 3419                    **P. O.,**              Shawnee, Okla.
*Received for registration*    4-16    *191* 4   *from*
                    Shawnee Indian Agency

*addressed to*                    George Thorpe
                          Sacred Heart  Okla

                              ⎰To addressee in person
*Receipt desired*    *Delivery restricted* ⎱To addressee or order

    1    *class postage prepaid.*      *Postmaster, per*        P

**********

Letter ⎱ No. **3441**
Parcel ⎰

P. O.,   Shawnee, Okla.

Received for registration   4-16   191 4   from
Shawnee Indian Agency

addressed to   James V Blandin
Mayetta Kans

Receipt desired   Delivery restricted   ⎰ To addressee in person
⎱ To addressee or order

1   class postage prepaid.   Postmaster, per   P

\*\*\*\*\*\*\*\*\*\*

Letter ⎱ No. **3442**
Parcel ⎰

P. O.,   Shawnee, Okla.

Received for registration   4-16   191 4   from
Shawnee Indian Agency

addressed to   Richard Rice Sr
Mayetta Kans

Receipt desired   Delivery restricted   ⎰ To addressee in person
⎱ To addressee or order

1   class postage prepaid.   Postmaster, per   P

\*\*\*\*\*\*\*\*\*\*

Letter ⎱ No. **3443**
Parcel ⎰

P. O.,   Shawnee, Okla.

Received for registration   4/16   191 4   from
Shawnee Indian Agency

addressed to   Samuel Blandin
Mayetta Kans

Receipt desired   Delivery restricted   ⎰ To addressee in person
⎱ To addressee or order

1   class postage prepaid.   Postmaster, per   P

\*\*\*\*\*\*\*\*\*\*

Letter ⎫
~~Parcel~~ ⎬ No. **3444**                    P. O.,                 Shawnee, Okla.

*Received for registration*   4-16   191 4   *from*

Shawnee Indian Agency

*addressed to*                   Lenora Blandin

Mayetta Kans

*Receipt desired*   *Delivery restricted*   ⎰ *To addressee in person*
                                            ⎱ *To addressee or order*

1   *class postage prepaid.*        *Postmaster, per*        P

**********

Letter ⎫
~~Parcel~~ ⎬ No. **3381**                    P. O.,               Shawnee  Okla

*Received for registration*   4-15   191 4   *from*

Shawnee Indian Agency

*addressed to*                   Robert Beaubien

Wanette   Okla

*Receipt desired*   *Delivery restricted*   ⎰ *To addressee in person*
                                            ⎱ *To addressee or order*

1   *class postage prepaid.*        *Postmaster, per*        P

**********

Letter ⎫
~~Parcel~~ ⎬ No. **3382**                    P. O.,               Shawnee  Okla

*Received for registration*   4-15   191 4   *from*

Shawnee Indian Agency

*addressed to*                   Joseph Butrand[sic]

Wanette  Okla

*Receipt desired*   *Delivery restricted*   ⎰ *To addressee in person*
                                            ⎱ *To addressee or order*

1   *class postage prepaid.*        *Postmaster, per*        P

**********

**Letter**
~~Parcel~~ ∫ *No.* **3383**          *P. O.*,          Shawnee  Okla

*Received for registration*     4-15     *191* 4   *from*
                    Shawnee Indian Agency

*addressed to*          Mary Beaubien

*Receipt desired*  ____  *Delivery restricted*  { To addressee in person
                                                { To addressee or order

   1   *class postage prepaid.*     *Postmaster, per*      P

**********

**Letter**
~~Parcel~~ ∫ *No.* **3384**          *P. O.*,          Shawnee  Okla

*Received for registration*     4-15     *191* 4   *from*
                    Shawnee Indian Agency

*addressed to*          Clara Beaubien
                        Wanette Okla

*Receipt desired*  ____  *Delivery restricted*  { To addressee in person
                                                { To addressee or order

   1   *class postage prepaid.*     *Postmaster, per*      P

**********

**Letter**
~~Parcel~~ ∫ *No.* **3409**          *P. O.*,          Shawnee, Okla.

*Received for registration*     4-16     *191* 4   *from*
                    Shawnee Indian Agency

*addressed to*          Tena Heck
                        Shawnee  Okla

*Receipt desired*  ____  *Delivery restricted*  { To addressee in person
                                                { To addressee or order

   1   *class postage prepaid.*     *Postmaster, per*      P

**********

Letter ⎫
Parcel ⎰ *No.* **3410**                              P. O.,        Shawnee, Okla.

*Received for registration*     Apr 16      191 4   *from*

Shawnee Indian Agency

*addressed to*                   Nancy Wilson

Shawnee   Okla

⎧ *To addressee in person*

*Receipt desired*     *Delivery restricted* ⎨ *To addressee or order*

1    *class postage prepaid.*          *Postmaster, per*        P

**********

Letter ⎫
Parcel ⎰ *No.* **3411**                              P. O.,        Shawnee, Okla.

*Received for registration*     4-16      191 4   *from*

Shawnee Indian Agency

*addressed to*                   Tony Wentworth

Shawnee Okla

⎧ *To addressee in person*

*Receipt desired*     *Delivery restricted* ⎨ *To addressee or order*

1    *class postage prepaid.*          *Postmaster, per*        P

**********

Letter ⎫
Parcel ⎰ *No.* **3412**                              P. O.,        Shawnee, Okla.

*Received for registration*     4-16      191 4   *from*

Shawnee Indian Agency

*addressed to*                   Harry Johnson

Shawnee Okla

⎧ *To addressee in person*

*Receipt desired*     *Delivery restricted* ⎨ *To addressee or order*

1    *class postage prepaid.*          *Postmaster, per*        P

**********

Sac & Fox – Shawnee Estates
1911-1919 Volume VI

**Letter**
~~Parcel~~ *No.* **3254**                P. O.,                Shawnee  Okla
*Received for registration*        4/4        191 4   *from*
Shawnee Indian Agency

*addressed to*            Addie [?]avand[?]
El Paso  Tex

⎧ *To addressee in person*
*Receipt desired*        *Delivery restricted*  ⎨ *To addressee or order*

1   *class postage prepaid.*        *Postmaster, per*        [Initials Illegible]

**********

**Letter**
~~Parcel~~ *No.* **3255**                P. O.,                Shawnee  Okla
*Received for registration*        4/4        191 4   *from*
Shawnee Indian Agency

*addressed to*            [?]mp  Ch[illegible]
Paden  Okla

⎧ *To addressee in person*
*Receipt desired*        *Delivery restricted*  ⎨ *To addressee or order*

1   *class postage prepaid.*        *Postmaster, per*        [Initials Illegible]

**********

**Letter**
~~Parcel~~ *No.* **3256**                P. O.,                Shawnee  Okla
*Received for registration*        4/4        191 4   *from*
Shawnee Indian Agency

*addressed to*            Thomas Butler
Paden Okla

⎧ *To addressee in person*
*Receipt desired*        *Delivery restricted*  ⎨ *To addressee or order*

1   *class postage prepaid.*        *Postmaster, per*        [Initials Illegible]

**********

89

Letter ⎱
Parcel ⎰ No. 3257                         P. O.,            Shawnee  Okla

Received for registration      4/4        191 4  from

Shawnee Indian Agency

addressed to          Li[??]ly Cortana

Cobb  Okla

⎰To addressee in person

Receipt desired     Delivery restricted  ⎱To addressee or order

1    class postage prepaid.         Postmaster, per        [Initials Illegible]

**********

Letter ⎱
Parcel ⎰ No. 3258                         P. O.,            Shawnee  Okla

Received for registration      4/4        191 4  from

Shawnee Indian Agency

addressed to          Ellen Hood

Norman  Okla

⎰To addressee in person

Receipt desired     Delivery restricted  ⎱To addressee or order

1    class postage prepaid.         Postmaster, per        [Initials Illegible]

**********

Letter ⎱
Parcel ⎰ No. 3537                         P. O.,            Shawnee  Okla

Received for registration      4/25       191 4  from

Shawnee Indian Agency

addressed to          Thurman Ogee

Gerty  Okla

⎰To addressee in person

Receipt desired     Delivery restricted  ⎱To addressee or order

1    class postage prepaid.         Postmaster, per        [Initials Illegible]

**********

**Letter** ⎫
~~Parcel~~ ⎰ *No.* **3538**          **P. O.,**          Shawnee  Okla

*Received for registration*          4/25          191 4   *from*

Shawnee Indian Agency

*addressed to*          Clarence Ogee

Bliss,  Ida

⎧ *To addressee in person*
*Receipt desired*          *Delivery restricted* ⎩ *To addressee or order*

1   *class postage prepaid.*          *Postmaster, per*          [Initials Illegible]

**\*\*\*\*\*\*\*\*\*\***

**Letter** ⎫
~~Parcel~~ ⎰ *No.* **3539**          **P. O.,**          Shawnee  Okla

*Received for registration*          4/25          191 4   *from*

Shawnee Indian Agency

*addressed to*          Mary Ogee

Shawnee Okl

⎧ *To addressee in person*
*Receipt desired*          *Delivery restricted* ⎩ *To addressee or order*

1   *class postage prepaid.*          *Postmaster, per*          [Initials Illegible]

**\*\*\*\*\*\*\*\*\*\***

**Letter** ⎫
~~Parcel~~ ⎰ *No.* **3589**          **P. O.,**          Shawnee  Okla

*Received for registration*          4/26          191 4   *from*

Shawnee Indian Agency

*addressed to*          John D Bear

Washunga   Okla

⎧ *To addressee in person*
*Receipt desired*          *Delivery restricted* ⎩ *To addressee or order*

1   *class postage prepaid.*          *Postmaster, per*          [Initials Illegible]

**\*\*\*\*\*\*\*\*\*\***

Letter ⎱
~~Parcel~~ ⎰ No. **3335**              P. O.,              Shawnee  Okla

*Received for registration*      4/10      191 4   *from*

Shawnee Indian Agency

*addressed to*        Steve Negahnquit

Trousdale  Okla

⎰To addressee in person
*Receipt desired*      *Delivery restricted* ⎱To addressee or order

1    *class postage prepaid.*        *Postmaster, per*       [Initials Illegible]

\*\*\*\*\*\*\*\*\*\*

Letter ⎱
~~Parcel~~ ⎰ No. **3281**              P. O.,              Shawnee  Okla

*Received for registration*      4/7      191 4   *from*

Shawnee Indian Agency

*addressed to*        Geo A Beaubien

Shawnee  Okla

⎰To addressee in person
*Receipt desired*    ✓ *Delivery restricted* ⎱To addressee or order

1    *class postage prepaid.*        *Postmaster, per*       [Initials Illegible]

\*\*\*\*\*\*\*\*\*\*

Letter ⎱
~~Parcel~~ ⎰ No. **3282**              P. O.,              Shawnee  Okla

*Received for registration*      4/7      191 4   *from*

Shawnee Indian Agency

*addressed to*        John C Myers

Carson  Okla

⎰To addressee in person
*Receipt desired*    ✓ *Delivery restricted* ⎱To addressee or order

1    *class postage prepaid.*        *Postmaster, per*       [Initials Illegible]

\*\*\*\*\*\*\*\*\*\*

Letter ⎫
~~Parcel~~ ⎬ *No.* **3283**          *P. O.,*          Shawnee  Okla

*Received for registration*     4/7     *191* 4  *from*
                    Shawnee Indian Agency

*addressed to*              Mary Armstrong
                         Trousdale  Okla

                                     ⎧ *To addressee in person*
*Receipt desired*  ✓ *Delivery restricted* ⎩ *To addressee or order*

1   *class postage prepaid.*        *Postmaster, per*     [Initials Illegible]

**********

Letter ⎫
~~Parcel~~ ⎬ *No.* **3284**          *P. O.,*          Shawnee  Okla

*Received for registration*     4/7     *191* 4  *from*
                    Shawnee Indian Agency

*addressed to*              Mary Bostick
                         M^cComb[sic]  Okla

                                     ⎧ *To addressee in person*
*Receipt desired*  ✓ *Delivery restricted* ⎩ *To addressee or order*

1   *class postage prepaid.*        *Postmaster, per*     [Initials Illegible]

**********

Letter ⎫
~~Parcel~~ ⎬ *No.* **3285**          *P. O.,*          Shawnee  Okla

*Received for registration*     4/7     *191* 4  *from*
                    Shawnee Indian Agency

*addressed to*              John B Beaubien
                         M^cComb  Okla

                                     ⎧ *To addressee in person*
*Receipt desired*  ✓ *Delivery restricted* ⎩ *To addressee or order*

1   *class postage prepaid.*        *Postmaster, per*     [Initials Illegible]

**********

Letter ⎫
Parcel ⎰ *No.* **3286**　　　　　　　　**P. O.,**　　　Shawnee  Okla
*Received for registration*　4/7　　191 4　*from*
　　　　　　Shawnee Indian Agency

*addressed to*　　　　　Jos Watkins
　　　　　　Topeka  Kans

　　　　　　　　　　⎧*To addressee in person*
*Receipt desired* ✓ *Delivery restricted* ⎨*To addressee or order*

1　*class postage prepaid.*　　*Postmaster, per*　　[Initials Illegible]

**********

Letter ⎫
Parcel ⎰ *No.* **3980**　　　　　　　　**P. O.,**　　　Shawnee  Okla
*Received for registration*　6/6　　191 4　*from*
　　　　　　Shawnee Indian Agency

*addressed to*　　　　　W M Montan
　　　　　　Lexington  Okla

　　　　　　　　　　⎧*To addressee in person*
*Receipt desired* ✓ *Delivery restricted* ⎨*To addressee or order*

1　*class postage prepaid.*　　*Postmaster, per*　　[Initials Illegible]

**********

Letter ⎫
Parcel ⎰ *No.* **3981**　　　　　　　　**P. O.,**　　　Shawnee  Okla
*Received for registration*　6/6　　191 4　*from*
　　　　　　Shawnee Indian Agency

*addressed to*　　　　　Charles [Illegible]
　　　　　　Lexington  Okla

　　　　　　　　　　⎧*To addressee in person*
*Receipt desired* ✓ *Delivery restricted* ⎨*To addressee or order*

1　*class postage prepaid.*　　*Postmaster, per*　　[Initials Illegible]

**********

Letter ⎫
~~Parcel~~ ⎬ No. **3982**                    **P. O.,**              Shawnee  Okla

*Received for registration*          6/6          191 4    *from*

Shawnee Indian Agency

*addressed to*                    Mrs [?]ami Moutaw

Lexington  Okla

⎧ *To addressee in person*
*Receipt desired*   ✓ *Delivery restricted*  ⎨ *To addressee or order*

1   *class postage prepaid.*          *Postmaster, per*          [Initials Illegible]

**********

Letter ⎫
~~Parcel~~ ⎬ No. **3983**                    **P. O.,**              Shawnee  Okla

*Received for registration*          6/6          191 4    *from*

Shawnee Indian Agency

*addressed to*                    Joseph M Welch

Emmett    Kans

⎧ *To addressee in person*
*Receipt desired*   ✓ *Delivery restricted*  ⎨ *To addressee or order*

1   *class postage prepaid.*          *Postmaster, per*          [Initials Illegible]

**********

Letter ⎫
~~Parcel~~ ⎬ No. **3984**                    **P. O.,**              Shawnee  Okla

*Received for registration*          6/6          191 4    *from*

Shawnee Indian Agency

*addressed to*                    Mary D Ley

Emmett  Kans

⎧ *To addressee in person*
*Receipt desired*   ✓ *Delivery restricted*  ⎨ *To addressee or order*

1   *class postage prepaid.*          *Postmaster, per*          [Initials Illegible]

**********

Sac & Fox – Shawnee Estates
1911-1919   Volume VI

Letter ⎫
Parcel ⎬ No. **3985**                     P. O.,              Shawnee  Okla
*Received for registration*    6/6      191 4   *from*
                       Shawnee Indian Agency

*addressed to*                    Sich[?]y  Smith
                                Dover Kans

*Receipt desired*  √ *Delivery restricted*  ⎰ To addressee in person
                                            ⎱ To addressee or order

   1    *class postage prepaid.*       *Postmaster, per*      [Initials Illegible]

**********

Letter ⎫
Parcel ⎬ No. **3986**                     P. O.,              Shawnee  Okla
*Received for registration*    6/6      191 4   *from*
                       Shawnee Indian Agency

*addressed to*               Eliza Edward nee Smith
                                Maud  Okla

*Receipt desired*  √ *Delivery restricted*  ⎰ To addressee in person
                                            ⎱ To addressee or order

   1    *class postage prepaid.*       *Postmaster, per*      [Initials Illegible]

**********

Letter ⎫
Parcel ⎬ No. **3938**                     P. O.,              Shawnee  Okla
*Received for registration*    6/3      191 4   *from*
                       Shawnee Indian Agency

*addressed to*               Mr  [or Mrs]    Alford
                                Carlsb[???] Okla

*Receipt desired*  √ *Delivery restricted*  ⎰ To addressee in person
                                            ⎱ To addressee or order

   1    *class postage prepaid.*       *Postmaster, per*      [Initials Illegible]

**********

96

Letter ⎱ No. **3939**
Parcel ⎰

P. O.,  Shawnee  Okla

Received for registration   6/3   191 4   from

Shawnee Indian Agency

addressed to   Susie Wilson

Shawnee  Okl

Receipt desired   V   Delivery restricted   ⎰ To addressee in person
⎱ To addressee or order

1   class postage prepaid.   Postmaster, per   [Initials Illegible]

**********

Letter ⎱ No. **3940**
Parcel ⎰

P. O.,  Shawnee  Okla

Received for registration   6/3   191 4   from

Shawnee Indian Agency

addressed to   Edgar Creek

Norman Okla

Receipt desired   V   Delivery restricted   ⎰ To addressee in person
⎱ To addressee or order

1   class postage prepaid.   Postmaster, per   [Initials Illegible]

**********

Letter ⎱ No. **3978**
Parcel ⎰

P. O.,  Shawnee  Okla

Received for registration   6/3   191 4   from

Shawnee Indian Agency

addressed to   Nancy Smith Tellig[sic]

Kansas City Mo

Receipt desired   V   Delivery restricted   ⎰ To addressee in person
⎱ To addressee or order

1   class postage prepaid.   Postmaster, per   [Initials Illegible]

**********

Letter }
Parcel } *No.* **3979**                          P. O.,              Shawnee  Okla

*Received for registration*      6/3        191 4    *from*

Shawnee Indian Agency

*addressed to*                          Albert McClane

Topeka  Kans

{To addressee in person

*Receipt desired*  ✓ *Delivery restricted* {To addressee or order

1      *class postage prepaid.*          *Postmaster, per*        [Initials Illegible]

\*\*\*\*\*\*\*\*\*\*

Letter }
Parcel } *No.* **3987**                          P. O.,              Shawnee  Okla

*Received for registration*      6/6        191 4    *from*

Shawnee Indian School

*addressed to*                          Frank Smith

Maud  Okla

{To addressee in person

*Receipt desired*  ✓ *Delivery restricted* {To addressee or order

1      *class postage prepaid.*          *Postmaster, per*        [Initials Illegible]

\*\*\*\*\*\*\*\*\*\*

Letter }
Parcel } *No.* **3988**                          P. O.,              Shawnee  Okla

*Received for registration*      6/6        191 4    *from*

Shawnee Indian Agency

*addressed to*                          Martha Smith

Maud  Okla

{To addressee in person

*Receipt desired*  ✓ *Delivery restricted* {To addressee or order

1      *class postage prepaid.*          *Postmaster, per*        [Initials Illegible]

\*\*\*\*\*\*\*\*\*\*

Sac & Fox – Shawnee Estates
1911-1919   Volume VI

Letter ⎱
Parcel ⎰ *No.* 3989                    **P. O.,**         Shawnee  Okla

*Received for registration*     6/6      *191* 4  *from*
                    Shawnee Indian Agency

*addressed to*                Nellie Bourassa
                          Maud  Okla

                                  ⎧ *To addressee in person*
*Receipt desired*  ✓ *Delivery restricted*  ⎩ *To addressee or order*

  1   *class postage prepaid.*        *Postmaster, per*      [Initials Illegible]

---

## TEMPORARY BULK RECEIPT.

Post Office,

**REGISTRY DIVISION,**

                                      , *190*

*RECEIVED this day, of*   Shawnee Indian

          School

  20      ⎱ *Letters* ⎱  *for Registration.*
          ⎰ *Parcels* ⎰

Present this to-morrow and the regular individual
receipt will be given.

                    CM Cade Jr.     , *P. M.,*

          *Per*      [Initials Illegible]

# DEPARTMENT OF THE INTERIOR

## UNITED STATES INDIAN SERVICE.

Shawnee Indian Agency.

Shawnee, Oklahoma,

April 14, 1914.

Mr. Jno. A. Buntin,

Superintendent,

Building.

Sir:

The following letters were registered this date:

Jim Bobb, Jr. Waynona[sic], Okla.
Belethia,[sic] Hood, Shawnee, Okla.
Riley Hood, Shawnee, Okla.
Edw Fox, Carlisle, Pa.
Geo Butler, Stroud, Okla.
Emily Holloway, Wanette, Okla.
Robert Beaubien, Wanette, Okla.
Henrietta A. Clark, 674 W. 35 Place Los Angeles, Cal.,
Clara Beaubien, Wanette, Okla.
Mr. Edw Butler, Stroud, Okla.,
Mary Beaubien, Wanette, Okla.,
Joseph Bertrand, Wanette, Okla.,
Eliza Beaubien, Wanette, Okla.,
Arch Armstrong, St. Marys, Kansas,
W. H. Collister, 27th & Jackson Ave., Kansas City, Mo.,
Ben Beaubien, Wanette, Okla.,
W. H. True, St. Marys, Kansas,
Mrs. W. C. Boyer, Purcell, Okla,
Hah-mah-com-se, c/o Thos J. Pritchett, Ft. Cobb.

Respectfully,

4-LHW-14.                                        Examiner of Inheritance.

Distribution of
estate for
deposit.

**RECEIVED**
APR 27 A.M.
SAC & FOX AGENCY,
OKLAHOMA.

RECEIVED
APR 20 1928
SHAWNEE INDIAN
AGENCY

Sac and Fox Indian School,
Stroud, Okla., Apr. 17. 1914.

R. L. Russell, Supt.,
  Sac and Fox Sanatorium,
    Toledo, Iowa.

Sir:-

I hand you herewith check No. 3653 drawn upon the First National Bank of Chandler, Okla., in your favor, in the sum of check No. 700 drawn upon the First National Bank of Stroud, Oklahoma in your favor for $33.00 to be deposited as follows:

| | |
|---|---|
| Emma Hunter | $16.50 |
| Gertrude Hunter | 16.50 |

These funds were derived[sic] from the distribution of the estate of Robert Hunter and represents their shares thereof.

I shallbe[sic] pleased to have you sign the receipt on the duplicate of this letter and return it to this office.

Very respectfully,

Horace J Johnson

Supt. & S. D. A.

AM
Enc. check and duplicate letter.

Received the above mentioned check and have credited same to Indian Accounts as indicated.

RL Russell
Supt. & S. D. A.

Distribution of
estate for
deposit.

Sac and Fox Indian School,
Stroud, Okla., Apr. 17. 1914.

J. A. Buntin, Supt.,
    Shawnee Indian School,
        Shawnee, Oklahoma.

Sir:-

I hand you herewith check No. 702 on a/c No 808 drawn upon the First National Bank of Stroud, Oklahoma in your favor for $314.61 to be deposited to the credit of Indian Accounts as follows:

Pe-ah-ma-ske ---------------- $104.87
Albert Ketch-show-no ---------209.74
Total ------------------314.61

These funds were derived from the distribution of the estate of Neoma Sullivan and represents their shares thereof.

I shall be pleased to have you sign the receipt on the duplicate of this letter and return it to this office.

Very respectfully,

Horace J Johnson

Supt. & S. D. A.

AM
Enc. check and duplicate letter.

Received the above mentioned check and have credited same to Indian Accounts as indicated.

John A Buntin
Supt. & S. D. A.

Distribution of
estate for deposit.

**RECEIVED**

APR 21 A.M.

SAC & FOX AGENCY,
Sac and Fox Indian School,
OKLAHOMA.

Stroud, Okla., Apr. 17, 1914.

First National Bank,
   Chandler, Oklahoma.

Gentlemen:-

     Enclosed herewith you will find check No. 699 drawn upon the First National Bank of Stroud, Oklahoma in your favor for $49.47 which I shall be pleased to have you credit to Indian Accounts as follows:

| Acct. No. | Name | Amount. | Distribution |
|---|---|---|---|
| 377 | Harrison Hunter | $16.49 | of estate. #822 |
| 379 | Daniel S. Hunter | 16.49 | "     #822 |
| 676 | Henry Hunter | 16.49 | "     #822 |

     Please sign the receipt on the duplicate of this letter and return it to this office.
     A return penalty envelope is enclosed for this purpose.

Very respectfully,
Horace J Johnson
Supt. & S. D. A.

AM
Enc. check, envelope &
   duplicate letter.

     Received the above mentioned check and have credited same as indicated

_____Roy Dawson_____

## TEMPORARY BULK RECEIPT.

Post Office, ...............................................

### REGISTRY DIVISION,

....................................... , *190*

*RECEIVED this day, of*   Shawnee Indian .................

103

Agency

18    $\left.\begin{array}{c}\textit{Letters} \\ \textit{Parcels}\end{array}\right\}$   for Registration.

Present this to-morrow and the regular individual receipt will be given.

CM Cade Jr.    , *P. M.,*

*Per*        [Initials Illegible]

\*\*\*\*\*\*\*\*\*\*

4-16-14

Registered:

Mrs. Josephone[sic] Roberts,
Tecumseh, Kansas.

---

Shawnee, Okla.,

May 7, 1914.

Mr. W.A. Eahart,
Clerk in Charge,
Building.

Dear Sir:

The following registered letters were mailed this date:

Case of JOHN B. JACKSON:
Minot Jackson, Powhattan, Kans. R.R. No. 1,
Jimmie Jackson,     "     "     "
Joe Moose, Sacred Heart, Okla.,
Stephen Ne-gahn-quit, Trousdale, Okla.,
Me-nah-nee, Quackee, Mayetta, Kansas,
Louise Sacto, Mayetta, Kansas.

Respectfully,

(Signed)    WARNER L. WILMETH,

Examiner of Inheritance.

5-LHW-7.

Shawnee, Oklahoma,

May 22, 1914.

Mr. John A. Buntin,
Superintendent,
Building.

Sir:

The following registered letters were dispatched by this office, this date:

Heirship of KATE MAY PEARCE:

Mr. Chris T. Pearce, Noble, Oklahoma,
Mr. Theodore Abraham Pearce, Noble, Oklahoma,
Mr. George Van Pearce, Norman, Oklahoma.

Respectfully,

5-LHW-22.

Warner L. Wilmeth
Examiner of Inheritance.

---

Shawnee, Okla.,

May 5, 1914.

Mr. W.A. Eahart,

Clerk in Charge,

Building.

Dear Sir:

The following registered letters were mailed today in the case of M-ta-ma-pa-ha-kw-we, or Thos Pas-ka-wee:

Frank Paw-ka-wee, c/o Indian Farmer, Miami, Okla.,
Mrs. Sallie Moxley, R.R. No. 5, Miami, Oklahoma,
Susie Walker, Hammon, Oklahoma,
Sherman Walker, Hammon, Oklahoma.

Respectfully,
(Signed)      WARNER L. WILMETH,
5-LHW-5.                    Examiner of Inheritance.

---

Shawnee, Oklahoma,

April 25, 1914.

Mr. Jno. A. Buntin,
Superintendent,
Building.

Sir:

The following letters were registered this date:

HEARING OF LOUIS OGREE[sic]:

Thurman Ogee, Gerty, Oklahoma,
Carl Ogee, Pocatello, Idaho,
Clarence Ogee, Bliss, Idaho,
Mary Ogee, Shawnee, Oklahoma.

Respectfully,

(Signed)   Warner L. Wilmeth,

Examiner of Inheritance.

---

Shawnee, Oklahoma,

April 27, 1914.

Mr. Jno. A. Buntin,
Superintendent,
Building.

Sir:

The following letters were registered this date:

CASE OF JOSEPH LEWIS ACTON:
James Burnett, Sacred Heart, Okla.,
Antoine Burnett, Pawhuska, Okla.,
Andrew Curley, Kaw, Okla.,
John E. Bear, Washinga[sic], Okla.,
Adam Pappan, Newkirk, Okla.,
Nack-nach-kuck, Sacred Heart, Okla.,
John B. Bruno        "        "
Joseph Rhodd         "        "
Steve Negahnquit, Trousdale, Okla.,
Peter Curley, Sacred Heart, Okla.,

Ellen Rhodd, Konowa[sic], Oklahoma,
Joel Delonais, Pawhuska, Oklahoma,
Fannie Mayberry or Canalis, Pawhuska, Okla.,

CASE OF MADELINE ACTON:
Mary Acton, Sacred Heart, Oklahoma,
Joseph Moose    "        "        "
Steve Negahnquit, Trousdale, Oklahoma,
James Acton,              "         "

Respectfully,

(Signed.)    Warner L. Wilmeth,

Examiner of Inheritance.

---

The Following Registered Letters

Mailed

April 11th, 1914.

| | |
|---|---|
| Mr. W.M. Moutaw | Lexington, Okla. |
| Mr. William H. Clark | Cleveland, Okla. |
| Mr. L. B. Higbee | Lexington, Okla. |
| Laura Bertrand Patrick | Roswell, N. M. |
| Lucy Cruse, | Roswell, N. M. |
| Geo. E. Carpenter | Lexington, Okla., |
| Peter WASHINGTON | Shawnee, Okla.  R.  No. 3. |

WARNER L. WILMETH,
Examiner of Inheritances.

---

# DEPARTMENT OF THE INTERIOR
## UNITED STATES INDIAN SERVICE.

Shawnee Indian Agency.
Shawnee, Oklahoma,
April 15, 1914.

Mr. Jno. A. Buntin,
Superintendent,
Building.

Sir:

107

Sac & Fox – Shawnee Estates
1911-1919   Volume VI

The following letters were registered to the following parties, this date:

Harry Johnson, Shawnee, Oklahoma.
Andrew Cummings, Maud, Oklahoma,
George Thorpe, Sacred Heart, Oklahoma,
Mrs. Julia Bourassa, Tecumseh, Kansas,
Cyrus W. Bayliss, R.No. 1, Maud, Oklahoma,
A. Bourassa, Tecumseh, Kansas.
Mrs. Jennie Best, Sedalia, Missouri,
Priscilla T. Bayliss, Ossawottomie[sic], Kans. I.A. Hospital,
John Bourassa, Mekusukey[sic], Oklahoma,
Maggie Bourassa, Mekusukey, Oklahoma,
Hiram Thorpe, Sac & Fox Agency, Stroud, Oklahoma,
Tena Heck, Shawnee, Oklahoma,
Frank Thorpe, Sacred Heart, Oklahoma,
Tony Wentworth, Route No. 4., Shawnee, Oklahoma,
Henry Cummings, Maud, Oklahoma,
Adeline Rhodd, Sacred Heart, Oklahoma,
Nancy Wilson, R. No. 4., Shawnee, Oklahoma,
James Warrior, Tecumseh, Oklahoma, R.No. 2,
Ruth Warrior, R. No. 2, Tecumseh, Oklahoma,
Frank A. Bourbonnais, Delia, Kansas,
Laura I. Nadeau, R. No. 1, Maud, Oklahoma,
Idlewild R. Hutton, St. Louis, Missouri,
Richard Rice, Sr., Mayetta, Kansas,
John Pamdosh, Sacred Heart, Oklahoma,
James Morse, Sacred Heart, Oklahoma,
Steve Ne-gahn-quit, Trousdale, Oklahoma,
S. H. Vinson, Mekusukey, Oklahoma.
James V. Blandin, Mayetta, Kansas,
Samuel Blandin, Mayetta, Kansas,
Lenora Blandin, Mayetta, Kansas,
Daniel O'Bright, Oklahoma City, Oklahoma.

Respectfully,
Warner L. Wilmeth
Examiner of Inheritance.

4-LHW-15.

Funds.

Sac and Fox Indian School,
Stroud, Okla/,[sic] May 16, 1914.

Claud Chandler,
Shawnee, Oklahoma.

108

---

Sir:-

I enclose herewith checks No. 737 and 738 drawn upon the First National Bank of Stroud, Oklahoma and check No. 3713 drawn upon the First National Bank of Chandler, Oklahoma, in favor of Albert D. Kenyon, Jennie Cofer and Richard Duncan for $9.20, $10.20 and $4.70, respectively. The same are to cover mileage and witness fees in Heirship cases of Lena Seaborn and Abby Redrock.

I shall be pleased to have you deliver same to proper parties.

Very respectfully,

Supt. & S. D. A.

AM
Enc. checks.

---

Mileage &
Witness
Fees.

Sac and Fox Indian School,
Stroud, Okla., May 16, 1914.

J. A. Buntin, Supt.,
    Shawnee Indian School,
        Shawnee, Oklahoma.

Sir:-

I enclose herewith check No. 735 drawn upon the First National Bank of Stroud, Oklahoma in favor of Minnie Mathews for $5.10. Please deliver the same to her and advise her that covers mileage and witness fees on the Walter Matthews Heirship.

Very respectfully,

Supt. & S. D. A.

AM
Enc. check.

DEPARTMENT OF THE INTERIOR

Law-Heirship
  I C F               Office of Indian Affairs.

Notices to heirs.         Washington

MAY **26** 1914

Mr. Horace J. Johnson,

    Supt. Sac & Fox Agency, Okla.

Dear Mr. Johnson:

        Inclosed you will find copy of a formal letter to be sent to each of the heirs or interested parties, in heirship cases, when a final determination of the heirs has been made by the Department, informing them of said finding and the interest each of the heirs takes in every case.  You are requested to ascertain how many copies you will need for your agency and submit a formal request to the Department for same.

                    Respectfully,

              ( Signed ) E. B. Meritt

Incl.                       Assistant Commissioner.

                  **********

[Transcription of formal letter]

# DEPARTMENT OF THE INTERIOR

## UNITED STATES INDIAN SERVICE.

........................................, 19......

........................................

........................................

........................................

    The heirs of ........................................ deceased ........................................

Allottee No. ..............., were determined by the Secretary of the Interior, under the Act of June 25, 1910 (36 Stats. 855) ..............................., 19.......and are entitled to inherit in this estate as follows:

    Name of heir.                     Interest in estate.

Amount of funds credited to estate, $........................

Respectfully,

........................................................................

**********

Law-
  Heirship
  I C F

Sac & Fox Indian School,
Stroud, Okla., June 1, 1914.

Notice to heirs.

Commissioner of Indian Affairs,

WASHINGTON, D. C.,

Sir:-

I have the honor to acknowledge receipt of the above noted communication and in reply thereto to request that I be furnished with 2000 blanks, form 5-108a, formal letter to be sent to each of the heirs or interested parties in heirship cases, when a final determination of the heirs has been made by the Department, informing them of said finding and the interest each of the heirs takes in every case.

I believe that the above is a very conservative estimate of the blanks we will need at this Agency.

Very respectfully,

Horace J Johnson

WMH.
Supt. & S. D. A.,

**********

DEPARTMENT OF THE INTERIOR

Law-Heirship
  I C F
Office of Indian Affairs.

Notices to heirs.
Washington

MAY **26** 1914

Mr. John A. Buntin,

Supt. Shawnee Agency, Okla.

Dear Mr. Buntin:

Inclosed you will find copy of a formal letter to be sent to each of the heirs or interested parties, in heirship cases, when a final determination of the heirs has been made by the Department, informing them of said finding and the interest each of the

111

heirs takes in every case.  You are requested to ascertain how many copies you will
need for your agency and submit a formal request to the Department for same.

Respectfully,

( Signed ) E. B. Meritt

Incl.                                                          Assistant Commissioner.

**********

[Transcription of formal letter]

# DEPARTMENT OF THE INTERIOR
**UNITED STATES INDIAN SERVICE.**

................................................, 19........

......................................................................................

......................................................................................

...........................................

The heirs of ............................................................................ deceased .................................

Allottee No. ......................, were determined by the Secretary of the Interior, under the
Act of June 25, 1910 (36 Stats. 855) ................................................, 19........and are entitled to
inherit in this estate as follows:

Name of heir.                                             Interest in estate.

Amount of funds credited to estate, $.............................

Respectfully,

.......................................................................................

---

[The letter below typed as given]

Norman  Okla R.F.D. #6<br>
June 2  1914

J.A. Buntin
My friend
Our rental money is paid since last fall and held ever since.  the business is business
by law, but as long as law set side case never will be done business, until law takes up
case and settled in business way.  I believe Honorable Franklin K. Lane Secretary of

the Interior he told truth on his letter says I am friend to the Indians and I was chosen by president in white house to sit up, and watch to keep the wolves away from the Indians, and he loves to do justice with Indians, and he like to see the Indians treated by justice and should be done things at once not to delay. Now my friend, Mr Buntin you have had hunting up of a legal hiers of Davis Pooler since last falls and still you had all the papers at Anadorko a waiting for hearing of Davis Pooler's legal hiers and you had been saying in this way last two month; as long as you had papers delay at Anadarko this case never be settled. it is your business to write Supt at Anadarko and have him call his hearing at once. I think this is a slow business I ever did have, going on nine month never done any thing with papers; yet, not even hearing never had call, yet you said you had all paper up there Anadarko;

James Clark

---

Shawnee, Oklahoma,

June 22, 1914.

Mr. James A. Odel[sic],

      Principal in Charge,

         Building.

Dear Sir:

      The following registered letters were mailed this date:

CASE OF NAHK-SA:

Joseph Op-tos-ke, Sacred Heart, Oklahoma,
Mrs. Joseph Op-tos-ke,     "       "

Two . . . . . . . . . . . . . . . .20¢.

Respectfully,
Warner L. Wilmeth
Examiner of Inheritance.

6--LHW-22.

---

Shawnee, Oklahoma,

June 20, 1914.

Mr. J. H[sic]. Odle,
Principal in Charge,
B u i l d i n g.

Sir:

The following registered letters were mailed by this office, this date:

CASE OF OWEN GOBBLER:
Boletha Hood, Shawnee, Okla.,
Nancy Hood,          "          "
Jennie Charley,       "          "
Webster Tyner, c/o Beletha[sic] Hood, Shawnee, Okla.

Four . . . . . . . . . . . . . . . . . . 40¢.

Respectfully,

Warner L. Wilmeth
Examiner of Inheritance.

6-LHW-20.

---

Shawnee, Oklahoma,

June 17, 1914.

Mr. James A. Odle,

Principal in Charge,

B u i l d i n g.

Sir:

In addition to those reported, the following registered letters were mailed by this office, this date;

CASE OF LILLIE FORMAN:
Nancy Hood, Shawnee, Okla.,
Jennie Charley, Shawnee, Okla.,
Annie Sampson, Shawnee, Okla.,
Nancy Wilson, Shawnee, Okla.,
Webster Alford, Haskell Institute, Lawrence Kansas.

Respectfully,
Warner L Wilmeth
Examiner of Inheritance.

5-LHW-17.

---

Shawnee, Oklahoma,

June 20, 1914.

Mr. J. A. Odle,
Principal in Charge,
B u i l d i n g.

Sir:

In addition to report this AM, the following registered letters were mailed this date:

CASE OF ELIZABETH DIMBLER[sic]:
Francis P. Dimler, St. Marys, Kansas,
Mike Dimler,            "            "
Martin Shocman, Wanette, Oklahoma
R. Mitchner, St. Marys, Kansas,
John Grotz, Wanette, Oklahoma.

CASE OF KE-SHE-SHE:
O-ke-mah, Bacerac, State of Senora, Mexico.
SIX . . . . . . . . . . . . . .60¢.

Respectfully,
Warner L. Wilmeth
Examiner of Inheritance.
6-LHW-20.

---

Shawnee, Oklahoma,

June 17, 1914.

Mr. James A. Odle,
Principal in Charge,
Building.
Sir:

The following registered letters were mailed by this office this date:

CASE OF JOSEPHENE BOURASSA:
Ellen Bourassa Wiley, Maud, Oklahoma,

ROBERT J. RIORDAN:
Rachel Hale, Shawnee, Oklahoma,
Mary Armstrong, Trousdale, Okla.,
Garcie[sic] Dewitt, Noble, Oklahoma,

115

John Bennett, Norman, Oklahoma,
Robert Bennett, Norman, Oklahoma,
G.C. Woodrow, Norman, Oklahoma.

QUACK-EY:
Me-nah-nee, Holton, Kansas,
F.A. Bourbonnais, Mayetta, Kansas,
James V. Blandin, Mayetta, Kansas,
Stephen Negahnquit, Trousdale, Oklahoma.

MYRA NAHK-SA:
Kah-dot Pe-mo, Mayetta, Kansas,
Mary Wam-me-go, Mayetta, Kansas,
J.V. Blandin, Mayetta, Kansas,
Stephen Negahnquit, Trousdale, Okla.

Respectfully,

(Signed.)  WARNER L. WILMETH.
Examiner of Inheritance.

6-LHW-17.

---

Shawnee, Oklahoma,

June 19, 1914.

Mr. James A. Odle,
    Principal in Charge,
        B u i l d i n g.
Sir:

The following registered letters were mailed by this office this date:

Case of ELIZA SACTO:

Joe Moose, Sacred Heart, Okla.,
Stephen Negahnquit, Trousdale, Okla.,
J.V. Blandin, Mayetta, Kansas,
Mary Sacto Studyvin, Miami, Okla. RR No. 2,
Louise Sacto Bent, Darlington, Okla.,
John Pe-an, Miami, Okla.,
Joe Sacto,          "        "
Agnation Sacto, "        "
Eight. . . . . . . . . . . . . . . . . . . . .  80¢.

Yours respectfully,
Warner L. Wilmeth
Examiner of Inheritance.

6-LHW-19.

Distribution
of estate for
deposit.

Sac and Fox Indian School,
Stroud, Okla., June 24, 1914.

First National Bank,
Chandler, Oklahoma.

Gentlemen:-

Inclosed herewith you will find checks No. 16 and 3807, drawn upon the
Prague National Bank of Prague, Oklahoma and the First National Bank of Chandler,
Oklahoma, in your favor for $425.00 and $89.68, respectively, to be deposited to the
credit of Indian accounts as follows:

| Acct. No. | Name. | Amount. | Transfer |
|-----------|-------|---------|----------|
| 348 | Jane Foster | $425.00 | of Acct. #3002 |
| 610 | Amos Black, Jr. | 44.84, Division of estate.⎤ acct # |
| 611 | Bertha Black | 44.84,    "     "     " ⎦ 661 |

Please sign the receipt on the duplicate of this letter and return it to this
office in the accompanying envelop which requires no postage.

Very respectfully,

Horace J Johnson

Supt. & S. D. A.

AM
Enc. checks, envelope and
duplicate letter.

Received the above mentioned checks and have credited same as
indicated.

First National Bank, Chandler, Okla

Roy Dawson

ALL O WAY PEA SE, Absentee Shawnee allottee
No.489.

BETSEY LITTLE BEAR………………..$1.50.


Pd 5/25/14


\*\*\*\*\*\*\*\*\*\*


ALL-O-WAY-PEA-SE, deceased Absentee Shawnee
Allottee No. 489

SHONEY LITTLE BEAR…………….$1.50

Pd 5/25/14


\*\*\*\*\*\*\*\*\*\*


OWEN GOBBLER, deceased Absentee Shawnee
Allottee No. 410

--------------------            Paid 6/27/14

BOLETHA HOOD………………………….$1.50

ck 2829


\*\*\*\*\*\*\*\*\*\*

Paid 6/12/14

THOMAS WILLIAMS……………..$1.00

Witness in the Heirship Case   ck 7809

-of-

BLACK WING, Absentee Shawnee allottee No.443.

W. L. W.

\*\*\*\*\*\*\*\*\*\*

OWEN GOBBLER, deceased Absentee Shawnee
Allottee No. 410

-------                  Paid 6/27/14
NANCY HOOD..............................$2.00

**********        ck 5830

OWEN GOBBLER, deceased Absentee Shawnee
Allottee No. 410
-------
Paid 6/27/14
BETSIE LITTLE BEAR....................$2.00

ck 2831

**********

LILLY FORMAN, deceased Absentee Shawnee
allottee No. 322.
-----------
ANNIE SAMPSON. .............. $1.50

Paid 6/29/14
ck 2834

---

Distribution
of estate for
deposit

First National Bank,
   Chandler, Okla.

Gentlemen:-

R E C E I V E D

JUL 1 1914

SAC AND FOX INDIAN SCHOOL, OKLA.
Sac and Fox Indian School,
Stroud, Okla  June 29, 1914.

Enclosed herewith you will find check No. 3807 drawn upon the First National Bank of Chandler, Chandler, Oklahoma, in your favor for $89.68 to be deposited to Indian accounts as follows:

| Acct. No. | Name. | Amount. | Transfer |
|---|---|---|---|
| 610 | Amos Black Jr. | $44.84 | Division of estate |
| 611 | Bertha Black | 44.84 | "    "    " |

Please sign the receipt on the duplicate of this letter and return it to this office in the accompaning[sic] envelop which requires no stamp.

Very Respectfully

Horace J Johnson
SP                                             Supt. & S. D. A.
Enc. check, envelop and
   duplicate letter.

Received the above mentioned check and have credited same as indicated.

First National Bank, Chandler, Okla

Roy Dawson

---

# DEPARTMENT OF THE INTERIOR

### UNITED STATES INDIAN SERVICE.

Shawnee Indian Agency,
Shawnee, Oklahoma,
June 30th, 1914.

Received of JOHN A. BUNTIN, Superintendent and Special Disbursing Agent, the sum of Seventeen and No/100 ($17.00) Dollars, which amount has been paid by him as registry fees on 170 letters, as evidenced by 170 receipts which he holds.

C. M. CADE, Jr. POSTMASTER,
Per_____

---

DEPARTMENT OF                                        **MEMORANDUM**
THE INTERIOR        VOUCHER FOR TRAVELING EXPENSES
U. S. INDIAN SERVICE
Form approved by the Comptroller of
the Treasury May 15, 1909

The United States.

To          John A. Buntin,                        , Dr.

Address,      Shawnee, Oklahoma
                (City or town.)                    (State or territory.)

For ACTUAL traveling expenses as per itemized statement forming a part of this account, incurred in the discharge of official duty from ........................., 19    , to ............................, 19   , under written authorization from ........................., dated ............................, 19   , which is attached to this or to

voucher No. ............, to account for ................ quarter, 19   , for the purpose of  registering letters to Indians to appear as witnesses on Heirship Cases.

| DATE<br>19 14. | ITEMS.<br>Use extra sheets (Form 5-335 b), if necessary, and bring total to this blank. | Sub-<br>voucher. | DOLLARS. | Cts. |
|---|---|---|---|---|
| June 30th | For Registry Fees paid on 170 letters, mailed out | | | |

120

| | | |
|---|---|---|
| for parties to appear as witnesses on Heirship Hearing Cases, @ 10¢ Each, ---------------------- | | 17 00 |
| (Receipt of Postmaster attached.) | | |
| AMOUNT CLAIMED............................. | | **17 00** |

swear

personal

Sup't & S. D. A.

sworn                     Shawnee, Oklahoma              30th

June,                  14.

A true Copy of Original Voucher, except as to affidavit.

Sup't & S. D. A.

2907           June 30th, 1914           17.00   TREASURER OF U.S.

**********

MEMORANDUM.

## CASH.

*Voucher No.* 85 , 4th *Quarter, 19* 14.

FOR

## TRAVELING EXPENSES

IN FAVOR OF

JOHN A. BUNTIN

*For $* 17.00

*Paid by* JOHN A. BUNTIN
(Name.)

Sup't & Spl. Disbg. Agent.
(Official title.)

SHAWNEEOKLAHOMA.[sic]
(Agency or school.)

Any disbursing or other officer of the United States or other person who shall knowingly present, or cause to be presented, any voucher, account, or claim to any officer of the United States for approval or payment, or for the pur-pose of securing a credit in any account with the United States, relating to any matter pertaining to the Indian Service, which shall contain any material misrepresentation of fact in regard to the amount due or paid, the name or character of the article furnished or received, or of the service rendered, or to the date of purchase, delivery, or performance of service, or in any other particular, shall not be entitled to payment or credit for any part of said voucher, account, or claim; and if any such credit shall be given or received, or payment made, the United States may recharge the same to the officer or person receiving the credit or payment and recover the amount from either or both, in the same manner as other debts due the United States are collected; PROVIDED, That where an account contains more than one voucher the foregoing shall apply only to such vouchers as contain the misrepresentation; AND PROVIDED FURTHER, That the officers and persons by and between whom the business is transacted shall be presumed to know the facts in relation to the matter set forth in the voucher, account, or claim; AND PROVIDED FURTHER, That the foregoing shall be in addition to the penalties now prescribed by law, and in no way to affect proceedings under existing law for like offenses. That, where practicable, this section shall be printed on the blank forms of vouchers provided for general use. (Act March 1, 1883 § 8. 22 Stat. 451: Ace July 4. 1884. § 8: Cir. 113 Ind O.)

DEPARTMENT OF THE
INTERIOR,
U. S. INDIAN SERVICE.

**WITNESS & INTERPRETER FEES OF**

NOT TO BE SIGNED IN DUPLICATE.

Form approved by the Comptroller of the Treasury October 30, 1907.

### VOUCHER FOR ~~OPEN MARKET PURCHASES FROM~~ INDIANS.

### IN HEARINGS FOR DETERM~~INATION OF HEIRS~~ OF DECEASD[sic] ALLOTTEES.

Submission of vouchers on this form without consulting instructions printed on back hereof risks delay in settlement.

*WE, THE SUBSCRIBERS, severally acknowledge to have received of* ____ John A. Buntin ____
_____, *the sums set opposite our respective names, in full payment of the amounts due us for* Witness or Interpreter Fees , *at the rate of* _____ *per* _____ , *delivered during the* Fourth *Quarter, 19*14 , *at* Shawnee Agency, Oklahoma , *and we certify that said sums are correct.*

| NO. | NAME. | NO. OF Dec'd Allottee | AMOUNT PAID. | | DATE OF CASH PAYMENT, OR DATE AND NUMBER OF CHECK. 1914 | SIGNATURE OF PAYEE. To be signed, whether payment is made in cash or by check. | MARK. | REMARKS, AND WITNESS TO SIGNATURE BY MARK. |
|---|---|---|---|---|---|---|---|---|
| 1 | Mary Armstrong | 255 & 258 | 1 | 00 | April 20 2194 | Mary Armstrong | | |
| 2 | Geo. Kishketon | 171 | 1 | 50 | May 22 2736 | Geo. Kishketon | | |
| 3 | Geo. Kishketon | 160 | 1 | 50 | 2736 | Geo. Kishketon | | |
| 4 | Joseph Moose | 523 | 1 | 00 | May 22 2733 | Joseph Moose | | |
| 5 | Joseph Moose | 50 | 1 | 00 | 2733 | Joseph Moose | | |
| 6 | Joseph Moose | 1173 | 2 | 00 | 2733 | Joseph Moose | | |
| 7 | Wah pe pah | 160 | 1 | 00 | 2737 | Wah pe pah | Her X mark | |
| 8 | Betsey Little Bear | 489 | 1 | 50 | May 25 2740 | Betsey Little Bear | | F E Perkins |
| 9 | Shoney Little Bear | 489 | 1 | 50 | 2741 | Shoney Little Bear | His X mark | F E Perkins |
| 10 | Joseph Moose | 82 | 2 | 00 | May 28 2743 | Joseph Moose | | |
| 11 | Stephen Negahnquit | 82 & 748 | | | | Stephen Negahnquit | | |
| 12 | Peter Curley | 748 | 2 | 00 | 2745 | Peter Curley | His mark | F E Perkins |
| 13 | Andrew Curley | 748 | 2 | 00 | 2746 | Andrew Curley | His mark | F E Perkins |
| 14 | George Kishketon | 29 | 1 | 50 | June 3 2786 | George Kishketon | | |
| 15 | George Kishketon | 143 | 1 | 50 | June 4 2791 | George Kishketon | | |
| 16 | Ah ko the | 29 | 1 | 00 | 2792 | Ah ko the | His mark | F E Perkins |
| 17 | Joe Murdock | 154 | 1 | 50 | June 5 2795 | Joe Murdock | | |

# Sac & Fox – Shawnee Estates
## 1911-1919   Volume VI

| | | | | | | | | |
|---|---|---|---|---|---|---|---|---|
| 18 | Joseph Moose | 1057 | 2\|00 | 6-6-14 2800 | Joseph Moose | | | |
| 19 | Nicholas Trombla | For affidavit | 1\|00 | 2801 | Nicholas Trombla | | | |
| 20 | Stephen Negahnquit | 1057 | 2\|00 | 2801 | Stephen Negahnquit | | | |
| 21 | Do | 1057 | \|50 | 2803 | Do | | | |
| 22 | Nicholas Trombla | 83 | 1\|50 | 6-11-14 2808 | Nicholas Trombla | | | |
| 23 | Thomas Williams | 443 | 1\|00 | 6-12-14 2809 | Thomas Williams | His mark | F E Perkins | |
| 24 | George Kishketon | 143 | 2\|00 | 6-28-14 2826 | George Kishketon | | | |
| 25 | Do | 114 | 1\|50 | 2826 | Do | | | |

forward                    .37        Service                           Service was

I CERTIFY on honor that the foregoing account is correct as to ~~quantities~~ delivered, that the ~~articles were in~~ performed on dates & for the purpose specified. ~~good condition and of quality equal to the requirements of the specifications.~~

*(To be signed by an employee)*.......................................................

I CERTIFY on honor that the foregoing account is correct and just; ~~that the supplies specified were delivered to me in good condition,~~ the Service ~~that they~~ were necessary and have been, or will be, used for Determination of Heirs of Deceased Allottees  and that the ^ ~~purchases~~ were made under authority dated  March 24 (28965)  , 1901 4, which is attached to this or to voucher No.  8  to account for  Fourth quarter. 1914.

Checks drawn on  U.S. Treasurer

.....................................

.....................................
(Official title.)

\*\*\*\*\*\*\*\*\*\*

124

## CASH.

*Voucher No.* 85

4th   *Quarter, 19*14.

FOR

SERVICES AS WITNESS OR
INTERPRETER IN HEARINGS TO
DETERMINE HEIRS OF DEC'D ALLOTTEES
~~OPEN-MARKET PURCHASES~~

~~FROM INDIANS.~~

AMOUNT, $ _____

Paid by _____ John A. Buntin _____

_____
(Official title.)

_____
(Agency or school.)

Any disbursing or other officer of the United States or other person who shall knowingly present, or cause to be presented, any voucher, account, or claim to any officer of the United States for approval or payment, or for the purpose of securing a credit in any account with the United States, relating to any matter pertaining to the Indian Service, which shall contain any material misrepresentation of fact in regard to the amount due or paid, the name or character of the article furnished or received, or of the service rendered, or to the date of purchase, delivery, or performance of service, or in any other particular, shall not be entitled to payment or credit for any part of said voucher, account, or claim; and if any such credit shall be given or received, or payment made, the United States may recharge the same to the officer or person receiving the credit or payment and recover the amount from either or both, in the same manner as other debts due the United States are collected; PROVIDED, That where an account contains more than one voucher the foregoing shall apply only to such vouchers as contain the misrepresentation; AND PROVIDED FURTHER, That the officers and persons by and between whom the business is transacted shall be presumed to know the facts in relation to the matter set forth in the voucher, account, or claim; AND PROVIDED FURTHER, That the foregoing shall be in addition to the penalties now prescribed by law, and in no way to affect proceedings under existing law for like offenses. That, where practicable, this section shall be printed on the blank forms of vouchers provided for general use. (Act March 1, 1883 § 8. 22 Stat. 451: Ace July 4. 1884. § 8: Cir. 113 Ind. O.)

[Copy of Instructions for the above voucher.

### INSTRUCTIONS.

1. No vacant lines should be left between names on this voucher, and the unused space below the last entry should be ruled diagonally across the page, the roll footed up and the total placed in the space provided for that purpose.

2. The total of column "Amount paid" must show only the amounts actually paid. The amount of each payment which the agent expects to make will be extended to this column when the roll is prepared. If then, for any reason, payment is not made, the amount will be cancelled by drawing a red-ink line through it and excluded from the total.

3. Each signature by mark must be attested in the remarks column by one witness.

4. This voucher must not be signed in duplicate. Two copies should be made, *except as to signatures;* one to be forwarded to the Indian Office with the original and the other to be placed in the agency files.

5. In order that the appropriation from which the voucher is payable may be readily determined, the certificate of the agent must show exactly for what purpose the articles are required, and if for more than one purpose, the amount expended for each must be stated.

7. Certificates of interpreters are not required.

8. The original authority must in each case be attached to the original voucher, unless it has been attached to some other voucher for expenses incurred thereunder. In the latter event a reference must be made in the spaces provided therefor to the voucher with which the authority may be found. The same course will be pursued with memorandum vouchers sent to the Office of Indian Affairs, except that *copies* of the authorities will be attached or referred to thereon.

*********

125

DEPARTMENT OF THE
INTERIOR,
U. S. INDIAN SERVICE.

Form approved by the Comptroller of the Treasury October 30,1907.

NOT TO BE SIGNED IN DUPLICATE.

**WITNESS & INTERPRETER FEES OF**

VOUCHER FOR ~~OPEN MARKET PURCHASES FROM~~ INDIANS.

IN HEARINGS FOR DETER~~MINATION OF HEI~~RS OF DECEASED ALLOTTEES.

Submission of vouchers on this form without consulting instructions printed on back hereof risks delay in settlement.

*WE, THE SUBSCRIBERS, severally acknowledge to have received of*  JOHN A. BUNTIN

SUPT. AND SPECIAL DISBG. AGT.*, the sums set opposite our respective names, in full*
*payment of the amounts due us for* Witness or Interpreter Fees*, at the rate of* _____ *per* _____,
*delivered during the* Fourth *Quarter, 19*14 *, at* Shawnee Agency, Oklahoma *, and we*
*certify that said sums are correct.*

| NO. | NAME. | NO. OF Dec'd Allottee | AMOUNT PAID. | DATE OF CASH PAYMENT, OR DATE AND NUMBER OF CHECK. 1914 | SIGNATURE OF PAYEE. To be signed, whether payment is made in cash or by check. | MARK. | REMARKS, AND WITNESS TO SIGNATURE BY MARK. |
|---|---|---|---|---|---|---|---|
| | AMOUNT BROUGHT FORWARD | | 37 00 | | | | |
| 26 | Boletha Hood | 410 | 1 50 | 6-27-14 2829 | Boletha Hood | [Thumb Print] | F E Perkins |
| 27 | Nancy Hood | 410 | 2 00 | 2830 | Nancy Hood | [Thumb Print] | F E Perkins |
| 28 | Betsey Little Bear | 410 | 2 00 | 2831 | Betsey Little Bear | [Thumb Print] | F E Perkins |
| 29 | Sam Bosley | 56 | 2 00 | 2832 | Sam Bosley | | F E Perkins |
| 30 | Annie Sampson | 322 | 1 50 | 6-29-14 2834 | Annie Sampson | [Thumb Print] | F E Perkins |
| 31 | Pah nah kah tho | 154 | 1 00 | 2835 | Pah nah kah tho | [Thumb Print] | F E Perkins |
| 32 | Ah ki kuck | 154 | 1 00 | 2836 | Ah kis kuck | [Thumb Print] | F E Perkins |
| 33 | Pe qua | 154 | 1 00 | 2837 | Pe qua | [Thumb Print] | F E Perkins |
| 34 | Joe Murdock | 154 | 1 50 | 2828 | Joe Murdock | | F E Perkins |
| 35 | Stephen Negahnquit | 1173 | 2 00 | 6-30-14 2911 | Stephen Negahnquit | | F E Perkins |
| | TOTAL | | 52 50 | | | | |

I CERTIFY on honor that the foregoing voucher is correct as to ~~quantities and prices~~, Service performed - Service was performed on dates that the ^ articles were in good condition and of quality equal to ~~the requirements of the specifications~~ and for the purpose specified.  *(To be signed by an employee)*.............................................................

I CERTIFY on honor that the foregoing account is correct and just; that the ~~supplies~~ specified were delivered to me in good condition; that they were necessary and have been, ~~will be~~, used for Determination of Heirs of Deceased Allottees and that the ^ p~~ayments~~ were made under authority dated __March 24 (28965)__, 1914, which is attached to this or to voucher No.__8__ to account for __Fourth__ quarter. 1914.

Checks drawn on _____U.S. Treasurer_____       ......................................

......................................

(Official title.)

**********

Any disbursing or other officer of the United States or other person who shall knowingly present, or cause to be presented, any voucher, account, or claim to any officer of the United States for approval or payment, or for the purpose of securing a credit in any account with the United States, relating to any matter pertaining to the Indian Service, which shall contain any material misrepresentation of fact in regard to the amount due or paid, the name or character of the article furnished or received, or of the service rendered, or to the date of purchase, delivery, or performance of service, or in any other particular, shall not be entitled to payment or credit for any part of said voucher, account, or claim; and if any such credit shall be given or received, or payment made, the United States may recharge the same to the officer or person receiving the credit or payment and recover the amount from either or both, in the same manner as other debts due the United States are collected; PROVIDED, That where an account contains more than one voucher the foregoing shall apply only to such vouchers as contain the misrepresentation; AND PROVIDED FURTHER, That the officers and persons by and between whom the business is transacted shall be presumed to know the facts in relation to the matter set forth in the voucher, account, or claim; AND PROVIDED FURTHER, That the foregoing shall be in addition to the penalties now prescribed by law, and in no way to affect proceedings under existing law for like offenses. That, where practicable, this section shall be printed on the blank forms of vouchers provided for general use. (Act March 1, 1883 § 8, 22 Stat. 451; Ace July 4, 1884, § 8; Cir. 113 Ind. O.)

## CASH.

*Voucher No.* __11__

__Fourth__ ___*Quarter, 19*__14.

FOR

SERVICES AS WITNESS OR
INTERPRETER IN HEARINGS TO
DETERMINE HEIRS OF DEC'D ALLOTTEES
~~OPEN-MARKET PURCHASES~~

~~FROM INDIANS.~~

AMOUNT, $ __52.50__

Paid by _____ JOHN A. BUNTIN _____

Sup't & Spl. Disbg. Agent.
(Official title.)

Shawnee, Oklahoma.
(Agency or school.)

[The Instructions on page 125 were also with this voucher.]
**********

# DEPARTMENT OF THE INTERIOR
## UNITED STATES INDIAN SERVICE

⒜

............Shawnee Indian Agency,............

*THE COMMISSIONER OF INDIAN AFFAIRS,*   Shawnee, Okla. July 9th, 1914 , *191* ..

*WASHINGTON, D. C.*

*Sir:*

*Authority is respectfully requested to expend, during the fiscal year 1915 , from*

| | | | |
|---|---|---|---|
| *(1)* Determining Heirs of Deceased Indian Allottees, 1915, | | $ | 40 00 |
| *(2)* | | $ | |
| *(3)* | | $ | |
| *(4)* | | $ | |

*for the following:*

| OBJECT. (HERE TABULATE SEPARATELY ITEMS FOR AGENCY, SCHOOL, POLICE, ETC., SHOWING PURPOSE OF EACH,) (Do not crowd this space—use leading sheets, Form 5-262 c, if necessary.) | UNIT PRICE. | AMOUNT. |
|---|---|---|
| <u>Agency</u> | | |
| To expend in paying disinterested witnesses in attending hearings of Deceased Indian Allottee, - - - - - - - - - - - - - - - - - - - - - - | | |
| It often occurs that the heirs of deceased allottees are without funds to expend in securing competent disinterested witnesses to testify at the hearing.  It frequently happens that a witness must be called from a point 25 or 30 miles from the Agency.  It is only fair and right this witness should have reasonable compensation for his time and to meet his expenses.  It is not my intention to pay witness fees only in such cases as where the service of the disinterested witness is such as that merits a fee. | | |
| TOTAL. | | 40 00 |

*Any explanation concerning this proposed expenditure must be made in a separate letter.*

| | |
|---|---|
| **DO NOT WRITE IN THIS SPACE.** | *Very respectfully,* |
| *Authority granted for $*_____ | |
| | ............John A. Buntin............ |
| ---------------------------------------- | |
| (Date.) | ...Sup't & Spcl. Disbg. Agent... |
| | (Official designation.) |

\*\*\*\*\*\*\*\*\*\*

DEPARTMENT OF THE
INTERIOR,
U. S. INDIAN SERVICE.

Form approved by the Comptroller of the Treasury October 30, 1907.

(triplicate)

**WITNESS & INTERPRETER FEES OF**

NOT TO BE SIGNED IN DUPLICATE.

VOUCHER FOR OPEN MARKET PURCHASES FROM INDIANS.

IN HEARINGS FOR DETERMINATION OF HEIRS OF DECEASED ALLOTTEES.

Submission of vouchers on this form without consulting instructions printed on back hereof risks delay in settlement.

*WE, THE SUBSCRIBERS, severally acknowledge to have received of* __JOHN A. BUNTIN__

__Supt. & Spcl. Disbg.Agt.__*, the sums set opposite our respective names, in full payment of the*
*amounts due us for* Witness or Interpreter Fees*, at the rate of _____ per _____ , delivered*
*during the* __first__ *Quarter, 19*15 *, at* __Shawnee Agency, Oklahoma__ *, and we certify that said*
*sums are correct.*

| NO. | NAME. | NO. OF Dec'd Allottee | AMOUNT PAID. | | DATE OF CASH PAYMENT, OR DATE AND NUMBER OF CHECK. 1914 | SIGNATURE OF PAYEE. To be signed, whether payment is made in cash or by check. | MARK. | REMARKS, AND WITNESS TO SIGNATURE BY MARK. |
|---|---|---|---|---|---|---|---|---|
| 1 | Joe Murdock | 213 | 1 | 50 | Aug. 22 2976 | Joe Murdock | | |
| 2 | Ah-kis-kuck | 213 | 1 | 00 | 2977 | Ah-kis-kuck | [Thumb Print] | FEPerkins |
| 3 | George Kishketon | 215 | 1 | 50 | Aug. 24 2978 | George Kishketon | | |
| 4 | George Kishketon | 509 | 1 | 50 | 2978 | George Kishketon | | |
| 5 | George Kishketon | 215 | 1 | 50 | Sep. 23 3355 | George Kishketon | | |
| 6 | George Kishketon | 517 | 1 | 50 | 3355 | George Kishketon | | |
| | TOTAL PAID | | 8 | 50 | | | | |

I CERTIFY on honor that the foregoing voucher is correct as to ~~quantities~~ service, ~~delivered, that the articles were in~~ service was performed, on
dates & for the purpose specified. ~~good condition and of quality equal to the requirements of the specifications.~~

*(To be signed by an employee)*.................................................................

I CERTIFY on honor that the foregoing account is correct and just; ~~that the supplies specified were delivered to me in good condition;~~ that they were necessary and have been, ~~or will be,~~ used for the service service was performed on dates & for purpose specified Determining Heirs of Deceased Allottees and that the purchases were made under authority date (76486) July 30th, 1914

190   , which is attached to this or to voucher No.   24   to account for   first   quarter. 1915.

Checks drawn on   U.S. Treasurer   ...........................................

...........................................
(Official title.)

**********

Any disbursing or other officer of the United States or other person who shall knowingly present, or cause to be presented, any voucher, account, or claim to any officer of the United States for approval or payment, or for the purpose of securing a credit in any account with the United States, relating to any matter pertaining to the Indian Service, which shall contain any material misrepresentation of fact in regard to the amount due or paid, the name or character of the article furnished or received, or of the service rendered, or to the date of purchase, delivery, or performance of service, or in any other particular, shall not be entitled to payment or credit for any part of said voucher, account, or claim; and if any such credit shall be given or received, or payment made, the United States may recharge the same to the officer or person receiving the credit or payment and recover the amount from either or both, in the same manner as other debts due the United States are collected; PROVIDED, That where an account contains more than one voucher the foregoing shall apply only to such vouchers as contain the misrepresentation; AND PROVIDED FURTHER, That the officers and persons by and between whom the business is transacted shall be presumed to know the facts in relation to the matter set forth in the voucher, account, or claim; AND PROVIDED FURTHER, That the foregoing shall be in addition to the penalties now prescribed by law, and in no way to affect proceedings under existing law for like offenses. That, where practicable, this section shall be printed on the blank forms of vouchers provided for general use. (Act March 1, 1883 § 8. 22 Stat. 451: Ace July 4, 1884, § 8: Cir. 113 Ind. O.)

# CASH.

*Voucher No.*   24

First   *Quarter,* ~~190~~ 1915

FOR
SERVICES AS WITNESS OR
INTERPRETER IN HEARINGS TO
DETERMINE HEIRS OF DEC'D ALLOTTEES
~~OPEN-MARKET PURCHASES~~
~~FROM INDIANS.~~

AMOUNT, $  8.50

Paid by   JOHN A. BUNTIN

Sup't & Spl. Disbg. Agent.
(Official title.)

Shawnee, Oklahoma.
(Agency or school.)

[The Instructions on page 125 were also with this voucher.]

\*\*\*\*\*\*\*\*\*\*

## DEPARTMENT OF THE INTERIOR
### OFFICE OF INDIAN AFFAIRS
### WASHINGTON

Authority is hereby granted for you to expend, during the fiscal year 1914 , the sum of $ 40.00    from the appropriation

| | | DO NOT WRITE IN THIS SPACE |
|---|---|---|
| *(1)* Determining Heirs of Deceased Indian Allottees, 1915,   $40.00 | | $ |
| *(2)* | $ | $ |
| *(3)* | $ | $ |
| *(4)* | $ | $ |

*for the following:*

| OBJECT. | UNIT PRICE. | AMOUNT. |
|---|---|---|
| Agency | | |
| To expend in paying disinterested witnesses in attending hearings of Deceased Indian Allottees, - - - - - - - - - - - - - - - - - - - - - - - - - | | 40 00 |
| From "Determining Heirs of Deceased Indian Allottees, 1915." | | |
| TOTAL. | | 40 00 |

TO:

Sup't. & Spcl. Disbg. Agent.
(Title or name.)

Shawnee Indian School
(School.)

Shawnee, Oklahoma.
(Post Office.)

JUL 30 1914

COPY.—To be filed by the disbursing officer with proper voucher in his copy of memorandum account.

*(Signed) C. F. Hauke*

# DEPARTMENT OF THE INTERIOR

RECEIVED

Distribution
of estate for
deposit.

**UNITED STATES INDIAN SERVICE.** JUL 25 1914

SAC AND FOX INDIAN SCHOOL, OKLA.

Sac and Fox Indians School,
Stroud, Okla., July 20, 1914.

Superintendent,
Pottawatomie Agency,
Mayetta, Kansas.

Sir:-

I enclose herewith check No. 778 drawn upon the First National Bank of Stroud, Oklahoma in your favor for $23.10, to be deposited to the credit of Maud Kakaque, the same being her share of the Maw-mel-lo-haw estate.

Please sign the receipt on the duplicate of this letter and return it to this office.

Very respectfully,

Horace J Johnson

Supt. & S. D. A.

AM
Encl. check & duplicate letter.        7/23, 1914

Received the above mentioned check and have credited same as indicated.

G.L. Williams

SUPERINTENDENT.

# DEPARTMENT OF THE INTERIOR

RECEIVED

Distribution of
estate

**UNITED STATES INDIAN SERVICE.** JUL 24 1914

SAC AND FOX INDIAN SCHOOL, OKLA.

Sac and Fox Indian School,
Stroud, Okla., July 21, 1914.

J. A. Buntin, Supt.,
Shawnee Indian School,
Shawnee, Oklahoma.

Sir:-

I enclose herewith check No. 786 drawn upon the First National Bank of Stroud, Oklahoma, in your favor for $235.71, to be deposited to the credit of George Littlebear. The same represents his share of the Carrie J. Littlebear estate.

Please sign the receipt on the duplicate copy of this letter and return it to this office.

Very respectfully,

Horace J Johnson

Supt. & S. D. A.

AM
Enc. check and duplicate letter.

Received the above mentioned check and have credited same as indicated.

John A. Buntin
Supt. & S. D. A.

---

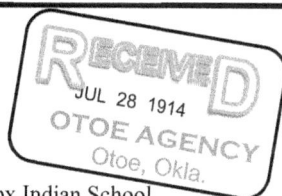

Distribution
of estate.

Sac and Fox Indian School,
Stroud, Okla., July 22, 1914.

George A. Hoyo, Supt.,
Otoe Indian School,
Otoe, Oklahoma.

Sir:-

Enclosed herewith you will find check No. 789 drawn upon the First National Bank of Stroud, Oklahoma in your favor for $5.52, to be credited to Indian accounts as follows:

| | | |
|---|---|---|
| Sophie Roubidoux, | $2.76, | Distribution of |
| Sevinah Roubidoux, | 2.76 | estate from Acct. 806. |

Please sign the receipt on the duplicate of this letter and return it to this office.

Very respectfully,

Horace J Johnson
Supt. & S. D. A.

AM
Encl. check and duplicate letter.

Received the above mentioned check ~~and have credited same~~ as indicated.

George A Hoyo

\*\*\*\*\*\*\*\*\*\*

Distribution
of estate.

RECEIVED
JUL 28 1914
OTOE AGENCY
Otoe, Okla.

Sac and Fox Indian School,
Stroud, Okla., July 25, 1914.

George A. Hoyo, Supt.,
Otoe Indian School,
Otoe, Oklahoma.

**RECEIVED**
AUG 1 1914
SAC AND FOX INDIAN SCHOOL, OKLA.

Sir:-

Enclosed herewith you will find check No. 3832 drawn upon the First National Bank of Chandler, Oklahoma, in your favor for $3.56, to be credited to Indian Accounts as follows:

| | | |
|---|---|---|
| Sophie Roubidoux, | $1.78, | Distribution of |
| Sevinah Roubidoux, | 1.78 | estate from Acct. 664. |

Please sign the receipt on the duplicate of this letter and return it to this office.

Very respectfully

Horace J Johnson

Supt. & S. D. A.

AM
Encl. check and
duplicate letter.

Received the above mentioned check ~~and have credited same to Indian accounts as~~ indicated.

George A Hoyo

134

Checks for
delivery to
Indians.

Sac and Fox Indian School,
Stroud, Okla.  Aug. 5, 1916.

Mr. O. J. Green, Supt.,
        Shawnee Indian School,
                Shawnee, Oklahoma.

Dear Sir:

Inclosed please find Checks No. 301 and 302 in the sum of $26.66 payable to the order of Pe-ah-ma-ske and $53.34 payable to the order of Albert Keach-Shawnno.  Both checks are drawn upon the National Bank of Commerce, Tulsa, Oklahoma and are for Lease rental on the allotment of Neoma Sullivan to whose estate these men are heirs.

Deliver these checks to the payees and oblige,

Very Respectfully,

MJ
enclose checks as above.

Superintendent.

---

Sac & Fox Indian School,
Stroud, Okla., Aug. 19, 1914.

L. A. Dorrington,
        Special Agent,
                Stroud, Okla.,

Dear Sir:-

With reference to the statement made by Andrew Conger that he has not received any money from inherited lands, that he thinks the heirs have been determined, that he has called at the office to see about the same but that the Superintendent would pay no attention to him, except to tell him that he had nothing coming, I have the honor to state that Andrew Conger has had heirship funds.  He has not had, however, all the heirship funds that he will get when the heirs of the various estates in which he is interested have been determined.  He is interested in the Hattie Conger, Jasper Conger, Jay Conger and William Conger estates.  Hearings have been held in these cases. These hearings were held on March 20, 1914 and reports thereon mailed to the Indian Office under date of May 21st., 22nd., 23rd., and 25th., 1914. No declaration has as yet, so far as I am aware, been made in these cases.

A declaration was made in the matter of the Silas Conger estate under date of July 19, 1913, in Indian Office Letter, Land 73333-1911, and subsequent correspondence. The part of the funds of Silas Conger, to which Andrew Conger was entitled, were placed to the credit of Andrew Conger under date of December 6, 1913, and steps were immediately taken looking towards the expenditure of this money in the erection of a barn and the repair of a house on Andrew Conger's own allotment. A barn costing $444.00, plans of which were furnished the Indian Office, was erected, and payment made therefor June 22, 1914. Repairs on the house of Andrew Conger in the sum of $325.00 were also made from these funds, and payment made therefor June 22, 1914.   Andrew Conger's share of the Silas Conger estate was $793.00, consequently the payment for the house and barn almost exhausted his account. He had left $25.93, plus the interest which had accrued on his bank account from January 1st. to June 30, 1914, amounting to $16.85.   On June 29, 1914 I requested authority to turn over to him for unrestricted use the $25.93. At that time we did not know what the interest accruals were, consequently a request to turn over these funds to him was not made. The check for $25.93 was drawn July 13, 1914 and paid to him at the time of his first visit to the office after that date. I do not know just what date this was, but I am certain that it was not very many days subsequent to the date on which the check was drawn.

Andrew Conger has an allotment of his own of 160 acres. His wife also has an allotment of 160 acres, and is interested in several heirship pieces of land. He and she have had since I have been in charge here $3627$\frac{76}{}$, consequently it does not appear to me that Conger has any cause for complaint, the more so on account of the fact that the funds on these heirship pieces are drawing interest at the rate of 4 1/2% per annum, with no taxes thereon.

Very respectfully,

Horace J Johnson

HJJ/WMH.                                        Supt. & S. D. A.

Sac & Fox Indian School,
Stroud, Okla., Aug 19, 1914.

Mr. L. A. Dorrington,
    Special Agent,
        Stroud, Okla.,

Dear Sir:-

Referring to the statement of Elbert Mack that he cannot get his inherited money, I have the honor to say that this statement is absolutely false, as the records show.

So far as our information here goes, Elbert Mack is an heir to only one piece of land upon this reservation, that being the allotment of his father, Edgar Mack. A hearing was held in this case of Edgar Mack, and a declaration made by the Secretary under date of February 27, 1914. This declaration was received here March 14, 1914. The estate was distributed March 17, 1914, and Elbert Mack's share placed to his credit in the First Nation Bank of Chandler, Okla., account No. 564. After the burial expenses, probate fees, and witness fees were paid in this estate, there remained for Elbert Mack the sum of $5.82. This money was paid to him under authority contained in paragraph 38 of the Regulations for the handling of Individual Indian Money, under date of May 25, 1914, so that at this time Elbert Mack has no funds, actual or prospective, he already having drawn on July 20th. the[sic] July 1st. lease rental on his own allotment amounting to $87.50. He has also withdrawn his share of the tribal trust funds.

                            Very respectfully,

                            Horace J Johnson
HJJ/WMH.                    Supt. & S. D. A.,

---

Sac & Fox Indian School,
Stroud, Okla., Aug 19, 1914.

Mr. L. A. Dorrington,
    Special Agent,
        Stroud, Okla.,

Dear Sir:-

Referring to the complaint of Alex Jefferson that his Oil & Gas lease money was paid last October, that he did not get it until April, that it was in the bank all the time, but that when it was paid to him he did not get any interest. I have to say that Alex Jefferson has an Oil & Gas Mining lease on eighty (80) acres of the Nancy Curtis allotment, of which he is the sole heir. The Oil & Gas lease rental was paid on this allotment October 10, 1913, as Jefferson states. With these Oil and Gas lease rentals it is necessary to get special authority from the Indian Office before they can be paid out, and up to the first of the present year, in order to lessen the correspondence and simplify the work, I had been asking for authority to pay out Oil & Gas lease rentals only about once every three months. On October 4, 1913, six days before Alex Jefferson lease rental was paid in, I requested authority from the Indian Office to pay out Oil & Gas lease rentals to about sixty lessors. Of course a request for Alex Jefferson was not in this list, for the reason that his money had not been paid in. No other authority to pay out lease money was made by me until February 15, 1914, when I again requested authority to pay out Oil and Gas lease rentals to all lessors who had such funds, there being thirty-four in number, among whom was Alex Jefferson, and his wife, Sarah Jefferson. The authority to make this payment was received in the office here on March 12, 1914, and on March 18, 1914 a check was drawn payable to the order of Alex Jefferson for the amount of his rental, viz: $92.00

Relative to his statement that this money had been in the bank all this time, but that when it was paid to him he did not get any interest, I have to say that I do not know whether or not this particular money was in the bank or not as at that time owing to the fact that we did not have sufficient bonded capacity we were carrying cash on hand to the amount of $6000.00. However, if this particular money was in the bank it was in the bank to my official credit, and the interest thereon is not payable to the individual Indians but to me for deposit to the credit of the tribe at large. Indian monies deposited in the bank to my official credit during the six months ending June 30, 1914, earned $162.85, which is now carried as, Indian Monies, Proceeds of Labor, and is applicable for expenditure for various purposes at this Agency.

In this connection a little information with reference to Alex Jefferson may be pertinent. Alex Jefferson is 36 years of age. He is a fee simple patentee to the extent of having one-half of his allotment patented to him on account of the expiration of the trust period. This one-half of his allotment consisted of eighty (80) acres. He sold this. The other half of his allotment he also sold, the deed being approved April 25, 1910. He has had his share of the tribal trust funds amounting to $1178.22. His and his wife's family consists of ten (10) members, and their annuity money has averaged during the last ten years not less than #275.00 per annum. His wife's allotment is leased for agricultural purposes and she receives therefor $325.00 per annum. During the last two years he and his wife have had #592.00 Oil and Gas lease rental, so that altogether it does not appear that either Jefferson or his wife have suffered because they did not get their Oil & Gas lease rental sooner, and it does not appear but that the lease rental which he mentions was paid to him with reasonable promptness.

Very respectfully,

H.J.J.

Supt. & S. D. A.

HJJ/WMH.

---

Shawnee Indian Agency,
Shawnee, Oklahoma,

August 19th, 1914.

Mr. Frank Martelle,

Wamego, Kansas.

Dear Sir:-

Replying to your letter of August 17th, 1914, this is to advise you that I have this day sent treasurer check No. 3293 for $105.55 to the Postmaster at Wamego, for proper delivery to you. This money represents your share in the estate of William Martelle, deceased.

At the time you receive this check the Postmaster will require you to sign a receipt for the same.   I enclose you herewith copy of the letter written to the Postmaster which may serve as a means of identifying yourself to said Postmaster.

Yours respectfully,

Sup't. & Spcl. Disbg. Agent.

FEP

Encl.

---

[The next three letters typed as given]

Wamego  Kans

June 27  1912

Mr. Buntin
Dear Sir
I would like to know what is the delay in that real estate deal of ours I have not received my share of Money yet from same  please inform me in regard to the matter as i wish to go away soon find stamp for reply
yours Truly
Frank Martell

\*\*\*\*\*\*\*\*\*\*

Wamego  Kans

July 21  1913

Mr J. A Buntin
Dear Sir

what about our signing of deed did it not go through  would like to know what is the delay   i have not heard a word from it since those interested are asking me abaout it every week  let me know as soon as you can

Yours Truly

Frank Martell

\*\*\*\*\*\*\*\*\*\*

140

Wamego  Kans

August 17 1914

Mr John A Buntin
Dear Sir
it is true that i live in Wamego and have lived here for 11 years  this is my hone it is true  I am away a great deal of the time I cannot tell where the rest of them are at present,  Sophia can inform you where they are
Yours Truly
Frank Martelle

**********

Shawnee Indian Agency,
Shawnee, Oklahoma,

August 19, 1914.

Postmaster,

Wamego, Kansas.

Sirs:-

I enclose you herewith check No. 3293 for $105.55 drawn in favor of Frank Martelle, which I will thank you very much to deliver to this party.  Mr. Martelle should have a copy of this letter by which to identify himself to you.  Also please require such other identification as you think best.

I also enclose you a receipt for this check which I will thank you to have Mr. Martelle sign when you deliver the check to him.  Kindly return the receipt properly signed in the enclosed return penalty envelope.

Thanking you in advance to attend to this matter promptly, I am,

Yours respectfully,

Supt. & Spcl. Disbg. Agent.

FEP
Encls.

Sac & Fox Indian School,
Stroud, Okla., Aug. 20, 1914.

Mr. L. A. Dorrington,
    Special Agent,
        Stroud, Okla.,
Dear Sir:-

Referring to the complaint of Clarence Logan that he cannot get his heirship money, that he believes the heirs have been determined, that the Superintendent told him the last time he inquired about it, that he, the Superintendent, did not know what the matter was, it was up to Washington, and that as soon as they heard from it, he the Superintendent, would give him, Clarence Logan, a check for his part, I have to say that this statement is partially correct and partially incorrect.

Clarence Logan is interested in the estates of Hattie Logan, his mother, and John A. Logan, his father. The heirs of Hattie Logan were declared by the Secretary under date of November 23, 1912, and Clarence Logan has had his share, which is one-half, of the agricultural and Oil & Gas lease rentals that have been derived from this allotment. The allotment is leased for agricultural purposes for $87.50 per annum. It is also leased for Oil & Gas Mining purposes, the lease having been approved and accepted by the lessee September 25, 1912. Since that date Clarence Logan has received $204.00 for his share of the Oil & Gas rentals. There is nothing due on this lease at this time.

The heirs of John A. Logan were declared by the Department under date of June 22, 1914. The declaration reached this office under date of June 27, 1914. The estate was distributed to the several heirs under date of July 20, 1914. A request for authority to pay Clarence Logan his share of the estate was made under date of July 22, 1914. In Ed-Industries 63260-14, 81920-14, dated Aug. 7, 1914, which authority was received in this office on Aug. 11, 1914, authority was given me to make this payment to Clarence Logan, and it was made under date of August 17, 1914. A check was drawn payable to the order of Clarence Logan in the sum of $204.07, the same being his share of the accrued rentals after deducting the probate and witness fees.

There is no Oil & Gas Mining lease upon the allotment of John A. Logan.

Clarence Logan has been advised from time to time as to the status of this latter case, and was told that as soon as we had a declaration from the Secretary and authority to pay him his share of the estate it would be paid. The records show that this has been done with no unnecessary delay.

Very respectfully,

Horace J Johnson

HJJ/WMH.

Supt. & S. D. A.

RECEIVED

**DEPARTMENT OF THE INTERIOR** AUG 27 1914

UNITED STATES INDIAN SERVICE SAC AND FOX INDIAN SCHOOL, OKLA.

Otoe Agency, Otoe, Oklahoma.

August 22, 1914

Mr. Horace J. Johnson,

Supt. & Spec'l Disb. Agent,

Stroud, Oklahoma.

Dear Sir:

Richard Robedeaux is in the office and wishes to know if the estate of Teresa Robedeaux has been determined.

Very respectfully,

George A. Hoyo
Supt. & Spec'l Disb. Agent.

\*\*\*\*\*\*\*\*\*\*

Estate of
Teresa
Robedeaux.

Sac and Fox Indian School,
Stroud, Okla., Aug. 27, 1914.

George A. Hoyo, Supt.,
Otoe Indian School,
Otoe, Oklahoma.

Sir:-

Referring to your letter of the 22nd inst., concerning the estate of Teresa Robedeaux, I have to advise that I do not know of any one by that name enrolled under this jurisdiction.

Very respectfully,

Supt. & S. D. A.

AM

---

REFER IN REPLY TO THE FOLLOWING:                                ADDRESS ONLY THE
Education -                                          COMMISSIONER OF INDIAN AFFAIRS
Industries   **DEPARTMENT OF THE INTERIOR,**
88032-14         OFFICE OF INDIAN AFFAIRS,      **RECEIVED**
C H S                WASHINGTON,                    SEP 1 1914
                                        AUG 29 1914
                                            SAC AND FOX INDIAN SCHOOL, OKLA.

Mr. Horace J. Johnson,

Supt. Sac and Fox School.

My dear Mr. Johnson:

In compliance with your request of August 10, 1914 authority is hereby granted you to sign and approve checks upon the accounts of the following names Indians in the amounts given:

Charley Howard Small, account No. 234, $3.01, to be deposited to the account of Charley Howard Small, account No. 2001.

Heirs of Rhoda Mansur, account No. 268, $3.52, to be deposited to the credit of Heirs of Rhoda Mansur, account No. 2002.

Heirs of Hester Pennock, in the amount of $2.37 to be deposited to the credit of Heirs of Hester Pennock, account 2003.

Heirs of John and Jane Wolf, account No. 297, in the sum of $1.67, to be deposited to the credit of Heirs of John and Jane Wolf, account No. 2004.

Heirs of Jerome Wolf, account No. 809, in the amount of $1.91, to be deposited to the credit of the Heirs of Jerome Wolf, account No. 530.

Heirs of Hannah Mansur, account No. 817, in the sum of $4.64, to be deposited to the credit of Heirs of Hannah Mansur, account No. 2009.

Heirs of Florence Bigwalker, account No. 821 in the sum of $2.93, to be deposited to the credit of Heirs of Florence Bigwalker, account No. 2010.

Very truly yours,

EB Meritt
8-AFC-27                                             Assistant Commissioner.

---

**DEPARTMENT OF THE INTERIOR**
Agricultural
lease rental            **UNITED STATES INDIAN SERVICE**

                              Sac and Fox Indian School,
                              Stroud, Okla., Sept. 2, 1914.
J. A. Buntin, Supt.,
   Shawnee Indian School,
      Shawnee, Oklahoma.

Sir:-

I enclose herewith check No. 2427 drawn upon the First National Bank of Stroud, Okla., in your favor for $19.55 to be deposited to the credit of Florien Littlebear, the same being her share of the agricultural lease rental derived from the allotment of Oliver P. Morton.

Please sign the receipt on the duplicate of this letter and return it to this office.

                              Very respectfully,
                              Horace J Johnson
                              Supt. & S. D. A.
AM
Encl. check and duplicate
      letter.

Received the above mentioned check and have credited same as indicated.

                        _____John A Buntin_____
                              Supt. & S. D. A.

JEANNE  GO-DO-PEA-SE, deceased ABSENTEE SHAWNEE

ALLOTTEE NO. 509.

--ooOoo--

GEORGE KISHKETON……………..$1.50.
as Interpreter.

July 3, 1914.                                                        Total……..$1.50
Paid 8/24/14

\*\*\*\*\*\*\*\*\*\*

Estate of Nee-co-ta-tom-se,
Deceased Absentee Shawnee allotee[sic] No. 517.

George Kishketon, Interpreter………………….$1.50

Pd   9/23-14

\*\*\*\*\*\*\*\*\*\*

Little Fish, dec.

Hearing fee paid

5-29-1917  =  $15$\frac{00}{}$
\*\*\*\*\*\*\*\*\*\*

Mary Mihardy   -   Hearing fee
Paid 2/9/17

Little Fish -   Hearing fee
Paid _____

Madeline Acton.
Paid  2/11/1917

Peter Shipshewana
Paid 2/17/17

\*\*\*\*\*\*\*\*\*\*

Wah the pe wes ka ka

$15$\frac{00}{}$ hearing fee paid
Sept 14 1917

$15$^{00}$ hearing fee
Paid Sept. 15-1917

Thomas J. Lazelle    Ge pa no tha,
15$^{00}$ hearing fee
Paid 9-15-17

**********

Ne-sa pea-se
2/20/1917

---

Authority.

Sac & Fox Indian School,
Stroud, Okla., Sept. 3, 1914.

Commissioner of Indian Affairs,

WASHINGTON, D. C.,

Sir:-

I have the honor to enclose herewith thirty-one requests for authority to sign and approve checks on various accounts, in the amounts stated therein, to settle witness fees and mileage due interested parties who testified at the hearings to determine the heirs of the different Sac and Fox allottees, also those disinterested parties who were brought by the interested parties.

In some cases several hearings were held during one day and the same persons testified at all the hearings. The witness fees and mileage of these persons have been equally divided among the estates in which they testified.

Under date of September 2, 1914 I requested authority to settle indebtednesses amounting to $106.70, to pay witness fees and mileage of disinterested parties summonsed by the Government in various hearings held to determine the heirs of Sac and Fox allottees, in accordance with the Regulations made to carry out an Act of Congress approved June 24, 1910 and amended by various Acts to date, and as shown in schedule, which schedule was submitted with the request for authority.

The enclosed requests, except in four cases, that of Mary Plumb, Benjamin Butler, Levi Barker and Lydia Walker, cover witness fees and mileage of all witnesses who testified in all cases during the period between January 1, 1914 and June 30, 1914 inclusive, for determining heirs of deceased allottees where there are any funds in the estate with which to make settlement of these fees. These requests cover cases where

147

determinations of heirs have been had and where they have not been had.   The hearings in the four above mentioned cases were held prior to January 1, 1914, and the reason we did not request authority to settle the witness fees and mileage connected with these cases at the time when requests were submitted to settle similar fees in other cases held during the same period in which these hearings were held is that there was no funds, or at any rate not sufficient funds, to the credit of the estates to liquidate same.

I should not have submitted requests in those cases where determinations had not been had only for the reason that I thought it advisable to clean up everything at one time.  In most cases where the determination of heirs has been definitely settled the estates have been divided amongst the heirs and there is now to the credit of the estate only a sufficient sum to pay the witness fees and mileage.

None of the witnesses for whom requests authorizing payment are being submitted herewith, so far as I know, have been paid by outside persons for appearing to give testimony, and none of them have been paid by the Government r through this office from funds belonging to the several estates in which they testified for doing this.

I shall be obliged if these requests for authority can be given early consideration.

Very respectfully,<br>Horace J Johnson<br>Supt. & S. D. A.

WMH.

---

C O P Y

Law-
Heirship-
 5769-14
92715-14
  L L

Condition Heirship Work.

Mr. Warner L. Wilmeth,

      Examiner of Inheritance, Shawnee, Oklahoma.

My Dear Mr. Wilmeth:

I am in receipt of your report of August 24, 1914, from which it appears that the work of determining the heirs of deceased Indian allottees at Shawnee Agency is nearing completion; that there are bout twelve cases in which the testimony will have to be taken at the Potawatomi Agency, Kansas, for the reason that most of the parties affected live in that locality.

Upon the completion of the work at Shawnee Agency, you will proceed to the Potawatomi Agency, Kansas, for the purpose of holding hearings to determine the heirs in the twelve cases, and you will also determine the heirs of all deceased Indian allotteez[sic] of the Potawatomi Agency.

You should give the Superintendent of the Potawatomi Agency sufficient advance notice of your intended arrival so that a number of notices of hearings may be issued by him thereby causing no unusual delay in the work.

Mr. G. L. Williams, Superintendent of the Potawatomi Agency, Kansas, has this day been advised of your assignment to his Agency and also instructed to take you up on his pay-roll from the date of your leaving Shawnee. Your stenographer will also accompany you to Potawatomi.

You are instructed to notify this Office by wire of the date of your leaving Shawnee.

Yours very truly,

Signed     E.B. Meritt,

9-AS-4               Assistant Commissioner.

**********

Law-Heirship-
 L L

Assignment
Examiner of          DEC -1 1914
Inheritance.

Mr. H. J. Johnson,

Supt., Sac & Fox School, Oklahoma.

My Dear Mr. Johnson:

Referring to the matter of determining the heirs of deceased Indian allottees, you are informed that Mr. Warner L. Wilmeth, Examiner of Inheritance, who is now on duty at the Potawatomi Agency, Kansas, will, upon the completion of the heirship work at that place, report at your Agency for the purpose of holding hearings to determine the heirs of deceased Indian allottees under your jurisdiction.

Mr. Wilmeth reports that he will finish this work about January 15, 1915. He has been instructed to notify you when he may be expected, giving sufficient advance notice so as to enable you to have a number of notices of hearings issued, thereby causing no unusual delay in the work.

You are further instructed to take Mr. Wilmeth up on your pay-roll from the date of his departure from the Potawatomi Agency, Kansas, and pay his salary and expenses from that date.

Copy of Mr. Wilmeth's appointment as Examiner of Inheritance, and his assignment to the Sac & Fox Agency, Oklahoma, are herewith enclosed for your information.

Mr. Frank A. Winsor, who is assisting Mr. Wilmeth, as a stenographer and typewriter, will accompany him, and instructions regarding the payment of the salary and expenses of Mr. Wilmeth are given in the case of his stenographer.

C o p y of Mr. Winsor's appointment and his assignment to the Sac & Fox Agency, Oklahoma, are also enclosed herewith.

Yours very truly,

( S )  E.B. Meritt

--
11-AS-24                                  Assistant Commissioner.

L- LL

LG-2-3-15.

TELEGRAM

Stroud, Okla., Jan. 7, 1915.

Indian Office

_____Washington, D. C._____

Hearings have been held in all heirship cases under this jurisdiction. Detail of examiner and stenographer appears entirely unnecessary. See my letter January Fourth.

GNC                                    (S) Johnson, Supt.
Phoned 8:15 p.m.

**RECEIVED**
# DEPARTMENT OF THE INTERIOR JAN 25 1915
### UNITED STATES INDIAN SERVICE SAC AND FOX INDIAN SCHOOL, OKLA.

POTAWATOMI INDIAN AGENCY,

MAYETTA, KANSAS, January 22, 1915.

Mr. Horace J. Johnson,

Superintendent Sac and Fox Agency,

Stroud, Oklahoma.

Dear Mr. Johnson:

My stenographer and myself will arrive at Stroud, Oklahoma 8:33 a.m. Monday, January 25, 1915, and you are requested to have Government conveyance meet us at that time.

Respectfully,

Warner L. Wilmeth
Examiner of Inheritance.

1-FAW-22.

Law-
  Heirship
  L L

Assignment,                                    Sac & Fox Indian School,
Examiner of                                        Stroud, Okla., Jan. 4, 1915.
Inheritance.

Commissioner of Indian Affairs,
        WASHINGTON, D. C.,
Sir:-

Referring to the above noted communication dated December 1, 1914 in which I am advised that Mr. Warner L. Wilmeth, Examiner of Inheritance, is to report here for duty in connection with heirship hearings about January 15, 1915, I have the honor to state that this assignment appears to be entirely unnecessary as the force here is perfectly competent and able to handle the heirship matters which we have on hand.

My report for December 31, 1914, shows that we have only twenty-one Sac and Fox cases left upon which to submit reports, and that in all cases hearings have been held and testimony taken. In nearly all of them we have probably sufficient testimony upon which to base a report and no doubt such reports will be made upon at least half of them during the present month without any assistance from an Examiner of Inheritance.

Of the Iowa hearings only four have not as yet been held and they have been set and will be held on January 4, 1915. Only eleven of the deceased Iowa's, including the four whose hearings are to be held January 4th., are yet to be reported on and no doubt the greater part of the reports on deceased Iowa allottees will be in your Office by the end of the present month, consequently there will be very little if anything for an Examiner of Inheritance to do, and absolutely nothing for an extra stenographer if the Examiner of Inheritance does anything himself in the line of preparing reports after the testimony has been obtained.

It is possible that later on, perhaps in April or May, it may be necessary for the Office to detail a Special Agent or Examiner of Inheritance to visit this Agency to satisfy itself that we have socured[sic] all the available data with reference to deceased allottees as no doubt there will be perhaps a half-dozen cases in which sufficient reliable data, such as is desired by the Office, is not obtainable for the purpose of basing reports thereon.

In this connection attention is also invited to my letters of December 10, 1914 submitting reports as to heirship work for the month of November, 1914. A comparison of the November and December reports will indicate that we have submitted nine cases for final action during the month of December. We have at least six cases more that require only a single affidavit, providing we can get the right person, in order to make reports thereon.

In view of all the facts in the case I strongly recommend that no Examiner of Inheritance nor Stenographer be sent to this Agency at this time for the purpose of assisting in the determination of the heirs of deceased Indian allottees, as it is my opinion that it will be a waste of both time and money to do so. A month or six weeks or two months at the most will enable our own force to complete this work so far as it can be completed with the data available, and the Indians are not suffering on account of the delay in the work.

Very respectfully,

Horace J Johnson

HJJ/WMH.                                  Supt. & S. D. A.

---

Neoma
Sullivan
allotment.

Sac and Fox Indian School,
Stroud, Okla., Sept. 9, 1914.

J. A. Buntin, Supt.,
   Shawnee Indian School,
      Shawnee, Oklahoma.

Sir:-

Referring to your letter of the 3rd., inst., concerning the Neoma Sullivan allotment, you are advised that the same contains 160 acres which is leased for $160.00 per annum. The lease expires December 31st., next.

153

I am enclosing herewith check No. 425 drawn upon the Union Nation Bank of Chandler, Oklahoma, in your favor for $80.00 to be deposited to the credit of Indians as follows:

| | |
|---|---|
| Pe-ah-ma-ske, | $26.67 |
| Albert Ketch-show-no, | 53.33 |

These funds are derived from the above mentioned allotment in which Pe-ah-ma-ske has a one-third interest and Albert Ketch-show-no, a two thirds interest.

The lease is for agricultural purposes and the rental fell due July first.

Please sign the receipt on the duplicate of this letter and return it to this office.

Very respectfully,

Horace J Johnson

Supt. & S. D. A.

AM
Encl. check and duplicate letter,

Received the above mentioned check and have credited same as indicated.

        John A. Buntin
        Supt. & S. D. A.

___

Preston C. West
    Solicitor

DEPARTMENT OF THE INTERIOR

Office of the Solicitor

WASHINGTON

September 15, 1914.

The Secretary of the Interior.

    Sir:

At the instance of the Indian Office my opinion has been requested as to the proper construction of that provision in section 5 of the act of February 28, 1891 (26 Stat., 794), which reads:

That for the purpose of determining the descent of land to the heirs of any deceased Indian under the provisions of the fifth section of said act, whenever any male and female Indian shall have co-habited together as husband and wife according to the custom and manner of Indian life the issue of such co-habitation shall be, for the purpose aforesaid, taken and deemed to be the legitimate issue of the Indians so living together, and every Indian child, otherwise illegitimate, shall for purpose be taken and deemed to be the legitimate issue of the father of such child.

The Indian Office formulates its questions as follows:

1. Does this act make legitimate the issue of Indians who have not cohabited together as husband and wife according to the custom and manner of Indian life?

2. Is the issue of Indians who have not cohabited together as husband and wife according to the custom and manner of Indian life to be taken and deemed to be the legitimate issue of the father of such child for all purposes of descent; that is, can the father inherit from such child, can the child inherit by representing either of its parents, etc., or is the child to be deemed legitimate only for the purpose of inheriting from its father?

The act of February 28, 1891, is amendatory of the general allotment act of February 8, 1887 (24 Stat., 388). The original act provided that the laws of descent and partition in force in the State or Territory where the allotted lands are situated shall apply thereto after patents except "as herein otherwise provided." The various states had laws providing that the recognition by the father of an illegitimate child should render such child legitimate for purposes of inheritance, Some of those laws provided that mere recognition would accomplish that end, while others required written acknowledgment. Evidently the purpose of the act of 1891 was to provide a general rule more nearly fitted to the mode of life of the Indians to govern in this matter.

The first provision of section 5 is plain and explicit. It recognizes as legitimate the children of a marriage according to Indian custom. The additional clause, which is now under consideration, must be held to have intended something more than that. The clause reads: "and every Indian child, otherwise illegitimate, shall for such purpose be taken and deemed to be the legitimate issue of the father of such child." This is broad enough to include the children of Indians who have not cohabited together as husband and wife, and there is nothing to indicate that the plain purport of the words was not intended. I am of opinion, therefore, that it must be construed to include Indian children who would be illegitimate even under Indian laws and customs. The words, "such purpose," must refer back to the beginning of the section which reads, "That for the purpose of determining the descent of land to the heirs of any deceased Indian." The provision in question, therefore, makes these children legitimate for all purposes connected with the descent of land. In my opinion the father may inherit from such child, the legitimate issue of either parent may likewise inherit from such child, and the child may inherit by representing either of its parents.

This statute came before the Supreme Court of Wisconsin in the matter of House's Heirs, 112 Northwestern, 27, where the court after noting that it is evident that this clause was intended to include children who are illegitimate according to Indian custom as well as by the laws of the State or Territory, said:

> Recognition of this difference in their status by Indian custom and manner and the law of the state or territory makes the act inclusive of all Indian children not born in lawful wedlock according to the law of the state or territory of their residence. It seems that Congress, in the evident purpose of caring for all Indians as its wards, whether legitimate or illegitimate, framed this statute so as to include all Indian children, legitimate or illegitimate under the codes of the Indians or of the state or territory where they reside.

The same court again considered this statute in the case of Smith v. Smith, 123 Northwestern, 146, and the ruling theretofore made in the House case was reaffirmed.

Very respectfully,

(Signed) PRESTON C. WEST

Solicitor.

Copy for the Indian Office.

Distribution of
estate of
Oliver P. Morton.

Sac and Fox Indian School,
Stroud, Okla., Sept. 17, 1914.

J. A. Buntin, Supt.,
Shawnee Indian School,
Shawnee, Oklahoma.

Sir:-

I enclose herewith check No. 213 drawn upon the Union National Bank of Chandler, Oklahoma, in your favor for $15.37, to be deposited to the credit of Florien Littlebear, the same being her share of the estate of Oliver P. Morton.

Please sign the receipt on the duplicate of this letter and return it to this office.

Very respectfully,

Horace J Johnson

Supt. & S. D. A.

AM
Encl. check, envelop and
duplicate letter.

Received the above mentioned check and have credited same as indicated.

John A Buntin
Supt. & S. D. A.

---

Distribution of
estate of
Harry Hall.

Sac and Fox Indian School,
Stroud, Okla., Sept. 18, 1914.

First National Bank,
Chandler, Oklahoma.

Gentlemen:-

Enclosed herewith you will find check No. 886 drawn upon the First National Bank of Stroud, Oklahoma, in your favor for $235.58, to be deposited to the credit of Indian account as follows:

| Acct. No. | Name. | Amount. | Distribution of es- |
|---|---|---|---|
| 370 | Rachel Hall | $235.58 | tate from Acct. 820. |

Please sign the receipt on the duplicate of this letter and return it to this office in the accompanying envelop.

Very respectfully,

Horace J Johnson

Supt. & S. D. A.

AM
Encl. check, envelop and
    duplicate letter.

Received the above mentioned check and have credited same as indicated.

Roy Dawson

First National Bank, Chandler, Okla

Distribution
of estate of
Frank Davis.

OKLA.

Sac and Fox Indian School,
Stroud, Okla., Sept. 22, 1914.

First National Bank,
    Chandler, Oklahoma.

Gentlemen:-

Enclosed herewith you will find check No. 888 drawn upon the First National Bank of Stroud, Oklahoma, in your favor for $89.44, to be deposited to the credit of Indian accounts as follows:

| Acct. No. | Name. | Amount. | Distribution of |
|---|---|---|---|
| 471 | Frank B. Davis | $44.72 | estate from |
| 472 | Harry Davis | 44.72 | account No. 295. |

Please sign the receipt on the duplicate of this letter and return it to this office in the accompanying envelop.

Very respectfully,

Horace J Johnson

Supt. & S. D. A.

AM
Encl. check, envelop and
    duplicate letter.

Received the above mentioned check and have credited same as
indicated.          First National Bank, Chandler, Okla
                    Roy Dawson

---

Distribution
of estate of
Benjamin Butler.

                                        14

                                   OKLA.

Sac and Fox Indian School,
Stroud, Okla., Sept. 22, 1914.

First National Bank,
    Chandler, Oklahoma.

Gentlemen:-

Enclosed herewith you will find check No. 216 drawn upon the Union
National Bank of your city, payable to your order for $0.09 to be deposited to the
credit of Indian Account as follows:

| Acct. No. | Name. | Amount. | From acct. |
|-----------|-------|---------|------------|
| 3480 | Jane Foster | $0.09 | No. 1107. |

Please sign the receipt on the duplicate of this letter and return it to this
office in the accompanying envelop.

Very respectfully,

Horace J Johnson

Supt. & S. D. A.

AM
Encl. check, envelop and
    duplicate letter.

Received the above mentioned check and have credited same as
indicated.          First National Bank, Chandler, Okla
                    Roy Dawson

Distribution of
estate of Amos
Black.

14

OKLA.

Sac and Fox Indian School,
Stroud, Okla., Sept. 22, 1914.

First National Bank,
    Chandler, Oklahoma.

Gentlemen:-

Enclosed herewith you will find check No. 3921 drawn upon your bank, in your favor, for $1.45, to be deposited to the credit of Indian accounts as follows:

| Acct. No. | Name. | Amount. | Distribution of |
|---|---|---|---|
| 610 | Amos Black, Jr. | $0.73 | estate from |
| 611 | Bertha Black, | 0.73 | account No. 661. |

Please sign the receipt on the duplicate of this letter and return it to this office in the accompanying envelop.

Very respectfully,

Horace J Johnson

Supt. & S. D. A.

AM
Encl. check, envelop and
    duplicate letter.

Received the above mentioned check and have credited same as indicated.      First National Bank, Chandler, Okla
                                          Roy Dawson

NOTICE OF HEARING TO DETERMINE HEIRS

# DEPARTMENT OF THE INTERIOR
## UNITED STATES INDIAN SERVICE.

Sac & Fox Indian School,
Stroud, Okla., Sept. 23, 191 2.

Julia Mixon, Prague, Oklahoma,
M  Minnie Rider, Prague, Oklahoma,
George Thorp, Prague, Oklahoma,
Frank Thorp, Prague, Oklahoma,

160

Mary Wilson, Prague, Oklahoma,
James Thorp, Carlisle, Pa.,
Alexander Connolly, Stroud, Okla.,
Fannie Grayson, Okmulgee, Oklahoma,
Thomas P. Myers, Stroud, Okla., Guardian-ad-litem for Roscoe, Adaline,.
Edward, and William Lasley Thorp, minors.

Notice is hereby given that on the    4th   day of      November      ,
191 2, at   Sac and Fox Agency, Oklahoma      , I will take testimony to be
submitted to the Secretary of the Interior for the purpose of determining the heirs
of      Hiram P. Thorp      , deceased.

All persons having an interest in the estate of the decedent are hereby notified
to be present at the hearing and furnish such evidence as they desire.

Respectfully,

Horace J. Johnson

Superintendent.
Sac and Fox Indian Agency,
Stroud, Okla., Oct. 17, 1912.

I, the undersigned, an employe[sic] of the Sac and Fox Indian Agency,
Oklahoma, do solemnly swear that I delivered to the persons named below on the
date set opposite their names a copy of the above notice.

Julia Mixon _Could not be located_ , 1912.   Minnie Rider _Sept. 26___ , 1912.
George Thorp _Oct. 12_____ , 1912.   Frank Thorp _Sept. 28___ , 1912.
Mary Wilson _Oct. 2_____ , 1912.   Thomas P. Meyers _Oct 15_ , 1912

_____ Maurice R. Gayle _____

Subscribed and sworn to before me this   17   day of    Oct.      , 1912,
at Sac and Fox Agency, Oklahoma.

___Horace J Johnson_____
Supt. & S. D. A.

I certify that copy of the above notice of hearing was posted in three
conspicuous placed on the reservation and delivered to all persons whom it was
thought were interested and could be reached.  I further certify that Thomas P.
Meyers was regularly appointed by me as Guardian-ad-litem for Roscoe Thorp,
Adaline Thorp, Edward Thorp, William Lasley Thorp, minors and children of the
deceased.

___Horace J Johnson_____
Supt. & S. D. A.

Distribution
of estate of
Dosh Kakaque.

Sac and Fox Indian School,
Stroud, Okla., Sept. 23, 1914.

Bristow National Bank,
          Bristow, Oklahoma.

Gentlemen:-

Enclosed herewith you will find check No. 893 drawn upon the First National Bank of Stroud, Oklahoma, in your favor for $0.06 to be deposited to the credit of Indian account as follows:

| Acct. No. | Name. | Amount. | Distribution of |
|---|---|---|---|
| 2019 | Julia Black | $0.06 | estate from acct. 294. |

Please sign the receipt on the duplicate of this letter and return it to this office in the accompanying envelop.

Very respectfully,

Horace J Johnson

Supt. & S. D. A.

AM
Encl. check, envelop and
          duplicate letter.

Received the above mentioned check and have credited same as indicated.

___R.Steinhout___
9/Cashier

---

Distribution
of estate of
Maw-mel-lo-haw

RECEIVED
SEP 28 1914
SAC AND FOX INDIAN SCHOOL, OKLA.

Sac and Fox Indian School,
Stroud, Okla., Sept. 23, 1914.

A. R. Snyder, Supt.,
          Pottawatomie Agency,
                    Mayetta, Kansas.

Sir:-

I enclose herewith check No. 897 drawn upon the First National Bank of Stroud, Oklahoma, in your favor for $0.53 to be deposited to the credit of Maud Kakaque, the same being her share of the Maw-mel-lo-haw estate.

I also enclose check No. 896 drawn upon the same bank, in favor of Jesse Eakaque[sic] for $0.42 to be delivered to him, the same being his share of the above mentioned estate.

Please sign the receipt on the duplicate of this letter and return it to this office.

Very respectfully,

Horace J Johnson

Supt. & S. D. A.

AM
Encl. checks and duplicate letter.

Received check No. 896 and have credited same as indicated.

A.R. Snyder
Supt. & S. D. A.

**********

**RECEIVED**

SEP 28 1914

SAC AND FOX INDIAN SCHOOL, OKLA.

Distribution
of estate of
Maw-mel-lo-haw

Sac and Fox Indian School,
Stroud, Okla., Sept 23, 1914.

First National Bank,
Chandler, Oklahoma.

Gentlemen:-

Enclosed herewith you will find check No. 898 drawn upon the First National Bank of Stroud, Oklahoma, in your favor for $6.76, to be deposited to the credit of Indian accounts as follows:

| Acct. No. | Name. | Amount. | Distribution |
|---|---|---|---|
| 506 | Sarah Ellis, | $3.93 | of estate |
| 511 | Annie McKosato, | 0.94 | from account |
| 591 | Stella Ellis, | 0.94 | No. 296 |
| 593 | Jackson Ellis, | 0.96 | "   "   " |
| | Total -------------------- | 6.76 | |

Please sign the receipt on the duplicate of this letter and return it to this office in the accompanying envelop.

Very respectfully,

Horace J Johnson

Supt. & S. D. A.

AM
Encl. check, envelop and
duplicate letter.

Received the above mentioned check and have credited same to Indian accounts as indicated.

Roy Dawson

Distribution
of estate of
Dosh Kakaque.

RECEIVED
SEP 28 1914
SAC AND FOX INDIAN SCHOOL, OKLA.

Sac and Fox Indian School,
Stroud, Okla., Sept. 23, 1914.

First National Bank,
Chandler, Oklahoma.

Gentlemen:-

Enclosed herewith you will find check No. 894 drawn upon the First National Bank fo[sic] of Stroud, Oklahoma, in your favor, for $1.00, to be credited to Indian accounts as follows:

| Acct. No. | Name. | Amount. | Distribution |
|-----------|-------|---------|--------------|
| 610 | Amos Black, Jr. | $0.24 | of estate from |
| 611 | Bertha Black, | 0.24 | account 294 |
| 660 | Alice Hunter, | 0.52 | "   "   " |
| | Total -------------------- | 1.00 | |

Please sign the receipt on the duplicate of this letter and return it to this office in the accompanying envelop.

Very respectfully,

Horace J Johnson

Supt. & S. D. A.

AM
Encl. check, envelop and[sic]
duplicate letter.

Received the above mentioned check and have credited same as indicated.

First National Bank, Chandler, Okla
Roy Dawson

Distribution
of estate of
Maw-mel-lo-haw

14

Sac and Fox Indian School,
Stroud, Okla., Sept 23, 1914.

First National Bank,
Chandler, Oklahoma.

Gentlemen:-

Enclosed herewith you will find check No. 899 drawn upon your bank, in your favor for $1.43 to be deposited to the credit of Indian accounts as follows:

| Acct. No. | Name. | Amount. | Distribution |
|---|---|---|---|
| 265 | Edith Brown | $0.24 | of estate |
| 862 | Clara Benson, | 1.19 | from account 296 |
| | total -------------------- | 1.43 | |

Please sign the receipt on the duplicate of this letter and return it to this office in the accompanying envelop.

Very respectfully,

Horace J Johnson

Supt. & S. D. A.

AM
Encl. check, envelop and
duplicate letter.

Received the above mentioned check and have credited same as indicated.

H E Breeding

# DEPARTMENT OF THE INTERIOR

### UNITED STATES INDIAN SERVICE.

Fond dau Lac School,
Cloquet, Minnesota,
Sept. 24, 1914.

The Superintendent,

Sac & Fox Agency,

Stroud, Okla.

Dear Sir:-

Inclosed herewith please find approval of heirs of a deceased Indian belonging to your jurisdiction. The se[sic] papers were included with others sent me by the Indian Office.

Kindly acknowledge receipt.

Respectfully,

GM Cross
Supt. & Spl. Disb. Agent.

CED.

---

AFFIDAVIT OF DELIVERY.

Okmulgee, Oklahoma,

Sept. 27th 1912

I,[sic]   I, the undersigned, an employe[sic] of the  Union  Agency, Oklahoma, do solemnly swear that I delivered to the person named below on the date set opposite her name a copy of a notice of a hearing to be held at Sac and Fox Agency, Stroud, Oklahoma, on the 4th day November, in the year 1912, for the purpose of determining the heirs of Hiram Thorp, deceased.

Fannie Grayson,  Sept. 27th 1912.

C E Bearse
Asst Field Clerk

Subscribed and sworn to before me this 27 day of Sept 1912 at Okmulgee, Oklahoma.

__Lyda Compton__
Notary Public

My Com Exp.   __June 7, 1915;__

---

Distribution of estate
of Lottie Duncan.

**RECEIVED**

OCT 9 1914

SAC AND FOX INDIAN SCHOOL, OKLA.

Sac and Fox Indian School,
Stroud, Okla., Oct. 5, 1914.

First National Bank,
Stroud, Oklahoma.

Gentlemen:-

Enclosed herewith you will find check No. 912 drawn upon your bank, in your favor for $269.69 to be deposited to the credit of Indian account as follows:

| Acct. No. | Name. | Amount. | From Acct. |
|---|---|---|---|
| 877 | Dickson Mokohoko | $269.69 | No. 272 |

Please sign the receipt on the duplicate copy of this letter and return it to this office in the accompanying envelop.

Very respectfully,

Horace J Johnson

Supt. & S. D. A.

AM
Encl. check, envelop and
duplicate letter.

Received the above mentioned check and have credited same as indicated.

__H.E. Breeding__

\*\*\*\*\*\*\*\*\*\*

167

Sac & Fox – Shawnee Estates
1911-1919   Volume VI

Distribution
of estate of
Lottie Duncan.

Sac and Fox Indian School,
Stroud, Okla., Oct. 7, 1914.

First National Bank,
    Stroud, Oklahoma.

Gentlemen:-

Enclosed herewith you will find check No. 910 drawn upon the First National Bank of Stroud, Oklahoma, in your favor for $321.07 to be deposited to the credit of Indian account as follows:

| Acct. No. | Name. | Amount. | Distribution |
|---|---|---|---|
| 350 | John Crane | $25.69 | of estate from |
| 351 | Harry Crane | 25.69 | Acct. No. |
| 433 | Allen G. Thurman, | 269.69 | 272. |
| | Total ----------------------- | 321.07 | |

Please sign the receipt on the duplicate of this letter and return it to this office in the accompanying envelop.

Very respectfully,

Horace J Johnson

Supt. & S. D. A.

AM
Encl. check, envelop and
    duplicate letter.

Received the above mentioned check and have credited same as indicated.

First National Bank, Chandler, Okla
_____Roy Dawson_____

Distribution of
estate of Hiram
Gibbs.

Sac and Fox Indian School,
Stroud, Okla., Oct. 7, 1914.

First National Bank,
    Chandler, Oklahoma.

Gentlemen:-

Enclosed herewith you will find check No. 3969 drawn upon ~~the~~ your bank, in your favor for $1$^{59.84}$.84, to be deposited to the credit of Indian accounts as follows:

| Acct. No. | Name. | Amount. | Distribution of |
|-----------|-------|---------|-----------------|
| 610 | Amos Black, Jr. | $79.92 | estate from |
| 611 | Bertha Black, | 79.92 | Acct. No. 629. |

Please sign the receipt on the duplicate of this letter and return it to this office in the accompanying envelop.

Very respectfully,

Horace J Johnson

Supt. & S. D. A.

AM

Encl. check, envelop and
     duplicate letter.

Received the above mentioned check and have credited same as indicated.

First National Bank, Chandler, Okla

Roy Dawson

---

Garfield
Ellis Land
Sale.

Sac and Fox Indian School,
Stroud, Okla   Oct 20, 1914.

Warner L Wilmeth,
     Examiner of Inheritance,
          Shawnee, Okla.

Sir:-

Referring to your letter of the 7th inst., concerning the Garfield Ellis land sale, I have to advise that I do not find anything on record here concerning this sale.

However, a payment was made by certificates of deposit, no doubt you can ascertain from the banks which drew these certificates of deposit to whom payment was made. The certificates of deposit should bear the endorsement of the drawee.

If I find anything with reference to this matter I will communicate with you.

Very Respectfully,

HJJ/SP                                          Supt. & S. D. A.

**********

Heirship of        **DEPARTMENT OF THE INTERIOR**
Garfield Ellis,
Shawnee Agency,        **UNITED STATES INDIAN SERVICE**
Okla.
                     SHAWNEE INDIAN AGENCY,

                          SHAWNEE, OKLA., October 7, 1914.

Mr. Horace J. Johnson,

    Superintendent Sac and Fox Agency,

        Stroud, Okla.

Dear Sir:

        It appears from Office letter (Land 20392-1901; 22080-1901) which was addressed to Lee Patrick, United States Indian Agent, Sac and Fox Agency, Okla., under date of April 28, 1901, that the allotment of Garfield Ellis, deceased Absentee Shawnee allottee No. 107 was conveyed to George M. Morgan for the sum of $725.00, said deed being approved April 23, 1901. Two vouchers were returned by the Department to Superintendent Lee Patrick, one number 1604 for $600.00, issued Jan. 28, 1901, by H.T. Douglas President, and one number 1653 for $125,00 issued April 1901, by Joe Bowers. Assistant Cashier of the Shawnee National Bank, Shawnee, O.T., each payable to the order of Garfield Ellis. Said deed was approved by the Secretary of the Interior the Interior. Garfield Ellis, in accordance with the Shawnee Family Register died November 7, 1900, and, as you will note, this deed was not approved until April 23, 1901, and that the two certificats[sic] of deposit were not issued until January 28, 1901 and April 13, 1901, respectively, this being subsequent to the death of Garfield Ellis. There are no records at this Agency to show to whom this money was paid and you are requested to inform me whether or not the records of your Agency will throw any light upon this subject.

Daniel Chisholm, a son, and probably the only son of Garfield Ellis, who is now 21 years of age says that 7 or 8 years ago he received about $40.00 from some bank in Tecumseh, Oklahoma, but that he does not remember which bank it was, and that so far as he knows this is all of the estate that he received. It appears that this young man would, at least, have been entitled to one-half of the proceeds of the sale of this land.

You are requested to look into this matter immediately for the reason that I expect to leave here about October 20, 1914, and desire to have any information that can be furnished by you, in hand before leaving here.

Respectfully,
Warner L. Wilmeth
Examiner of Inheritance.

10-FAW-7

---

Heirship of Owen Gobbler, deceased Absentee
Shawnee allottee No. 410.

Webster Tyner, witness fees . . . . . . . . . . . . . . . . $1.50

**\*\*\*\*\*\*\*\*\*\***

MEMORANDUM.

VOUCHER FOR MISCELLANEOUS EXPENSES, SUCH AS RENT OF BUILDINGS, TELEPHONE SERVICE, GAS, ELECTRIC LIGHT, AND WATER SUPPLY. ETC.

**THE UNITED STATES,**        October 21, *19*14

*To*     Webster Tyner,     , *Dr.*

(Give post-office address.)    Skiatook, Oklahoma

| DATE 1914 | ENTER BELOW THE SUBJECT MATTER OF THE CLAIM, SHOWING OF WHAT IT CONSISTS. | AMOUNT. |
|---|---|---|
| Oct. 21 | For witness fee in Hearing held Oct. 21, 1914, go determine the legal heirs of Owen Gobbler, Absentte[sic] Shawnee Allotee No. 410, - - - - - - - - | 1 50 |
| | | |
| | | |
| | | |
| | TOTAL.............................. $ | 1 50 |

THE ABOVE IS A TRUE COPY OF ORIGINAL VOUCHER, EXCEPT AS TO CERTIFICATES.
PAID IN CASH, UNLESS OTHERWISE NOTED AT THE BOTTOM HEREOF.

---

Services procured under authority dated _____ July 30, (76486) ___, 1914, attached to
~~original or to~~ voucher No. ___24_____ to account for ___first_____ Quarter, 1915 , and in
accordance with sections _____ and _____ of the methods stated on original.

(Letter)    (Number)

Dated __October 21st, 1914__, 19        (Sgd.) JOHN A. BUNTIN

Sup't. & Spcl. Disbg. Agent.

Paid by Check No. ___3100__, dated _____ October 21,_____, 1914, for $1.50 __,
on _____ TREASURER OF UNITED STATES ____, to order of claimant.

**********

---

**MEMORANDUM.**

---

### CASH

*Voucher No.* 10-1ˢᵗ for 2nd *Quarter, 19*15

FOR

**MISCELLANEOUS EXPENSES.**

---

IN FAVOR OF

___Wester Tyner_____

*For $* 1.50 _____

*Paid by* ____JOHN A. BUNTIN_____

Supt. and Specl. Disb'g. Agent.
(Official title.)

Shawnee, Okla.
(Agency or School.)

Any disbursing or other officer of the United States or other person who shall knowingly present, or cause to be presented, any voucher, account, or claim to any officer of the United States for approval or payment, or for the purpose of securing a credit in any account with the United States, relating to any matter pertaining to the Indian Service, which shall contain any material misrepresentation of fact in regard to the amount due or paid, the name or character of the article furnished or received, or of the service rendered, or to the date of purchase, delivery, or performance of service, or in any other particular, shall not be entitled to payment or credit for any part of said voucher, account, or claim; and if any such credit shall be given or received, or payment made, the United States may recharge the same to the officer or person receiving the credit or payment and recover the amount from either or both, in the same manner as other debts due the United States are collected; PROVIDED, That where an account contains more than one voucher the foregoing shall apply only to such vouchers as contain the misrepresentation; AND PROVIDED FURTHER, That the officers and persons by and between whom the business is transacted shall be presumed to know the facts in relation to the matter set forth in the voucher, account, or claim; AND PROVIDED FURTHER, That the foregoing shall be in addition to the penalties now prescribed by law, and in no way to affect proceedings under existing law for like offenses. That, where practicable, this section shall be printed on the blank forms of vouchers provided for general use. (Act March 1, 1883 § 8, 22 Stat., 451; Ace July 4, 1884, § 8; Cir. 113 Ind. O.)

Agricultural
lease rentals
for deposit.

Sac and Fox Indian School,
Stroud, Okla., Nov. 5, 1914.

J. A. Buntin, Supt.,
Shawnee Indian School,
Shawnee, Oklahoma.

Sir:-

Enclosed herewith you will find check No. 2505 drawn upon the First
National Bank of Stroud, Oklahoma, in your favor for $62.50, to be deposited to the
credit of Florien Littlebear, the same being agricultural lease rentals derived from the
allotment of Carrie J. Littlebear, deceased.

Please sign the receipt on the duplicate of this letter and return it to this
office.

Very respectfully,

Horace J Johnson

Supt. & S. D. Λ.

AM
Encl. check, and
duplicate letter.

Received the above mentioned check and have credited same as indicated.

John A. Buntin
Superintendent.

---

# DEPARTMENT OF THE INTERIOR

Agricultural        **UNITED STATES INDIAN SERVICE.**
lease rentals
for deposit.
Sac and Fox Indian School,
Stroud, Okla., Nov. 5, 1914.

J. A. Buntin, Supt.,
Shawnee Indian School,
Shawnee, Oklahoma.

Sir:-

Enclosed herewith you will find check No. 2505 drawn upon the First National Bank of Stroud, Oklahoma, in your favor for $62.50, to be deposited to the credit of Florien Littlebear, the same being agricultural lease rentals derived from the allotment of Carrie J. Littlebear, deceased.

Please sign the receipt on the duplicate of this letter and return it to this office.

Very respectfully,

Horace J Johnson

Supt. & S. D. A.

AM
Encl. check and
    duplicate letter.

Received the above mentioned check and have credited same as indicated.

<u>John A. Buntin</u>
Superintendent.

---

Sac & Fox Indian School,
Stroud, Okla., Nov. 6, 1914.

Number of Hearings Held (Sac & Fox & Iowa).................................156
"     "   Reports Made   "   "   "   "     "   .................................126

Number of Reports to be made..................................... 30

W. M. Hodsdon.

\*\*\*\*\*\*\*\*\*\*

Aug  10

# DEPARTMENT OF THE INTERIOR
### UNITED STATES INDIAN SERVICE.

Number of Hearings held--------------------155
Number of Reports made--------------------113

\*\*\*\*\*\*\*\*\*\*

Sac & Fox – Shawnee Estates
1911-1919   Volume VI

Sac & Fox Indian Agency,
Stroud, Okla., May 20, 1914.

NUMBER OF HEIRSHIP HEARINGS HELD-------------154.
   "   "   "    "   Reported------------- 91
   "   "    "  DECLARATIONS BY SEC'Y.--- 75

W. M. Hodsdon.

---

# DEPARTMENT OF THE INTERIOR

## UNITED STATES INDIAN SERVICE

Otoe Indian School,
Otoe, Oklahoma.
Nov. 9, 1914

Sup't. H. J. Johnson,
    Sac and Fox Agency,
        Stroud, Oklahoma.

Dear Sir:-

    Charley Whitehorn is here this morning and says that sometime last spring he gave testimony as a disinterested witness in the hearing to determine the heirs of Mary Starr, and that he was promised a ten dollar witness fee for his services. He says that he was to get the money just as soon as the heirs to this estate were legally determined. Charley thinks the heirs have now been determined and he requests that his witness fee check be sent here for delivery.

    This letter is written at the request of Charley Whitehorn.

Very respectfully,
George A. Hoyo
Superintendent.

\*\*\*\*\*\*\*\*\*\*

Re
Charley
Whitehorn.

Sac and Fox Indian School,
Stroud, Okla Nov 11, 1914.

Supt George A Hoyo,
    Otoe, Okla.

175

Sir:-

Referring to your letter of the 9th inst. written at the request of Charley Whitehorn stating that he gave testimony in a hearing to determine the heirs of Mary Starr and was promised $10.00 witness fees for his services, I have to advise that the records of this office do not show that we held any hearing to determine the heirs of Mary Starr.

We did hold a hearing to determine the heirs of Helen Starr but no testimony was given in this case by Charley Whitehorn consequently he could not have been promised a fee for this purpose.

I do not remember of Charley Whitehorn giving testimony in any case however, if he can substantiate a claim that he did so I shall be pleased to give this matter further consideration.

Very Respectfully.

Hjj/SP                                   Supt. & S. D. A.

---

# SPECIAL

**RECEIVED**

Law-Heirship
  L  L                    DEPARTMENT OF THE INTERIOR       NOV 21 1914

SAC AND FOX INDIAN SCHOOL, OKLA.

Report as to                    Office of Indian Affairs
  Heirship work.

Washington

Mr. H.J. Johnson,                              November 13, 1914.

  Supt., Sac & Fox School.

Sir:

Referring to the matter of the determination of the heirs of deceased Indian allottees, you are requested to submit to this Office your report at the close of each month. For the sake of uniformity in the reports they should be submitted somewhat in the manner indicated:

> Number of cases on hand at the beginning of the month;
> Number of cases in which notices have been given for hearing to be held
>     during the month;
> Original hearings held during the month;
> Supplemental hearings held during the month;
> Number of cases submitted to this Office;

# Sac & Fox – Shawnee Estates
## 1911-1919   Volume VI

Number of cases returned by this Office for correction;
Number of cases returned by this Office for further evidence or re-hearings;
Unfinished cases upon which original hearings have been held, but cases still
on hand;
Number of cases in which no action has been taken;
Number of cases in which notice of final action has been received;
Number of letters written.

You are further advised that hereafter when heirship cases are returned for further evidence on material questions of fact, supplemental hearings n fifteen (15) days notice to parties at interest, should be held.

These instructions are not to be construed as applying to cases returned for clerical corrections or additional data that can be supplied from the records of the agency office.

Yours very truly,

E. B. MERITT,

11-AS-13                                                         Assistant Commissioner.

---

|  |  | *Voucher No.* | ? |
| --- | --- | --- | --- |

𝕯𝕰𝕻𝕬𝕽𝕿𝕸𝕰𝕹𝕿 𝕺𝕱                                                **MEMORANDUM**
𝕿𝕳𝕰 𝕴𝕹𝕿𝕰𝕽𝕴𝕺𝕽        VOUCHER FOR TRAVELING EXPENSES
U. S. INDIAN SERVICE
Form approved by the Comptroller of
the Treasury May 15, 1909

𝕿𝖍𝖊 𝖀𝖓𝖎𝖙𝖊𝖉 𝕾𝖙𝖆𝖙𝖊𝖘.

*To* _____ Warner L. Wilmeth _____ , *Dr.*

*Address,* ___ Sac and Fox Agency _____ Okla.
(City or town.)          (State or territory.)

For ACTUAL traveling expenses as per itemized statement forming a part of this account, incurred in the discharge of official duty from ...January 23.............., 1915 , to .....January 25..........., 1915, under written authorization from ...Indian Office ..........., dated ..December 1........., 1914 , which is attached to this or to voucher No. .....4...., to account for ....3ʳᵈ........... quarter, 1915 , for the purpose of  Holding hearings to determine heirs of deceased Sac and Fox Okla. allottees

| DATE *1915* | ITEMS. Use extra sheets (Form 5-335 b), if necessary, and bring total to this blank. | Sub-voucher. | DOLLARS. | Cts. |
| --- | --- | --- | --- | --- |
| Jan. 23 | Railroad fare Mayetta, Kansas to Topeka, Kansas |  |  | 42 |
| Jan. 23 | Checking baggage at Topeka, Kansas. |  |  | 10 |
| Jan. 23 | Railroad fare from Topeka, Kans. to Stroud, Okla. |  | 8 | 81 |
| Jan. 23 | Express on Typewriter, Mayetta, Kans. to Stroud, Okla. |  | 1 | 16 |
| Jan. 24 | Sleeping-car fare from Kansas City, Mo., to Stroud, Okla. Standard Lower |  | 2 | 00 |

177

| | | | | |
|---|---|---|---|---|
| Jan. 25 | Pullman porter.  Night Service | | | 25 |
| Jan. 26 | Storage of baggage for 1 day at Stroud, Okla. | | | 25 |
| Paid from | Fund, Determining Heirs Deceased Indian Allottees"1915 | | | |
| | AMOUNT CLAIMED.................................... | | 12 | 99 |

A true Copy of Original Voucher, except as to affidavit.

**********

Any disbursing or other officer of the United States or other person who shall knowingly present, or cause to be presented, any voucher, account, or claim to any officer of the United States for approval or payment, or for the pur-pose of securing a credit in any account with the United States, relating to any matter pertaining to the Indian Service, which shall contain any material misrepresentation of fact in regard to the amount due or paid, the name or character of the article furnished or received, or of the service rendered, or to the date of purchase, delivery, or performance of service, or in any other particular, shall not be entitled to payment or credit for any part of said voucher, account, or claim; and if any such credit shall be given or payment or credit for any part of said voucher, account, or claim; and if any such credit shall be given or received, or payment made, the United States may recharge the same to the officer or person receiving the credit or payment and recover the amount from either or both, in the same manner as other debts due the United States are collected: PROVIDED, That where an account contains more than one voucher the foregoing shall apply only to such vouchers as contain the misrepresentation: AND PROVIDED FURTHER, That the officers and persons by and between whom the business is transacted shall be presumed to know the facts in relation to the matter set forth in the voucher, account, or claim; AND PROVIDED FURTHER, That the foregoing shall be in addition to the penalties now prescribed by law, and in no way to affect proceedings under existing law for like offenses. That, where practicable, this section shall be printed on the blank forms of vouchers provided for general use. (Act March 1, 1883 § 8. 22 Stat. 451: Ace July 4. 1884. § 8: Cir. 113 Ind. O.)

MEMORANDUM.

# CASH.

*Voucher No.* __21__ , __3__rd __ Quarter, 19_15_

FOR

# TRAVELING EXPENSES

IN FAVOR OF

Warner L Wilmeth

*For $* __12.99__

*Paid by* _____ Horace J Johnson _____
(Name.)

Supt. & S. D. A.
(Official title.)

Sac and Fox Indian School  Oklahoma.
(Agency or school.)

Voucher No.        ?

𝔇𝔈ℙ𝔄ℜ𝔗𝔐𝔈𝔑𝔗 𝔒𝔣                              **MEMORANDUM**
𝔗ℌ𝔈 𝔍𝔑𝔗𝔈ℜ𝔍𝔒ℜ        VOUCHER FOR TRAVELING EXPENSES
U. S. INDIAN SERVICE
Form approved by the Comptroller of
the Treasury May 15, 1909

𝔗ℌ𝔢 𝔘𝔫𝔦𝔱𝔢𝔡 𝔖𝔱𝔞𝔱𝔢𝔰.

To            Frank A. Winsor                    , Dr.

_Address,_  Sac and Fox Agency          Okla.
                        (City or town.)                    (State or territory.)

For ACTUAL traveling expenses as per itemized statement forming a part of this account, incurred in the discharge of
official duty from ...January 23..........., 1915 , to ....January 25..........., 1915, under written authorization
from ...Indian Office ..........., dated ...December 1..........., 1914   , which is attached to this or to
voucher No. .....4...., to account for .....3rd........... quarter, 1915 , for the purpose of  Holding
Hearings to determine heirs of deceased Sac and Fox Allottees

| DATE 1915 | ITEMS. Use extra sheets (Form 5-335 b), if necessary, and bring total to this blank. | Sub-voucher. | DOLLARS. | Cts. |
|---|---|---|---|---|
| Jan. 23 | Railroad fare Mayetta. Kansas, to Topeka, Kansas | | | 42 |
| Jan. 23 | Railroad fare from Topek, Kans., to Stroud, Okla. | | 8 | 81 |
| Jan. 24 | Sleeping car fare from Kansas City, Mo., to Stroud, Okla. Standard Lower Berth | | 2 | 00 |
| Jan. 25 | Pullman porter. (Night Service) | | | 25 |
| Jan. 26 | Storage of baggage for 1 day at Stroud, Okla. | | | 25 |
| | Paid from Fund, "Determining Heirs Deceased Indian Allottees, 1915" | | | |
| | AMOUNT CLAIMED............................................ | | 11 | 73 |

A true Copy of Original Voucher, except as to affidavit.

1134        Feb 1        5        11.73        U. S. Treasurer

**********

179

MEMORANDUM.

## CASH.

*Voucher No.* 20 , 3rd Quarter, 19 15

FOR

## TRAVELING EXPENSES

IN FAVOR OF

Frank A Winsor

*For $* 11.73

*Paid by* Korace[sic] J Johnson
(Name.)

Supt. & S. D. A.
(Official title.)

Sac and Fox Indian School  Oklahoma.
(Agency or school.)

Law-
   Heirship
   L  L

Report as to
   Heirship work.

Sac & Fox Indian School,
   Stroud, Okla., Dec. 10, 1914.

Commissioner of Indian Affairs,
   Washington, D. C.,
Sir:-

Referring to the above noted circular letter dated November 13, 1914, I have the honor to make the following report on the Sac and Fox heirship work at this Agency for the month of November, 1914.

Number of cases on hand at the beginning of
the month.................................................................30
Number of cases in which notices have been given for
hearing to be held during the month................................... 0
Original hearings held during the month........................... 0
(Ex-parte affidavits were taken in several cases, however).
Supplemental hearings held during the month..................... 0
Number of cases submitted to Indian Office....................... 5
Number of cases returned by Indian Office for correction...... 0
Number of cases returned by Indian Office for further
evidence or re-hearings.................................................. 7
(The above includes all that have been heretofore returned,
and that were on hand on November 30th.)
Number of cases returned by Indian Office for further
evidence or re-hearings re-submitted to Indian Office during
month....................................................................... 0
Unfinished cases upon which original hearings have been
held, but cases still on hand............................................25
Number of cases In which no action has been taken............. 0
Number of cases in which notice of final action has been
received....................................................................95
Number of cases in Indian Office upon which no definite
no action has been taken................................................ 7
Number of letters written...............................................30

In connection with this report it may be well to make a little explanation with reference to the status of the heirship work at this Agency concerning the Sac and Foxes.

Hearings have been held in all Sac and Fox cases except two and these have been set for hearing during the present month. One of these died something like a month or six weeks ago and the other has no allotment but does have quite considerable personal estate.

We have considerable testimony in all the Sac and Fox cases upon which no report has been made and in some of them no doubt we have sufficient data upon which to base a report which will warrant the Office in making a declaration, but we do not have sufficientdata[sic] in all of them. There are a few in which there are contested points, still others in which it is necessary for us to get certified copies of court records, and still others which will necessitate our carrying on correspondence with other Agencies. We are handling all of these cases just as rapidly as possible consistent with the other work in the office and the best interests of the Indians. None of them I believe are suffering in consequence of any delay which is being occasioned by not being able to make a declaration, and except in one or two cases I believe the Indian heirs themselves are much better off not to have the funds so that they can make excuses for unnecessary expenditures which on account of their nature we find it rather difficult to disapprove.

I have heretofore reported to the Office that we would be able toclose[sic] up probably all heirship cases under this Agency sometime about December 30, 1914. We shall not quite be able to do this but I believe if left to ourselves we can close up practically everything by the end of January. There will be then perhaps a half-dozen cases in which we shall not have been able to secure sufficient data upon which to base a report and in all of these cases I believe it will be practically impossible for anybody to obtain reliable data for the purpose.

Three of the seven cases reported as being returned by the Indian Office for further evidence or re-hearings have at this date been returned to your Office, consequently we now have on hand a large amount of data and in many of which no doubt we have sufficient data upon which to base a report when we can get to do so. One Clerk is now spending about half or more of his time upon this work.

Very respectfully,

Horace J Johnson
Supt. & S. D. A.

HJJ/WMH.

---

Law-
　Heirship
　　L L

Report as to
　Heirship work.

Sac & Fox Indian School,
Stroud, Okla., Dec. 10, 1914.

Commissioner of Indian Affairs,
　　　　Washington, D. C.,
　Sir:-

Referring to the above noted circular letter dated November 13, 1914, I have the honor to make the following report on the Iowa heirship work at this Agency for the month of November, 1914.

Number of cases on hand at the beginning of
the month................................................................. 4
Number of cases in which notices have been given for
hearing to be held during the month................................... 0
Original hearings held during the month........................... 0
Supplemental hearings held during the month.................... 0
Number of cases submitted to Indian Office...................... 0
Number of cases returned by Indian Office for correction...... 0
Number of cases returned by Indian Office for further
evidence or re-hearings................................................ 3
(The above includes all that have been heretofore returned,
and that were on hand on November 30th.)
Number of cases returned by Indian Office for further
evidence or re-hearings re-submitted to Indian Office during
month...................................................................... 0
Unfinished cases upon which original hearings have been
held, but cases still on hand........................................... 4
Number of cases in which no action has been taken............. 4
Number of cases in which notice of final action has been
received....................................................................15
Number of cases in Indian Office upon which no definite
no action has been taken................................................ 0
Number of letters written............................................... 0

In connection with this report it may be well to make a little explanation with reference to the status of the heirship work at this Agency concerning the Iowas.

Hearings have been held in all Iowa cases except four. I had promised the Iowa Indians that I would hold these hearings on the first Monday in January and notices have been issued to that effect.

We have four unfinished Iowa cases on all of which we have considerable data but not enough to base a report thereon. We are expecting on Jan. 4th. when hearings are held in the remaining Iowa cases to make another attempt to get sufficient data for the purpose mentioned.

I have heretofore reported to the Office that we should be able to clear up all heirship cases by the end of the present calendar year but it seems that we shall not be able to do this. I believe, however, if left to ourselves by the close of January we shall be above to make final reports on all cases in which it is possible to secure sufficient data. The probabilities are, however, that there will be at least three cases, possibly more, upon which we shall not be able to get this data, neither do I believe that the data is obtainable. It is possible that developments may arise whereby it will be necessary that we have more correspondence with other Agencies, with reference to some of these Iowa cases, than I now anticipate and if this is the case the matter of final reports may be somewhat delayed. However, in no cases are the interests of the interested Indians suffering on account of any delay which is being occasioned by the failure to secure declarations of heirship, in fact I believe the Indians in these cases are being benefited thereby.

Very respectfully,

Horace J Johnson

HJJ/WMH.                                          Supt. & S. D. A.

---

Law- Heirship
    L  L

Sac & Fox Indian School,<br>Stroud, Okla., Jan. 4, 1915.

Report as to
    Heirship work.

Commissioner of Indian Affairs,
                        Washington, D. C.,
Sir:-

Referring to the above noted circular letter dated November 13, 1914, I have the honor to make the following report on the Sac and Fox heirship work at this Agency for the month of December, 1914.

Number of cases on hand at the beginning of
the month...................................................................25
Number of cases in which notices have been given for
hearing to be held during the month.................................. 2
Original hearings held during the month.......................... 2
(Ex-parte affidavits were taken in several cases also).
Supplemental hearings held during the month.................... 4
Number of cases submitted to Indian Office..................... 6
Number of cases returned by Indian Office for correction...... 0
Number of cases returned by Indian Office for further
evidence or re-hearings................................................ 0
(We have four cases on hand that were returned some time ago
upon which sufficient data has not be obtained.)

Number of cases returned by Indian Office for further
evidence or re-hearings re-submitted to Indian Office during
month................................................................................. 3
Unfinished cases upon which original hearings have been
held, but cases still on hand..............................................21
Number of cases in which no action has been taken............ 0
Number of cases in which notice of final action has been
received.........................................................................96
Number of cases in Indian Office upon which no definite
no action has been taken.................................................15
Number of letters written................................................25

Attention is invited to my letter of January 4, 1915 in which the necessity

and advisability of appointing an Examiner of Inheritance at this Agency is questions.

Very respectfully,

Horace J Johnson
HJJ/WMH.                                        Supt. & S. D. A.

---

Law-
    Heirship
    L  L                                   Sac & Fox Indian School,
                                           Stroud, Okla., Jan. 4, 1915.
Report as to
    Heirship work.

Commissioner of Indian Affairs,
              Washington, D. C.,
    Sir:-

        Referring to the above noted circular letter dated November 13, 1914, I have

the honor to make the following report on the Iowa heirship work at this Agency for

the month of December, 1914.

Number of cases on hand at the beginning of
the month............................................................... 4
Number of cases in which notices have been given for
hearing to be held during the month................................. 0
Original hearings held during the month.......................... 0
Supplemental hearings held during the month................... 0
Number of cases submitted to Indian Office...................... 0
Number of cases returned by Indian Office for correction...... 0
Number of cases returned by Indian Office for further
evidence or re-hearings................................................. 0
(We have three cases on hand that were returned some time
ago upon which sufficient data has not been obtained.)

Unfinished cases upon which original hearings have been
held, but cases still on hand............................................. 4
Number of cases in which no action has been taken............. 0
Number of cases in which notice of final action has been
received...................................................................15
Number of cases in Indian Office upon which no definite
no action has been taken................................................ 0
Number of letters written............................................ 21

My report for the month of November shows that no action has been taken
in four Iowa cases. I have stated in this report that there are no Iowa cases on which
no action has been taken. On Dec. 5, 1914 notices were issued for those four hearings
to be held on January 4, 1915 and they are to be held on this date, consequently there
are no Iowa cases on which action has not been taken.

Attention is invited to my letter of January 4, 1915 in which the necessity
and advisability of appointing an Examiner of Inheritance at this Agency is
questioned.

Very respectfully,

Horace J Johnson
HJJ/WMH.                                      Supt. & S. D. A.

Law-
    Heirship
    L L
                                      Sac & Fox Indian School,
                                      Stroud, Okla., Feb. 6, 1915.
Report as to
    Heirship Work.

Commissioner of Indian Affairs,
                Washington, D. C.,
    Sir:-

    Referring to the above noted circular letter dated November 13, 1914, I have
the honor to make the following report on the Sac and Fox heirship work at this
Agency for the month of January, 1915.

        Number of cases on hand at the beginning of
        the month...................................................................21
        Number of cases in which notices have been given for

hearing to be held during the month..................................... 0
Original hearings held during the month........................... 0
Supplemental hearings held during the month.................... 0
Number of cases submitted to Indian Office...................... 9
Number of cases returned by Indian Office for correction...... 0
Number of cases returned by Indian Office for further
evidence or re-hearings................................................. 0
(We had four cases on hand at the beginning of the month
that were returned some time ago upon which sufficient data
had not been received.)
Number of cases returned by Indian Office for further
evidence or re-hearings re-submitted to Indian Office during
month................................................................... 1
Unfinished cases upon which original hearings have been          2[sic]
held, but cases still on hand............................................. 1
Number of cases in which no action has been taken............. 0
Number of cases in which notice of final action has been
received...............................................................99
Number of cases in Indian Office upon which no definite
no action has been taken..............................................22
Number of letters written............................................42


Very respectfully,

Horace J Johnson
WMH.                              Supt. & S. D. A.

---

Law-
   Heirship
   L L                                Sac & Fox Indian School,
                                         Stroud, Okla., Feb. 6, 1915.
Report as to
   Heirship work.

Commissioner of Indian Affairs,
               Washington, D. C.,
Sir:-

Referring to the above noted circular letter dated November 13, 1914, I have the honor to make the following report on the Iowa heirship work at this Agency for the month of January, 1915.


Number of cases on hand at the beginning of
the month............................................................... 4

Number of cases in which notices have been given for
hearing to be held during the month.................................... 4
Original hearings held during the month........................... 4
Supplemental hearings held during the month..................... 1
Number of cases submitted to Indian Office....................... 4
Number of cases returned by Indian Office for correction...... 0
Number of cases returned by Indian Office for further
evidence or re-hearings................................................. 0
(We had three cases on hand at the beginning of the month
that were returned some time ago upon which sufficient date
had not been received.)
Number of cases returned by Indian Office for further
evidence or re-hearing re-submitted to Indian Office during
month.................................................................... 2
Unfinished cases upon which original hearings have been
held, but cases still on hand............................................ 5
Number of cases in which no action has been taken............. 0
Number of cases in which notice of final action has been
received......................................................................15
Number of cases in Indian Office upon which no definite
no action has been taken................................................ 6
Number of letters written............................................. 9

Very respectfully,

Horace J Johnson
Supt. & S. D. A. S. D. A.

WMH.

---

DEPARTMENT OF THE INTERIOR

OFFICE OF INDIAN AFFAIRS

__Sac and Fox_____Agency, November 14, 1914

The Commissioner of Indian Affairs,

WASHINGTON, D. C.

Sir:

I respectfully report as directed in Office letter of November    , 1914, on the
amount of funds which should be apportioned me for the remainder of the current
fiscal year, 1915:

Practically all this work
should be closed up here
( 1 ) Length of time estimated for completion
of present assignment or work........ by June 30, 1915.....
( 2 ) Amount required for expenses,     ...... $100$^{00}$..........
$75 of this is for Witness and
mileage fees.

188

made us[sic] as follows:

| | |
|---|---|
| Salaries of examiners, | ......... |
| Traveling expenses examiners, | ..$15$^{00}$.... |
| Salaries clerical assistants, | ......... |
| Traveling expenses clerical assistants, | . $10$^{00}$.... |
| Total salaries and expenses allowed, | Have never heard of any allowances ......... |
| Total salaries and expenses apportioned, | Have never heard of any apportionment ......... |

Have expended $93.[33]

Respectfully submitted,

Examiner or Superintendent.

\*\*\*\*\*\*\*\*\*\*

Law-Heirship
L L

Apportionment,
Determining
Heirs, 1915.

DEPARTMENT OF THE INTERIOR
OFFICE OF INDIAN AFFAIRS
WASHINGTON

NOV 5 1914

Mr. H.J. Johnson,

Supt., Sac & Fox School, Oklahoma.

Sir:

For the purpose of apportioning the amount of money required for expenses in determining heirship cases for the remainder of the current fiscal year, you are directed on receipt of this letter to submit a report in answer to the following questions:

( 1 )  Length of time you estimate necessary for completion of present assignment?  (If answered by a superintendent give estimated time of completing the work.)

( 2 )  Approximate amount required for expenses of present assignment (exclusive of salary and amount already apportioned you) but not extending beyond close of current fiscal year?

Elaborate the answer to this question by going into as full details as may be required for a thorough understanding on the part of this Office of your needs for the amount of expenses which you ask for the continuation of your work.

Superintendents who are handling heirship cases will make the specific report called for in this letter from Examiners of Inheritance, and on the same basis.

It is important that this information should be received in this Office as early as practicable in order that an apportionment may be made, commencing December 1, and Examiners and others interested be notified as promptly after that date as practicable.

For uniformity, blanks on which to make your report at inclosed. In case it is necessary to use more space than that allotted on the blank under the second question, you should add a second sheet so that your full explanation of the necessity for each item of expense may be so complete that it readily can be seen whether the amount asked for should be allowed. Be sure to give the amounts already allowed you, as well as amounts expended to date of report.

Yours truly,

E. B. MERITT,

Assistant Commissioner.

---

Sac and Fox Indian School,
Stroud, Okla., Nov. 18, 1914.

George A. Hoyo, Supt.,
Otoe Indian School,
Otoe, Oklahoma.

Sir:-

Referring to your letter of the 11th inst., concerning the estate of Po-ha-ga, I have to advise that Po-ha-ga is not known here by that name. If the name is known by another name and you will advise me thereof, and we can identify him, I shall be pleased to give you the desired information.

Very respectfully,

Supt. & S. D. A.

AM

\*\*\*\*\*\*\*\*\*\*

# DEPARTMENT OF THE INTERIOR

## UNITED STATES INDIAN SERVICE.

RECEIVED
NOV 14 1914
SAC AND FOX INDIAN SCHOOL, OKLA.

Otoe Indian School,

Otoe, Oklahoma.

Nov. 11, 1914

Sup't. H. J. Johnson,

Sac and Fox Agency,

Stroud, Oklahoma.

Dear Sir:-

Frank O. English, an Otoe Indian, wants to know if the heirs to the estate of Po-ha-ga have ever been legally determined. If so, he wants to know who the heirs are.

Please advise us and we will give him this information.

Very respectfully,
George A. Hoyo
Superintendent.

PEH

---

APPOINTMENT OF GUARDIAN-AD-LITEM.

Sac and Fox Indian School,
Stroud, Okla., Dec. 5, 1914.

Walter M. Hodsdon,
Sac and Fox Indian Agency,
Stroud, Okla.

Sir:-

In the matter of determining the heirs of Charley Mohee, deceased Iowa allottee No. 96, it appearing that there are certain minors, to wit:

Frank Burgess,
Roy Burgess
and       Mark Burgess

who are interested in the estate, you are hereby appointed in accordance with the regulations of the Indian Office as Guardian-Ad-Litem for the said minor heirs in the said estate, and you will see to it that the interests of the said minor heirs in the said estate are at all times protected until you are discharged from such obligation.

_____

Supt. & S. D. A. S. D. A.

\*\*\*\*\*\*\*\*\*\*

**NOTICE OF HEARING TO DETERMINE HEIRS**

_____

## DEPARTMENT OF THE INTERIOR

### UNITED STATES INDIAN SERVICE.

Sac and Fox Indian Agency,
Stroud, Okla., Dec. 5  191 4

Osmond Franklin, Avery, Okla.
M  Walter M. Hodsdon, Stroud, Okla.
     Guardian-Ad-Litem for Frank Burgess,
     Roy Burgess and Mark Burgess, minors.
David Thoee[sic], Perkins, Okla.
Joseph Springer, Perkins, Okla.
Frank Kent, Perkins, Okla.
Robert Small, Perkins, Okla.

Notice is hereby given that on the     4th   day of       January     , 1912, at       The Indian Mission, Perkins, Okla.       , I will take testimony to be submitted to the Secretary of the Interior for the purpose of determining the heirs of       Charley Mohee         , deceased.

All persons having an interest in the estate of the decedent are hereby notified to be present at the hearing and furnish such evidence as they desire.

Respectfully,
Horace J. Johnson
Superintendent.

*№* 1607   Tecumseh, Okla.,          Dec 15              1914

IN DISTRICT COURT.

Received this day of          **W. M. Hodsdon**

35¢                                              DOLLARS

~~to apply on judgment, interest and costs in case~~   certified copy of divorce proceeding

Thorp

VS          Thorp

F. W. Watts          Clerk

Case No.  62          By   Homer King          Deputy

Deposits.

---

RECEIVED

## DEPARTMENT OF THE INTERIOR

### UNITED STATES INDIAN SERVICE

POTAWATOMI INDIAN AGENCY,

MAYETTA, KANSAS, December 15, 1914.

Horace J. Johnson,

Superintendent Sac and Fox Agency,

Oklahoma.

Dear Mr. Johnson:

I have received orders from the Office to proceed from this place to the Sac and Fox Agency, Oklahoma, about January 15, 1915.

You are requested to post notices of hearing for each day in the week beginning with January 22, 1915. Inclosed you will find the form that I have been using.  In cases where there are minor heirs you are requested to appoint a guardian ad litem to represent these heirs at the hearing.

Respectfully,

Warner L Wilmeth
Examiner of Inheritance.

12-FAW-15.

---

## DEPARTMENT OF THE INTERIOR
### UNITED STATES INDIAN SERVICE.

Seneca School, Quapaw Agency,
Wyandotte, Oklahoma,
December 16, 1914.
-18-

Mr. Orval E. Green,

Supt. Shawnee Indian School,

Shawnee, Okla.

Dear Sir:

I have another Shawnee Indian heirship case on which I have been unable to get sufficient testimony to establish the heirs.  It is that of Newton and Nancy McNeer, Shawnee Reservee No. 206 of Johnson County, Kansas.

This Indian lived and had his reservation on Cedar Creek, Kansas, between Olatha and DeSota, Kansas.  From what testimony I have taken it appears that Newton McNeer died in the early '50's, probably survived by his wife, Nancy, who died soon afterwards.  As far as I can learn he had at least one child, a daughter named Mary, who first married a Shawnee Indian by the name of White and by this husband had two or three children, one whose names was probably William White and a daughter named Tennessee White.  It further appears that after the death of White, Mary married an Irishman by the name of Todd who, with his wife, came to the Indian Territory and settled on what is known a Hudson Creek, near what is known as the town of Fairland.

Mary had two children by the said Todd, a son and daughter named John and Fannie.  Fannie is now married to a White man by by[sic] the name of Crotzer.  These children were very young when their mother died, consequently do not know anything about their family history.  It is probable that Newton McNeer may have nad[sic] other children than the said Mary, but I have no testimony on this subject.

If from this information you could secure the testimony from some old Shawnee Indians that may have known this man McNeer, I would thank you to do so.

Very respectfully,

Ira C. Deaver
Superintendent.

D-A

Sac & Fox – Shawnee Estates
1911-1919   Volume VI

\*\*\*\*\*\*\*\*\*\*

Shawnee Indian School,

Shawnee, Oklahoma, January 18, 1915.

Supt. Ira C. Deaver,
   Seneca School, Quapaw Agency,
     Wyandotte, Oklahoma.

Dear Mr. Deaver:

    Replying to your letter of the 16th, making inquiry as to the heirs in connection with the estate of Newton and Nancy McNeer, Shawnee Reservee No. 206, of Johnson County, Kansas, I have handed your letter to Mr. Thompson Alford, one of the clerks most acquainted with the Indians in this locality, and he has looked up the files, and has also taken this matter up with some of the older Indians, and advises me we are unable to furnish you any information in this matter.

Very respectfully,

OJG/cx                                 Superintendent.

---

Heirship
hearings.

Sac and Fox Indian School,
Stroud, Okla  Dec 19, 1914.

Warner L Wilmeth,
   Examiner of Inheritance,
     Mayetta, Kans.

Sir:-

    I have your letter of the 15th inst., and have to advise that there will be no hearings to be held at this Agency as late as January 22, 1915.

    There are only six estates in which no hearings have been held. Two of these are set for December 30th and the other four for January 4th.

    I am advising the Indian Office to this effect.

Very Respectfully,

HJJ/SP                     Supt. & S. D. A.

Distribution of
estate of Robert
Hunter.

Sac and Fox Indian School,
Stroud, Okla., Dec. 21, 1914.

R L Russell, Supt.,
Sac and Fox Sanatorium,
Toledo, Iowa.

Sir:
I enclose herewith checks as follows:

935 payable to Harrison Hunter for twenty five cents
936 payable to Emma Hunter for Twenty four cents
and      937 payable to R L Russell, Supt. for forty eight cents.

Please deliver the two former to the person in whose favor they are drawn and

deposit the latter as follows:

| | | |
|---|---|---|
| Daniel S Hunter | $0.24 | from Acct #822 |
| Gertrude Hunter | 0.24 | from Acct #822 |

Please sign the receipt on the duplicate of this letter and return it to me.  The
checks represent an interest balance that had accrued to the estate when the
distribution checks were presented.
I shall also be obliged to you if you will see that the the[sic] two former ones

are cashed and placed in bank so that they will not be lost and never presented for

payment.

Very respectfully,
Horace J Johnson
Supt. & S. D. A.


Received this day the check for forty eight cents and have deposited it as requested.

_R L Russell_

Letter in Duplicate.
Enclose checks (3)

NOTICE OF HEARING TO DETERMINE HEIRS

# DEPARTMENT OF THE INTERIOR

## UNITED STATES INDIAN SERVICE.

Potawatomi Indian Agency,

Mayetta, Kansas.

January 5      , 191 5

M Betsey Little Bear,  Stroud, Okla.

Much-e-ne-ne, Shawnee, Okla.

------------------ etc.

Friends:

Notice is hereby given that on the      6th    day of      February      .
1915, at     10:00 a.m. Sac and Fox Agency      , I will take testimony to be
submitted to the Secretary of the Interior for the purpose of determining the heirs
of           Rosa Felix          , deceased.

Sac and Fox allottee No, 568

All persons having an interest in the estate of the decedent are hereby notified
to be present at the hearing and furnish such evidence as they desire.

Respectfully,

Superintendent.

The heirs are required to furnish at least two disinterested witnesses who are
competent to give testimony that will establish the right of these heirs to inherit in
this estate.

---

Heirship
hearings
Sac and Fox Agency
Okla.

# DEPARTMENT OF THE INTERIOR

## UNITED STATES INDIAN SERVICE.

POTAWATOMI  INDIAN AGENCY,

MAYETTA, KANSAS, January 15, 1915.

Mr. Horace J. Johnson,

Superintendent Sac and Fox Agency,

Stroud, Oklahoma.

Dear Mr. Johnson:

I am in receipt of Office letter of January 12, 1915, instructing me to proceed to your Agency on the completion of my work at this place.

I advised the Office of the substance of your letter of December 19, 1914, and in reply thereto I have received Office letter of the above mentioned date.

You are requested to immediately post notices of hearing in all heriship[sic] cases under your jurisdiction which are not completed, giving 30 days notice in each instance, and posting one case for each work day in the week.   You will be informed as to the date of my arrival.

Respectfully,
Warner L. Wilmeth
Examiner of Inheritance.

1-FAW-15.

---

REFER IN REPLY TO THE FOLLOWING:

Law-Heirship
129231-14
2049-15
2242-15
F W S

ADDRESS ONLY THE
COMMISSIONER OF INDIAN AFFAIRS

**DEPARTMENT OF THE INTERIOR,**

OFFICE OF INDIAN AFFAIRS,

WASHINGTON,

RECEIVED

JAN 12 1915

Examiner of Inheritance,
Sac & Fox Agcy, Okla.

Mr. Horace J. Johnson,

Supt., Sac and Fox School.

My dear Mr. Johnson:

Receipt is acknowledged of your letter of January 4, 1915, also of your telegram of January 7, 1915, with reference to the detail of an Examiner of Inheritance to carry on the heirship work at the Sac and Fox Agency, Oklahoma. You state that the detail of this Examiner appears entirely unnecessary.

You are advised that the assignment of an Examiner of Inheritance to your Agency is in pursuance of the policy of this Office to relieve the various Superintendents, so far as possible, of the heirship work at their respective agencies.  It is the purpose to have Examiners of Inheritance proceed from one jurisdiction to another, bringing the work at each up to date; and in furtherance of this purpose, Examiner of Inheritance Wilmeth has been detailed to your Agency.

Inasmuch as it is the desire of the Office that the heirship work be handled as special work, there seems to be no reason for rescinding the directions given in Office letter of December 1, 1914 (Law-Heirship 129231-14).

Very truly yours,

EB Meritt

1-ANB-10                                                   Assistant Commissioner

---

REFER IN REPLY TO THE FOLLOWING:                                   ADDRESS ONLY THE
Law-Heirship                                         COMMISSIONER OF INDIAN AFFAIRS
L. L.          **DEPARTMENT OF THE INTERIOR,**

**OFFICE OF INDIAN AFFAIRS,**
Fees determining                **WASHINGTON,**          RECEIVED
heirs.

Mr. Horace J. Johnson,
                                                          JAN 18 1915
Supt. Sac and Fox School.

My dear Mr. Johnson:

The liability records of this Office show approximately 25 cases at your Agency where heirs have been determined by the Secretary of the Interior and for which no fees have been paid to September 30, 1914.

The Office desires that where fees are collectible for the determination of heirs that the same be paid and taken up in the cash accounts as soon as practicable after the notice of determination of heirs has been received. Payment should be made from any funds on hand to the credit of the estate or if the decedent left no funds from which payment may be made you should endeavor to have the heirs pay the fee from any funds to their credit under your supervision, or from any private funds if they are willing to make payment.

Hereafter, whenever funds belonging to an estate are divided among the heirs you will note in the "Remarks" column of the Land Sales, Lease Roll, Bank Accounts or other appropriate voucher, the file number for determination of heirs, allotment number of the decedent and the quarter in which the fee for determination of heirs was taken up in the accounts. If paid from bank accounts, lease moneys or proceeds of land sales, the bank account number, lease number, etc., should also be given.

Please give this matter immediate attention and acknowledge receipt of this letter within four days of its receipt.

Very truly yours,

E. B. Meritt
1-ELW-15                                    Assistant Commissioner.

---

## DEPARTMENT OF THE INTERIOR
### UNITED STATES INDIAN SERVICE.

Sac and Fox Indian School,
Stroud, Okla  Jan 18, 1915.

Indian Office
   Washington  D. C.

16 heirship cases on hand on which no report has been made. Regular hearings have been held in all cases and testimony taken. In some the evidence is sufficient upon which to base a report and in nearly all it is incomplete in minor details only that necessitates looking up court records and getting testimony and record information from other Agencies.

If he means in all cases on which no report has been made this will unnecessarily delay his work thus causing extra expense and before doing so desire further instruction from the Office.

Phoned 5:30 P.M.                    (S) Johnson, Supt.
1/18/15
Govt.N.R.C.

Wilmeth requests by letter received today that I post notices in all incomplete cases giving 30 days notice.

---

200

**TELEGRAM**
Law-Heirship
6616-1915
F W S

Telegram
──────

**DEPARTMENT OF THE INTERIOR**
OFFICE OF INDIAN AFFAIRS
WASHINGTON

January 19, 1915.

*Mail to*

Johnson,

Superintendent,

Stroud, Oklahoma.

Your telegram eighteenth. For new hearings give thirty days' notice. For cases incomplete, in which hearings have been held, fifteen days' notice sufficient.

1-VR-19

*(Signed) E. B. Meritt*
............................................................................
Assistant    *Commissioner*

**CONFIRMATION OF TELEGRAM**

─────────────────────────────────────

Authority
to reimburse.

Sac and Fox Indian School,
Stroud, Okla. Jan. 22, 1915.

Commissioner of Indian Affairs,
Washington, D. C.

Sir:

Referring to another communication of even date herewith concerning the matter of the collection of probate fees on Indian estates, I have the honor to ask that authority be granted me to reimburse the estates mentioned below in the sum of $15.00 each for probate fees erroneously collected thereon.

|  |  | Collected |  |
|---|---|---|---|
| Susie Grant, | L-H 34323-1913, | 1/24/14, | $15.00 |
| Jane Johnson, | L-H 36466-1913, | 9/18/13, | 15.00 |

| | | |
|---|---|---|
| Laura Keokuk, L-H 55151-1913, | 8/ 1/13, | 15.00 |
| Phoebe Keokuk, L-H 55152-13, | | |
| 62288-13, | 8/ 1/13, | 15.00 |
| Charles Keokuk, L-H 55050-13, | | |
| 55614-13, | 9/29/13, | 15.00 |
| William Ingalls, L-H 63921-13, | 9/29/13, | 15.00 |

and also to reimburse the estate of Silas Conger in the sum of $15.00 for a double collection of probate fees such collection having been made on the Land and Timber Sales Roll and also from the bank account of the estate and whereas only one collection should have been made, and it is doubtful in my mind now if even this collection should have been made, as the hearing was held long prior to February 14, 1913. If no such fee at all should be collected from this estate, authority is requested to reimburse the estate in the sum of $30.00 instead of $15.00.

The error in double collection on the Silas Conger estate (Land-Heirship 34272-13) is a clerical one pure and simple, but the error in collection on the six other estates was occasioned by it being the understanding on the part of this office that collections should be made on all estates in which declarations were made, subsequent to June first instead of June 30th. We thought we had a letter from the Indian Office on file giving us instructions to that effect but dilligent[sic] search on our part fails to bring any such instructions to light and unless such were issued and received, I am unable to state how we came to have such an understanding.

Very respectfully,

HJJ/AM                                      Supt. & S. D. A.

---

Law-Heirship
L  L

Sac and Fox Indian School,<br>Stroud, Okla. Jan. 22, 1915.

Commissioner of Indian Affairs,
    Washington, D. C.

Sir:

Sac & Fox – Shawnee Estates
1911-1919   Volume VI

Referring to the above noted communication dated January 18, 1915, I have the honor to advise that my report on Heirship work for the period ending December 31, 1914 shows that we have received declarations by the Secretary in 111 Heirship cases, not including those of Mary Thurman which was held at Toledo, Iowa and Samuel Wilson which was held at Kickapoo Indian School, Horton, Kansas, copies of which declarations were furnished me. Our records also show that of these 111 cases, thirty one were received prior to the passage of the Act of February 14, 1913, fifteen prior to the passage of the Act of June 30, 1913 and one had no allotment. It is my understanding that no fee is to be collected in cases of this kind, consequently on December 31, 1914, if my understanding is correct, we should have collected fees in sixty four cases. As a matter of fact, my cash reports to and including that of December 31, 1914 show that we have collected fees in sixty eight cases and further, that we have collected fees twice in one case. We erroneously, it appears, collected fees on six cases in which declarations were made during the month of June, 1913. These fees were on the estates of Susie Grant, (Land-Heirship 34323-1913), Jane Johnson (Land-Heirship 364660-1913), Laura Keokuk (Land-Heirship 55151-1913), Phoebe Keokuk (Land-Heirship 35152-1913, 62288-1913), Charles Keokuk (Land-Heirship 55051-13, 55614-13), and William Ingalls (Land-Heirship 63921-1913). The estate on which we have collected twice is that of Silas Conger. Fees were taken from the Land and Timber Sales voucher and also from his bank account.

In a separate communication I shall ask for authority to reimburse these estates in the amounts which we have erroneously collected. The only estates so far as our records show on which declarations have been received prior to December 31, 1914, and fees not collected, are those of Charles C. Murray, Eliza White Kebolte, Flora Mokohoko, Judith Houston and Lena Seaborn. I have not had in my possession any funds belonging to the estate of Charles C. Murray, Flora Mokohoko and Judith Houston since the declaration was made, consequently I have not been able to make any collections. I have talked with the heirs and they have promised to settle the probate fees but so far it has not been done. The Eliza White Kebolte estate descends in equal shares to a white man and an Indian. The Indian has paid his share of probate fees and it is deposited in bank account No. 2016 to the credit of the estate of Eliza White Kebolts, until such time as I can make collection of the othe[sic] half of the fee. The

203

white man, however absolutely refuses to pay the fee or acknowledge that the Depattment[sic] has any jurisdiction whatever, over the estate.  Steos are being taken for the partitionment of the estate and on January 16th 1915 all the papers connected witht the partutuinent of the estate and on Jaunuary 16th 1915 all the papers connected with the partitionment of the estate of Eiza White Kebolte were forwarded for Office action.

With reference to the Lena Seaborn case, this has been long drawn out and it was only recently that a final declaration was had and correspondence looking  to the eventual distribution of the estate, instituted.  The probate fees were collected January 6, 1915,

This therefore leaves but four estates in which the fee has not been paid in none of which are there funds for the purpose.

Very respectfully,

HJJ/AM                                                          Supt. & S. D. A.

---

Distribution of
estate.

Sac and Fox Indian School,
Stroud, Okla. Jan. 22, 1913.

R. L. Russell, Supt.
  Sac and Fox Sanitarium,
            Toledo, Iowa.

Sir:

I enclose herewith check No. 985 drawn upon the First National Bank of Stroud, Oklahoma, in your favor, in the sum of $34.49 to be deposited as follows:

| | | |
|---|---|---|
| Jim Scott, | $18.10, | From Acct. 284 |
| Roy V. Thurman, | 8.20, | "    "    " |
| Jennie Thurman, | 8.19, | "    "    " |

These funds represent their shares of the personal estate of Gertrude Givens.

Please sign the receipt on the duplicate of this letter and return it to this office.

Very respectfully,

Horace J Johnson
Supt. & S. D. A.

AM
Encl. check and duplicate letter.

Received the above mentioned check and have credited same as indicated.

__RL Russell_____
Superintendent.

---

Law-Heirship
  L  L

Sac and Fox Indian School,
Stroud, Okla., Jan. 23, 1915.

Commissioner Indian Affairs,
        Washington, D. C.

Sir:

Referring to the next to the last paragraph of the above noted communication, dated Jan. 18, 1914, I have the honor to ask if the instructions given therein with reference to the insertion of data mentioned is to apply every time any money belonging to an estate is divided among the heirs or only to the first distribution of funds after a Declaration is received and the Probate Fees collected.

As I understand the instructions, we are to make the entry every time we divide any money belonging to an estate among the heirs but as we will have divisions of funds to make in practically every estate which has been settled at least twice a year and as such entries will entail extra work which appears unnecessary I have thought that perhaps I am mistaken in my construction of the instructions and shall be pleased to be advised as to it's[sic] correctness.

Very Respectfully,

Supt. & S. D. A.

---

Law-Heirship
   L.  L.

Fees determing[sic]
   heirs.

Shawnee Indian Agency,

Shawnee, Oklahoma.

January 26, 1915.

Commissioner of Indian Affairs,

   Washington, D. C.

Sir:

   I have the honor to acknowledge receipt of Office letter of January 18, 1915, with the above caption, relative to the collection of hearing fees in the matter of the determination of the heirs of Indian Allottees under this Agency.  I have carefully noted the desire of the Office in the matter of the collections of said fees.

   In this connection, I have the honor to state that every effort is being made to collect these fees at all times, and that notations are carefully made upon lease cards where payment is soon to be made, and the records of money coming in from other sources are similarly noted, in order that collection of said fees may not be overlooked.  Where certain moneys come in connected with the approved hearing, collection of the fees, if due, is made first before any other disbursement is made of it.

   There have been approximately 242 cases approved by the Department in the matter of the hearings held at this Agency; out of the 242 cases, there are about 135 cases come under the Act of June 30, 1913 (Public No. 4), out of these cases collections have been made in 47 cases amounting to $704.00 up to date, $1.00 being still due in one case.  This leaves 88 cases on which there have been no collections of the fees made.

   Instructions given in the Office letter of January 18, 1915, will be carefully followed out, and where there are no funds coming into certain estates, efforts will be made to collect the fees from private funds of the heirs.  Where collections have been made from the heirs out of their private funds, if they have any, I have found them willing to settle the fees in nearly all cases.

Very respectfully,

Superintendent.

Sac & Fox – Shawnee Estates
1911-1919   Volume VI

REFER IN REPLY TO THE FOLLOWING:
Law-Heirship
   L. L.

Fees determining
   heirs.

**DEPARTMENT OF THE INTERIOR,**

OFFICE OF INDIAN AFFAIRS,

WASHINGTON,

ADDRESS ONLY THE
COMMISSIONER OF INDIAN AFFAIRS

JAN 18 1915

Mr. Orville J. Green,

Supt. Shawnee School.

My dear Mr. Green:

The liability records of this Office show approximately 85 cases at your Agency where heirs have been determined by the Secretary of the Interior and for which no fees have been paid to September 30, 1914.

The Office desires that where fees are collectible for the determination of heirs that the same be paid and taken up in the cash accounts as soon as practicable after the notice of determination of heirs has been received. Payment should be made from any funds on hand to the credit of the estate or if the decedent left no funds from which payment may be made you should endeavor to have the heirs pay the fee from any funds to their credit under your supervision, or from any private funds if they are willing to make payment.

Hereafter, whenever funds belonging to an estate are divided among the heirs you will note in the "Remarks" column of the Land Sales, Lease Roll, Bank Accounts or other appropriate voucher, the file number for determination of heirs, allotment number of the decedent and the quarter in which the fee for determination of heirs was taken up in the accounts. If paid from bank accounts, lease moneys or proceeds of land sales, the bank account number, lease number, etc., should also be given.

Please give this matter immediate attention and acknowledge receipt of this letter within four days of its receipt.

Very truly yours,

EB Meritt
Assistant Commissioner.

1-ELW-15

207

Distribution of
estate.

RECEIVED

Sac and Fox Indian School,
Stroud, Okla. Jan. 28, 1915.

R. L. Russell, Supt.
  Sac and Fox Sanitarium,
            Toledo, Iowa.

Sir:

Referring to my telegram of the 25th inst., and your letter of the 26th, I am
enclosing herewith check No. 987 drawn upon the First National Bank of Stroud,
Oklahoma, payable to your order for $260.97 to be deposited as follows:

| | | |
|---|---|---|
| Jim Scott, | $136.89, | From Acct. #826 |
| Roy V. Thurman, | 62.04, | "      "      " |
| Jennie Thurman, | 62.04, | "      "      " |

These funds represent their shares of the personal estate of Lucy Thurman.

I shall be pleased to have you sign the receipt on the duplicate of this letter
and return it to this office.

Very respectfully,

Horace J Johnson
        Supt. & S. D. A.

AM
Encl. check, duplicate letter.

Received the above mentioned check and have deposited same as indicated.

RL  Russell
        Superintendent.

---

Distribution
of estate.

RECEIVED

FEB 3 1915

SAC AND FOX INDIAN SCHOOL, OKLA.
Sac and Fox Indian School,
Stroud, Okla. Jan. 29, 1915.

A. R. Snyder, Supt.
  Pottawatomie Agency,
        Mayetta, Kansas.

Sir:

Referring to your letter of the 8th inst concerning rentals due Me-ough-kaw from the allotment of Harvey Madison, I am enclosing herewith check No. 993 drawn upon the First National Bank of Stroud, Oklahoma, in your favor for $76.71 to be deposited to the credit of Me-ough-kaw.  This represents her share of the personal estate of Harvey Madison which covers all rentals that have accrued.

Relative to the last paragraph of your letter I have to advise that no steps have yet been taken looking to the division of the allotment of Harvey Madison.  The land lies in such way that the proper course to take seems to be the sale thereof.  If Me-ough-kaw cares to do so, I shall be pleased to prepare a petition for the sale of same, for her signature.

Please sign the receipt on the duplicate of this letter and return it to this office.

Very respectfully,<br>
Horace J Johnson<br>
Supt. & S. D. A.

AM
Encl. check & duplicate letter.

Received above mentioned check and have credited same as indicated

    A. R. Snyder       Supt. & S. D. A.

---

Deposit.

Sac and Fox Indian School,<br>
Stroud, Okla.   Jan. 30, 1915.

O. J. Green, Supt.,
  Shawnee Indian School,
    Shawnee, Oklahoma.

Sir:

I enclose herewith check No 4063 drawn upon the First National Bank of Chandler, Oklahoma, in your favor for $5.71 to be deposited to the credit of Florien Littlebear.  The same is drawn for the purpose of closing out her account here.

Please sign the receipt on the duplicate of this letter and return it to this office

.

Very respectfully,

Horace J Johnson
Supt. & S. D. A.

AM
Encl. check and duplicate letter.

Received the above mentioned check and have credited same as indicated.

_O. J. Green_____

Feb. 3, 1915                                              Superintendent.

**********

Agricultural
rental

Sac and Fox Indian School,
Stroud, Okla  Jan 30, 1915.

Supt. O. J. Green,
Shawnee, Okla.

Sir:-

I am enclosing herewith check number 2663 drawn on the First National Bank of Stroud, Oklahoma in your favor for $62.50 to be deposited to the credit of Florien Littlebear.

This is the December lease rental on the Carrie J Littlebear allotment.

Please sign the receipt on the duplicate of this letter and return it to this office.

Very respectfully,

Horace J Johnson
Supt. & S. D. A.

SP
Encl. duplicate letter
and check.

Received this__3__day of__Feb.__1915 the above mentioned check and have deposited same as requested.

_O.J. Green_____
SUP'T. & S. D. AGENT

**********

210

## DEPARTMENT OF THE INTERIOR

Distribution     **UNITED STATES INDIAN SERVICE.**
of estate.

*RECEIVED*
*MAR 18 1915*
*SAC AND FOX INDIAN SCHOOL, OKLA.*

Sac and Fox Indian School,
Stroud, Okla. March 10, 1915.

O. J. Green, Supt.
 Shawnee Indian School,
  Shawnee, Oklahoma.

Sir:

  I enclose herewith check No. 1065 drawn upon the First National Bank of Stroud, Oklahoma in your favor for $0.92 to be deposited to the credit of Florien Littlebear, the same being her share of the personal estate of Carrie J. Littlebear.

  Please sign the receipt on the duplicate of this letter and return it to this office.

    Very respectfully,

     Horace J Johnson
     Supt. & S. D. A.

AM
Encl. check and letter.

  Received the above mentioned check and have credited same as indicated.

      __OJ Green__
      Supt. & S. D. A.

    **********

*RECEIVED*
*MAR 18 1915*
*SAC AND FOX INDIAN SCHOOL, OKLA.*

Distribution
of estate.

    Sac and Fox Indian School,
    Stroud, Okla.  March 5, 1915.

O. J. Green, Supt.,
 Shawnee Indian School,
  Shawnee, Oklahoma.

Sir:

I enclose herewith check No. 35 drawn upon the Bristow National Bank of Bristow, Oklahoma, in your favor for $0.87 to be deposited to the credit of Florien Littlebear, the same being her share of the personal estate of Oliver P. Morton.

Please sign the receipt on the duplicate of this letter and return it to this office.

Very respectfully,

Horace J Johnson
Supt. & S. D. A.

AM
Encl. check and letter.

Received the above mentioned check and have credited same as indicated.

__O.J. Green_____
Supt. & S. D. A.

**********

Distribution
of estates.

Sac and Fox Indian School,
Stroud, Okla. March 3, 1915.

O. J. Green, Supt.
Shawnee Indian School,
Shawnee, Oklahoma.

Sir:

I enclose herewith check No. 302 drawn upon the Union Nation Bank of Chandler, Oklahoma in your favor for $0.17 to be deposited to the credit of Florien Littlebear, the same being her share of the personal estate of Oliver P. Morton.

I also enclose check No. 302 drawn upon the same bank, for the same amount, in favor of George Littlebear, for delivery to him, the same being his share of the above mentioned estate. As this check is very small I shall be obliged if you will cash it yourself and present it to a bank or if you will induce the payee to do so.

Very respectfully,

Horace J Johnson
Supt. & S. D. A.

AM
Encl. checks and letter.

212

Sac & Fox – Shawnee Estates
1911-1919   Volume VI

Received the above mentioned checks and have credited same as indicated.

March 6, 1915

_____O. J. Green_____
Supt. & S. D. A.

---

[The letter below typed as given]

White Cloud Kansas
Feb. 8, 1915.

**RECEIVED**

Mr. H. Johnson
  Ind. Spcl disb Ag't.
    Sac & Fox Agency
      Oklahoma.

FEB 11 1915

SAC AND FOX INDIAN SCHOOL, OKLA.

Dear Sir:

    I received a letter from down there telling me that I am one heir of the estate of Joe [?]aubray (decesed).   If there is any money due me will you kindly forward it to me at once?   Will I haulfto singe and affdivet to prove I am an heir

    Respectfuly Yours   James Norris

**********

Estate.

Sac and Fox Indian School,
Stroud, Okla. Feb. 11, 1915.

James Morris[sic],
  Whitecloud, Kansas.

Sir:

    Referring to your letter of February 8th you are advised that so far as I am aware, we have no estate belonging to the person which you mention.

Very respectfully,

Supt. & S. D. A.

HJJ/AM

---

Distribution
of estate.

Sac and Fox Indian School,
Stroud, Okla. Feb. 8. 1915.

O. J. Green, Supt.,
   Shawnee Indian School,
      Shawnee, Oklahoma.

Sir:

     I enclose herewith check No. 4087 drawn upon the First National Bank of Chandler, Oklahoma, in your favor, for $831.51, to be deposited to the credit of Albert Ketch-show-no, the same being the personal estate of Bion Sullivan.

     Please sign the receipt on the duplicate of this letter and return it to this office.

Very respectfully,

Horace J Johnson
Supt. & S. D. A.

AM
Encl. check and duplicate letter.

Received the above mentioned check and have deposited same as indicated.

Feb. 9, 1915          O. J. Green
                Supt. & S. D. A.

## DEPARTMENT OF THE INTERIOR
### OFFICE OF INDIAN AFFAIRS
### WASHINGTON

*Authority is hereby granted for the settlement of an indebtedness of*

$ __10.00_____ *, incurred during the* _____third_____ *quarter, 191 , as evidenced by*

*the following-described vouchers, which are* $\begin{cases} returned \\ retained \end{cases}$ *for file with your account:*

| VOU. | QR. | NAME OF CLAIMANT AND PURPOSE OF EXPENDITURE. | # | AMOUNT. |
|------|-----|---------------------------------------------|---|---------|
| | | Martha Wooten<br>    For use of room for three days in which to hold<br>hearings to Determine Heirs of deceased Iowa allottees<br><br>    A full explanation of the necessity for this service is given on<br>the voucher. The hearings were held in consequence to contents of<br>office letter [illegible] it being more [illegible] for both the Indians<br>and the Government to holds them where they were held than to<br>require the Indians to come to the agency.<br><br>    The Office is requested to designate the fund from which<br>payment is to be made. | | 10 00 |
| | | | TOTAL, | 10 00 |

*This sheet to be detached and retained by Disbursing Officer.*

TO:

Horace J Johnson
(Title or name.)

Sac and For Indian School
(School.)

Stroud, Oklahoma.
(Post Office.)

MAR 15 1915

COPY.—To be filed by the disbursing officer with proper voucher in his copy of memorandum account.

*(Signed) C.F. Hauke*

| *In this column will be indicated by use of one or more of the following numbers, the funds it is desired to use in making payment: | | |
|---|---|---|
| (1) "Determining Heirs Deceased Indian Allottees, | $10.00 | |
| (2)        1915" | $ | |
| (3) | $ | |
| (4) | $ | |
| (5) To be designated by the office  - - - - - - - - - - - - - - - - | $ | |

ADVERTISEMENT

### DEPARTMENT OF THE INTERIOR
#### UNITED STATES INDIAN SERVICE

Sac and Fox Indian School

Stroud, Okla.  Jan 4, 1915 , 191

Proposals on the blank below will be received at this office until＿＿＿＿＿＿o'clock ＿ m., ＿＿immediately＿＿＿, 191  , for furnishing the following articles or service for the period commencing＿＿January 4＿＿, 191 5  and ending＿January 6,＿, 1915

The right is reserved to reject any and all bids, to accept one part and reject the other, and to waive technical defects as the interests of the service may require.  Bidders are invited to be present.

Horace J. Johnson
(Agent or Superintendent.)

| ITEM No. | ARTICLES OR SERVICE REQUIRED. | Estimated shipping weight. (Pounds) | Price per unit. | TOTAL AMOUNT. |
|---|---|---|---|---|
| | | TO BE FILLED IN BY BIDDER. | | |
| 1 | Use of room for three days for conducting heirship hearings in the case of deceased Indian allottees. . . . . . . . . . . . . . . . . . . | | $3.33 1/3 | $10.00 |
| | | | | |
| | | | | |
| | | | | |
| | | | | |
| | | | | |
| | | | | |
| | Delivered f. o. b. ＿＿＿ (Insert place of delivery.) | | | |

## PROPOSAL.

The undersigned hereby agree to furnish the ＿＿＿＿Sac and Fox Indian School＿＿＿ in conformity with this proposal, and as per schedule attached, any or all of the foregoing articles or service at the prices affixed thereto, and will deliver the articles or service as above stated.

**No Member of Congress or other officer of the United States Government shall have any interest, direct or indirect, in this agreement. (35 Stats., 1109.)**

(S)  Martha Wooten
(Name.)

Perkins, Okla.
(P. O. address.)

Name of person affixing signature must be written by himself and his title must be given.

By＿＿＿＿＿＿＿＿＿＿＿＿

Title

## ACCEPTANCE.

*Approved and accepted as to items numbered* ＿＿＿1＿＿ *at the prices specified.*

Dated ＿ Jan 4 ＿, 1915               ＿＿＿Horace J. Johnson＿＿＿

\*\*\*\*\*\*\*\*\*\*

| Copies of this circular sent to the following persons: |
| --- |

---------------------------------------

_____ Martha Wooten _____
_____ Perkins, Oklahoma _____

**ABSTRACT OF PROPOSALS RECEIVED.**

☞ SEE INSTRUCTIONS TO AGENT. ☜

| Bidders | Bid. |
| --- | --- |
| | |
| | |
| Martha Wooten | $10 00 |
| | |
| | |
| | |
| | |

I certify that the above abstract is correct and the proposal herewith was the lowest upon the articles specified except _____

no other suitable place _____

available _____

which rejected because of _____

_____ Horace J. Johnson _____
*Agent or Superintendent.*

and posted in ___no___ public places.

\*\*\*\*\*\*\*\*\*\*

MEMORANDUM.

**VOUCHER FOR MISCELLANEOUS EXPENSES, SUCH AS RENT OF BUILDINGS, TELEPHONE
SERVICE, GAS, ELECTRIC LIGHT, AND WATER SUPPLY. ETC.**

THE UNITED STATES,                    Feb. 5, 1915.              *19*

*To*            Martha Wooten              *, Dr.*

(Give post-office address.)  Indian Mission Perkins, Okla.

| DATE 19 15 | ENTER BELOW THE SUBJECT MATTER OF THE CLAIM, SHOWING OF WHAT IT CONSISTS. | AMOUNT. |
|---|---|---|
| Jan. | **FOR AGENCY PURPOSES** | |
| 4/6 | To use of room for three days in which to hold Hearings | |
| | to determine heirs of deceased Iowa Allottees at $3.33 1/3 | 1000 |
| | per day | |

Paid from:"DETERMINING HEIRS DECEASED INDIAN ALLOTTEES" 1915"

    I certify that it was necessary to have a place in which to hold
Hearings to determine heirs of deceased allottees, Hearings for which
purpose were held January 4, 5 and 6, 1915, at the Indian Mission near
Perkins, Okla.

    I further certify that heretofore when we have held such Hearings at
Perkins we have used the church belonging to the Quaker Mission but
that on the occasion of those held as indicated herein, the church
building was not in condition so that it could be made comfortable.

    I further certify that Mrs. Wooten is the wife of the Missionary and
that in order for her to make room for us it was necessary for her to
move out her bed and some of her furniture each morning and move it
back at night so that her family could occupy the room during the night.

    I further certify that Mrs. Wooten furnished light and fuel for
keeping the room comfortable and was put to considerable
inconvenience to make things comfortable for us and for the Indian
witnesses who were present and that I believe the charge made for the
use of the room was very reasonable especially when the work
connected with the keeping of it in order is taken into consideration.

$ 1000

Supt. & S. D. A.

----TEN DOLLARS------------------Horace J Johnson

THE ABOVE IS A TRUE COPY OF ORIGINAL VOUCHER, EXCEPT AS TO CERTIFICATES.
PAID IN CASH, UNLESS OTHERWISE NOTED AT THE BOTTOM HEREOF.

Services procured under authority dated ........ Mar. 15, 1915 ., 19   , attached to
original or to voucher No. ....59......... to account for ..3..........Quarter, 1915 , and in
accordance with sections ..B... and ..4a... of the methods stated on original.
              Letter)      (Number)

Dated ------------------- , 19

Paid by Check No. ...1232... , dated .....March 16, 1915...... , 19  , for $10.00 ..,
on ................. U.S. Treasurer .................... , to order of claimant.

**********

## MEMORANDUM.

### CASH

*Voucher No.* __59__ , __3__ *Quarter, 19*15

FOR

### MISCELLANEOUS EXPENSES.

IN FAVOR OF

Martha Wooten

*For $* 10.00

*Paid by* Horace J Johnson

Supt. & S. D. A.
(Official title)

Sac and Fox Indian School
(Agency or School)

Oklahoma.

Any disbursing or other officer of the United States or other person who shall knowingly present, or cause to be presented, any voucher, account, or claim to any officer of the United States for approval or payment, or for the purpose of securing a credit in any account with the United States, relating to any matter pertaining to the Indian Service, which shall contain any material misrepresentation of fact in regard to the amount due or paid, the name or character of the article furnished or received, or of the service rendered, or to the date of purchase, delivery, or performance of service, or in any other particular, shall not be entitled to payment or credit for any part of said voucher, account, or claim; and if any such credit shall be given or received, or payment made, the United States may recharge the same to the officer or person receiving the credit or payment and recover the amount from either or both, in the same manner as other debts due the United States are collected; PROVIDED, That where an account contains more than one voucher the foregoing shall apply only to such vouchers as contain the misrepresentation; AND PROVIDED FURTHER, That the officers and persons by and between whom the business is transacted shall be presumed to know the facts in relation to the matter set forth in the voucher, account, or claim; AND PROVIDED FURTHER, That the foregoing shall be in addition to the penalties now prescribed by law, and in no way to affect proceedings under existing law for like offenses. That, where practicable, this section shall be printed on the blank forms of vouchers provided for general use. (Act March 1, 1883 § 8, 22 Stat, 451; Ace July 4, 1884, § 8; Cir. 113 Ind. O.)

---

Law-Heirship
13400-1915
  L  L
Assignment of
Examiner of Inher-
itance.

FEB **26** 1915

Mr. Ira C. Deaver,

   Supt. Seneca School,

My dear Mr. Deaver:

Referring to the matter of the determination of heirs of deceased Indian allottees, you are informed that Mr. Warner L. Wilmeth, Examiner of Inheritance, who is now on duty at the Sac and Fox Agency, will proceed to the Otoe Indian Agency for the purpose of holding hearing in several Sac and Fox cases, the evidence for which can only be furnished by parties residing at the latter place; and will then proceed to the Seneca School for the purpose of completing the heirship work there.

Examiner Wilmeth's stenographer, Mr. Frank A. Winsor, has also been directed to accompany him to Otoe and Seneca Agencies; and Mr. Wilmeth has been instructed to notify you when he may be expected at the Seneca School, giving sufficient advance notice so as to enable you to have a number of notices of hearings issued, thereby causing no unusual delay in the work.

You are further directed to take both Mr. Wilmeth and Mr. Winsor up on your payroll from the date of their departure from the Otoe Agency and pay their salaries and expenses, including traveling expenses from Otoe to Seneca, from that date until further instructions are sent you.

Very truly yours,

*(Signed) E. B. Meritt*

2-VR-25

Assistant Commissioner.

Carbon to Supt. Sac & Fox School.
 " " " Otoe   "
 " " Examiner Warner L. Wilmeth.

---

Distribution
of estate.

Sac and Fox Indian School,
Stroud, Okla. March 3, 1915.

O. J. Green, Supt.,
 Shawnee Indian School,
  Shawnee, Oklahoma.

Sir:

I enclose herewith check No. 1034 drawn upon the First National Bank of Stroud, Oklahoma, in your favor for $5.81 to be deposited as follows:

| Pe-ah-ma-ske, | $1.94 |
|---|---|
| Albert Ketch-show-no | 3.87 |

These funds represent their share of the personal estate of Neoma Sullivan.

Please sign the receipt on the duplicate of this check[sic] and return it to me.,

Very respectfully,

Horace J Johnson
Supt. & S. D. A.

AM
Encl. check, duplicate letter.

Received the above mentioned check and have deposited same as indicated.

O. J. Green
March 6, 1915                                Supt. & S. D. A.

---

Distribution
of estate.

RECEIVED
MAR 10 1915
SAC AND FOX INDIAN SCHOOL, OKLA

Sac and Fox Indian School,
Stroud, Okla. March 3, 1915

A. R. Snyder, Supt.,
    Pottawatomie Agency,
        Mayetta, Kansas.

Sir:

I enclose herewith check No. 1023 drawn upon the First National Bank of Stroud, Oklahoma, in your favor for $0.10 to be deposited to the credit of Maud Kakaque, the same being her share of the personal estate of Maw-mel-lo-haw.

I also enclose check No. 1025 drawn upon the same bank, in favor of Jesse Kakaque for $0.09, for delivery to him, the same being his share of the above mentioned estate. As this check is very small, I shall be obliged if you will cash it yourself and present it to a bank or if you will induce the payee to do so.

Please sign the receipt on the duplicate of this letter and return it to me.

Very respectfully,

Horace J Johnson
Supt. & S. D. A.

AM
Encl. checks, duplicate letter.

Received the above mentioned check and have credited same as indicated.

<u>A.R. Snyder</u>
Supt. & S. D. A.

---

Distribution
of estate.

Sac and Fox Indian School,
Stroud, Okla. March 10, 1915.

O. J. Green, Supt.
Shawnee Indian School,
Shawnee, Oklahoma.

Sir:

I enclose herewith check No. 1065 drawn upon the First National Bank of Stroud, Oklahoma in your favor for $0.92 to be deposited to the credit of Florien Littlebear, the same being her share of the personal estate of Carrie J. Littlebear.

Please sign the receipt on the duplicate of this letter and return it to this office.

Very respectfully,

Horace J Johnson
Supt. & S. D. A.

AM
Encl. check and letter.

Received the above mentioned check and have credited same as indicated.

- - - - - - - - - - - - - - - - - - - - -
Supt. & S. D. A.

Territory of Oklahoma )
                      ) SS.
Lincoln County        )

    We, the undersigned members of the Sac and Fox tribe of Indians, of lawful age and being first duly sworn, depose and say that we were well acquainted with Robert Hunter, deceased Sac and Fox allottee No. 509; that he died on or about June 10, 1901, leaving the following as his sole and only heirs:

    Henry Hunter, son,  aged 30 yrs. sharing 1/5 interest.
    Emma Hunter, dau.   "  26  "      "   1/5   "
    Harrison Hunter, son, " 18  "      "   1/5   "
    Gertrude Hunter, dau. " 15  "      "   1/5   "
    Daniel S. Hunter, son, "  8  "      "   1/5   "

    He left no wife, and no other children nor the issue of any deceased child or children than as above shown.

Witnesses:

| John RS Reeves | Alex Connolly |
|---|---|
| Charles F Welles | Edgar Mack  his X mark |

    Subscribed in my presence and sworn to before me this [?] day of June 190[?].

JUN 8 1911
My comm. expires.............................

    Charles F Welles
    Notary Public

**Cert. on file in Indian Office.**

---

## DEPARTMENT OF THE INTERIOR

Distribution of  **UNITED STATES INDIAN SERVICE**
estate for deposit.

Sac and Fox Indian School,
Stroud, Okla. March 17, 1915.

George A. Hoyo, Supt.
Otoe Indian School,
Otoe, Oklahoma.

Sir:

I enclose herewith check No. 1093 drawn upon the First National Bank of Stroud, Oklahoma, in your favor for $262.35 to be deposited as follows:

| | |
|---|---|
| Frank Burgess, | $87.45 |
| Roy Burgess, | 87.45 |
| Mary Burgess, | 87.45 |
| | Total . . . $262.35 |

These funds represent their share of the personal estate of Charles Mohee.

Please sign the receipt on the duplicate of this letter and return it to this office.

Very respectfully,

Horace J Johnson
Supt. & S. D. A.

AM
Encl. check envelope and
    duplicate letter.

MAR 22 1915

Received the above mentioned check and have credited same as indicated.

George A. Hoyo

---

# DEPARTMENT OF THE INTERIOR

Distribution
of estate for
deposit.

**UNITED STATES INDIAN SERVICE**

Sac and Fox Indian School,
Stroud, Okla. March 19, 1915.

George A. Hoyo, Supt.
    Otoe Indian School,
        Otoe, Oklahoma.

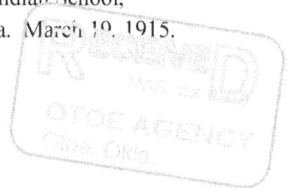

Sir:

I enclose herewith check No. 5048 drawn upon the First National Bank of Chandler, Oklahoma, in your favor for $429.30 to be credited as follows:

| | |
|---|---|
| John F. Falk, | $107.33 |
| Margaret Bassett | 107.32 |

Nora Pickering,                     160.98
Isaac Pickering,                     53.67

Please sign the receipt on the duplicate of this letter and return it to this office.

Very respectfully,

Horace J Johnson
Supt. & S. D. A.

AM
Encl. check.

MAR 22 '15

Received the above mentioned check and have credited same as indicated.

_George A. Hoyo_____
Supt. & S. D. A

---

Law-Heirship          DEPARTMENT OF THE INTERIOR
  L L
Sample card for          Office of Indian Affairs
record Depart-                         APR -2 1915
mental findings.          Washington

Mr. Horace J. Johnson,

Supt., Sac & Fox School.

My dear Mr. Johnson:

Find herewith a sample of the card to be used as permanent record of Departmental findings, determining the heirs of deceased Indians, and you are requested to make requisition for the number required for your agency. You are also requested, if you have not a proper filing case for the same, to make requisition therefor as soon as practicable, the same to be paid from "Determining heirs of deceased allottees, 1915,"

Very truly yours,

EB Meritt
3-VR-19                          Assistant Commissioner.

Sac & Fox – Shawnee Estates
1911-1919   Volume VI

# DEPARTMENT OF THE INTERIOR

Complaint of
Sophie Lincoln.

UNITED STATES INDIAN SERVICE

Sac and Fox Indian School,
Stroud, Okla., April 16, 1915.

E. M. Sweet, Jr.,
   U. S. Indian Inspector,
   Stroud, Oklahoma.

My Dear Mr. Sweet:
          Referring to your letter of today enumerating certain charges, or rather, complaints made against me by some of the Iowa Indians, I have the honor to reply as follows concerning the one made by Sophie Lincoln.
          Sophie Lincoln is the widow of Joe Embler, a deceased son of John Ford, or Hog-gra-ah-chey, as he is carried on our allotment roll.
          Hog-gra-ah-chey died several years ago and up to the time when I came here his presumed heirs had been drawing the lease rentals derived from his allotment. On account of legislation looking to determining of heirs of deceased Indians and the fear that payments might be wrongfully made I refused to pay out any heirship money until the heirs had been determined by the Department. My action in this respect has been upheld by the Office.
          The lease rentals accrueing[sic] on the Hog-gra-ah-chey allotment were among those held up. An effort was made to determine the heirs of Hog-gra-ah-chey and in December, 1913 I thought I had enough evidence upon which to base a report and did so. The Office, however thought otherwise and asked for more information. This was furnished in the course of time but as yet no determination has been had. I think Mr. Wilmeth also had instructions to hold a supplemental hearing in the case but of this I cannot be certain. At any rate the heirs of Hog-gra-ah-chey have not as yet been determined and though the funds are in my possession, their ownership has not as yet been decided.
          When the ownership is decided no doubt Sophie Embler will be found to have a one half interest in the estate and the money will be paid her or expended for her benefit. In the meantime it is drawing four and one half per cent interest and has no doubt made more for her in interest since it has been held than it ever will after she gets it in her hands.
          Both Sophie and Thomas Lincoln are thoroughly conversant with the matter and understand fully why it has not been paid to her. I have no doubt that I have explained it to them no less than a dozen times. They were also advised that they could expedite matters if they would be securing for us the date which the Office desired in order to make a declaration of heirs. They made no effort to do this.
                    Very Sincerely,

                              Supt. & S. D. A.

Hog-gra-ah-chey Account $357.02
Amount belonging to Sophie Embler $178.51

226

REFER IN REPLY TO THE FOLLOWING:                                        ADDRESS ONLY THE
Finance-Accounts.   **DEPARTMENT OF THE INTERIOR,**   COMMISSIONER OF INDIAN AFFAIRS
45720-15.                    **OFFICE OF INDIAN AFFAIRS,**
J. W. P.                            **WASHINGTON,**

MAY 4 1915

Fees determining heirs.

Mr. Horace J. Johnson,

    Supt. Sac and Fox School, Okla.

My dear Mr. Johnson:

    Answering your letter dated April 16, 1915, you are advised that upon
further consideration since writing letter dated March 2, 1915, stating that the
Office could not authorize you to reimburse the estates for heirship fees
erroneously paid, from fees collected for the determination of heirs in other
cases, it has been decided that it will be proper for you to reimburse the estates
from any funds in your hands collected as fees for the determination of heirs, and
you are authorized to restore the amounts to the credit of the estates mentioned in
Office letter of March 2, 1915, and pay to the several heirs of the deceased
Indians the amounts due them from the restored fees, provided they have no bank
accounts and are competent.   In case any of the Indians have individual Indian
money bank accounts, the amounts due them should be placed to their credit in
the bank and disbursed under proper authority.

               Very truly yours,

                   EB Meritt
4-EGK-30                            ~~Second~~ Assistant Commissioner.

Paid 6/1/15

---

Finance-Accounts
  11063-15
  J W P
Fees Determining
  Heirs

               Sac and Fox Indian School,
                 Stroud, Okla., April 16, 1915.

Commissioner Indian Affairs
   Washington, D. C.

Sir:

Referring to the above noted communication I have the honor to advise that the probate fees collected in the estates of

| | | |
|---|---|---|
| Jane Johnson, L-H 36466-1913 | 9-18-13 | $15.00 |
| Laura Keokuk, L-H 55151-1913 | 8- 1-13 | 15.00 |
| Phoebe Keokuk, L-H 55152-1913 | | |
| 52288-13 | 8- 1-13 | 15.00 |
| Charles Keokuk, L-H 55050-13 | | |
| 55614-13 | 9-29-13 | 15.00 |
| William Ingalls, L-H 63921-13 | 9-29-13 | 15.00 |
| Silas Conger(2) L-H 34272-13 | 9-8 -13 | 15.00 |
| | 12- 6-13 | 15.00,  and |
| Mary Roubidoux  L-H 90386-13 | 9-29-13 | 15.00 |

were deposited with the United States Treasurer to the credit of the United States during December, 1913.  The certificate from the Treasurer is numbered 1967 and is dated Jan. 25, 1914.

The fees in the Susie Grant case were deposited to the credit of the United States by Certificate No. 4294, dated March 30, 1914.

In this connection I have the honor to ask that the $135,99 erroneously collected as shown above be placed to my official account and that I be authorized to draw checks thereon to pay to the several heirs of the deceased allottees as indicated by the Secretary of the Interior the Interior in the declaration of heirs of the several estates, their proper share of the amounts erroneously collected.

Very respectfully,

Supt. & S. D. A.

HJJ/ND

---

REFER IN REPLY TO THE FOLLOWING:

Finance-Accounts.

11063-15.

J. W. P.

Fees determining
heirs.

**DEPARTMENT OF THE INTERIOR,**

OFFICE OF INDIAN AFFAIRS,

WASHINGTON,

MAR -2 1915

ADDRESS ONLY THE
COMMISSIONER OF INDIAN AFFAIRS

Mr. Horace J. Johnson,

Superintendent, Sac and Fox School, Okla.

Sac & Fox – Shawnee Estates
1911-1919   Volume VI

My dear Mr. Johnson:

Answering your letter dated January 22, 1915, relative to the collection of fees for the determination of heirs in the following cases, which should not have been collected, you are advised that the Office cannot authorize you to reimburse the estates from fees collected for the determination of heirs in other cases. However, if the money actually collected in these cases is still on hand, you may restore it to the credit of the respective estates. If the proceeds collected were deposited to the credit of the United States, you will advise the office of the number And date of the certificate of deposit, in order that the money may be placed to your official credit for return to the credit of the estates from which it was erroneously collected:

Collected

| | | |
|---|---|---|
| Susie Grant,  L-H 34323-1913 | 1-24-14 | $15.00 |
| Jane Johnson, L-H 36466-1912, | 9-18-13 | 15.00 |
| Laura Keokuk, L-H 55151-1913, | 8- 1-13 | 15.00 |
| Phoebe Keokuk, L-H 55152-12, | | |
| 62288-13 | 8- 1-13 | 15 00 |
| Charles Keokuk, L-H 55050-13, | | |
| 55614-13, | 9-29-13 | 15.00 |
| William Ingalls, L-H 63921-13, | 9-29-13 | 15.00 |

[end of letter]

---

[The letter below typed as given]

CHAS. L. MOORE                                                                GEO. H. MOORE

## C. L. MOORE & SON

DEALERS IN

NEW AND SECOND HAND GOODS

NORMAN, OKLA

May 29, 1915.

O.J. Green Esq.

Shawnee, Okla.

Dear sir:- Yours of recent date,with check for 64cts. received.  I must way that I am unable to give you the address of Rosalie G. Thompson,as I can not place the party.Francis E.Darling is probally my brother, who signs his name Edward Francis Darling,and is located on Route 6,Norman,Okla.

I understood that one,Fannie Sutherland claims heirship in the Lucius A Darling estate,inherited by being the wife of Francis L.Darling (my father) deceased (Francis L.Darling being a brother of Lucius Darling) In or during the latter part of Mr. Jno A.Buntins term in the office of which you now have charge, The Int.Department made a ruling that Fannie Sutherland was not the legal wife of Francis L.Darling deceased,and could not heir in the estate of Francis L.Darling.and it appears to me that, she can nit legally heirs any part of the Lucius Darling estate.

You will find enclosed herewith 25cts for which you will please place my name on the mailing list of the Scout,and oblige

Yours respectfully,

CLM

Rosa L Moore

119 E.Beal St. Norman, Okla.

---

Check for deposit

RECEIVED
JUN 12 1915
SAC AND FOX INDIAN SCHOOL, OKLA

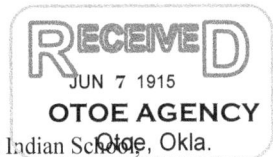

RECEIVED
JUN 7 1915
**OTOE AGENCY**
Otoe, Okla.

Sac and Fox Indian School
Stroud, Okla June 3, 1915.

Supt. George A Hoyo,
    Otoe, Oklahoma.

Sir:-

I am enclosing herewith check number 2846 drawn on the First National Bank of Stroud, Oklahoma in your favor for $4.58 which is to be deposited to the credit of Sophie Roubidoux.

This is reimbursement from the estate of Mary Roubidoux. Please sign the receipt on the duplicate of this letter and return it to this office.

Very respectfully,

Horace J Johnson
Supt. & S. D. A.

SP
Encl. Check
and letter.


Received this_7ᵗʰ_day of_June_1915 the above mentioned check and have
deposited same as requested.

_____George A. Hoyo_____
Supt. & S. D. A.

---

Check for
deposit

Sac and Fox Indian School,
Stroud, Okla. June 3, 1915.

First National Bank
Chandler, Oklahoma.

Gentlemen:-

I am enclosing herewith check number 2825 drawn on the First National
Bank of Stroud, Oklahoma in your favor for $15.00 which is to be deposited to Indian
Account as follows:

| Acct No. | Name | Amount | Reimbursement. |
|---|---|---|---|
| 383 | Orlando Johnson | $15.00 | Estate of Jane Johnson. |

Please sign the receipt on the duplicate of this letter and return it to this
office in the accompanying envelop which requires no stamp.

Very respectfully,

Horace J Johnson
Supt. & S. D. A.

SP
Check, letter and
envelop encl.


Received this_7_day of_June__1915 the above mentioned check and have
deposited same as requested.

First National Bank, Chandler, Okla
[Name Illegible] V.P.

---

Check for
deposit

Sac and Fox Indian School,
Stroud, Okla.  June 3, 1915.

First National Bank
   Chandler, Oklahoma.

Gentlemen:-

I am enclosing herewith check number 2840 drawn on the First National Bank of Stroud, Oklahoma in your favor for $5.00 which is to be deposited to Indian Account as follows:

| Acct No. | Name | Amount | Reimbursement. |
|---|---|---|---|
| 381 | Henry Ingalls | $5.00 | Estate of William Ingalls. |

Please sign the enclosed receipt on the duplicate of this letter and return it to this office in the accompanying envelop which requires no stamp.

Very respectfully,

Horace J Johnson
Supt. & S. D. A.

SP
Check, letter and
envelop encl.

Received this 7 day of June 1915 the above mentioned check and have deposited same as requested.

First National Bank, Chandler, Okla
[Name Illegible] V.P.

___

Heirship of
Anigre.

Sac and Fox Indian School,
Stroud, Okla.  June 11, 1915.

Warner L. Wilmeth,
   Examiner of Inheritance,
      Santee Indian Agency,
         Santee, Nebr.

My dear Mr. Wilmeth:

I acknowledge receipt of your letter of the 4th inst together with all the papers connected with your report on heirship in the Anigre case.  The papers have been properly placed in the files of this office.

Very truly yours,

Supt. & S. D. A.

HJJ/AM

---

Heirship
of
Hog-gra-ah-chey

Sac and Fox Indian School,
Stroud, Okla.  June 12, 1915.

Warner L. Wilmeth,
    Examiner of Inheritance,
        Santee, Nebr.

My dear Mr. Wilmeth:

I acknowledge receipt of your letter of the 5th ins. together with all the papers connected with your report on heirship in the Hog-gra-ah-chey case. The papers have been properly placed in the files of this office.

Very truly yours,

Supt. & S. D. A.

HJJ/AM

---

Sac and Fox Indian School
Stroud, Okla., June 17, 1915.

E. A. Upton
Examiner of Inheritance & S. D. A.
Otoe Indian Agency
Otoe, Oklahoma.

Sir:

Referring further to the heirship work at this Agency, and more particularly to your letter of June 10, 1915, I have to advise that before receiving the same I had posted for hearing the only case we have upon which a hearing has not been held. The notice was dated June 1 and a hearing set for July 1, 1915.

Very respectfully,

Supt. & S. D. A.

HJJ/ND

---

RECEIVED **DEPARTMENT OF THE INTERIOR**

JUN 12 1915     UNITED STATES INDIAN SERVICE

SAC AND FOX INDIAN SCHOOL, OKLA.

Otoe Indian Agency

Otoe, Oklahoma

June 10, 1915

Mr. Horace J. Johnson,

Supt. Sac & Fox Indian Agency,

Stroud, Oklahoma.

My dear Mr. Johnson:

With further reference to the heirship work at your agency and your letter regarding the same of May 29, 1915, you are advised that Mr. Wilmeth has been instructed by the Indian Office to forward to me such papers as he may have in connection with heirship cases at your agency and I understand, that Mr. Wilmeth has in his possession the papers in connection with several of such cases, and I am instructed to complete this work.

With reference to the case referred to in your letter in which the allottee has died since Mr. Wilmeth left your agency and any other such cases which may now be at your agency, I will be glad if you will post the same for hearing, setting the date of hearing thirty days from date of posting, so that the same may be hears as early as possible. I expect to complete the work at this agency on or about June 30 and will probably reach the Sac & Fox Agency near that date.

234

Very truly yours,

EAUpton

EAU js                                    Examiner of Inheritance & S. D. A.

---

( COPY )

Law-Heirship

L  L                    DEPARTMENT  OF  THE  INTERIOR

Office of Indian Affairs

Instructions,
 heirship                            Washington
hearings.

July 12, 1915.

To Superintendents and Examiners of Inheritance:

Hereafter in conducting heirship hearings, you are instructed to include in the testimony statements as to whether the decedent lived on his allotment, and whether any portion of the same could be termed a homestead.  In cases where a homestead right is involved is should be fully set out in your finding.

If the homestead right is limited in value by the law of the State governing the decedent, you should submit with your report, a certificate of appraisement showing the value of the lands termed as a homestead, or the lands on which the home and improvements are located.

In submitting your report on Form 5-107, you should follow the instructions on the reverse side of Sheet 3, and in each instance all the information indicated in the blank, concerning the immediate family of the decedent, and the names of the next of kin must be given whether or not all are heirs to the estate.  In other words, the immediate family must be shown regardless who are the heirs.  The Office desires this information in order that the same may be on record for future use in the identification of subsequent heirs to the estate, as well as for present use.

It is noticed that a number of the reports do not give the last "Annuity Roll No.", but state "no annuity to probate."  The Office desires that the "Annuity Roll No." be given in all cases where there is such a roll, and in cases where there is no annuity roll the lase census number should be given, in order that the Office may have a working basis if it becomes necessary to examine the records.

It is further noticed that a number of reports incorrectly give "State of domicile at time of death" as "living with his father-in law" or similar phrases.  This blank should be filled out in the name of the State in which the decedent was living at the time of his death.  This is important when any personal property is to be distributed as such is usually distributed under the laws of the State wherein the decedent was domiciled at the time of his death.

Respectfully,
E. B. MERITT,
Assistant Commissioner.

---

Notice of
Hearing.

Sac and Fox Indian School,
Stroud, Okla. July 13, 1915.

Ralph P. Stanion, Supt.,
   Pawnee Indian School,
      Pawnee, Oklahoma.

Sir:

Referring to your letter of the 30th ult., I am returning herewith notice of hearing to determine the heirs of Harriet Hissun, a deceased Indian. The same is properly signed.

Very respectfully,

Supt. & S. D. A.

AM
Encl. notice.

---

# DEPARTMENT OF THE INTERIOR
## UNITED STATES INDIAN SERVICE

Sac and Fox Indian Agency

Stroud, Oklahoma

July 16, 1915

Mr. Horace J. Johnson,
   Supt. Sac & Fox Indian Agency,
      Stroud, Oklahoma.

Dear Mr. Johnson:

For your information, I hand you the following list of heirship cases of your agency, which were received from Examiner Wilmeth in an unfinished condition. The

papers the cases were forwarded to the Indian Office on the dates opposite the allottee's names and the retained copies left at this agency for your files:

| | |
|---|---|
| Jerome Wolf | June 24, 1915 |
| ˣFlora Grass | July 1, 1915-not recd from Wilmeth |
| Luke Comley | July 3, 1915 |
| May Murray | July 7, 1915 |
| Kirwin Murray | July 7, 1915 |
| Bessie Davis | July 8, 1915 |
| Jennie Sampson | July 8, 1915 |
| Abbie Redrock | July 8, 1915 |
| Andrew Barker | July 8, 1915 |
| Theresa Big Ear | July 13, 1915 |
| Annie Nellie Grant | July 14, 1915 |
| John Grant | July 14, 1915 |
| Jane Ely | July 14, 1915 |
| James Wolf | July 15, 1915 |
| Jane Wolf | July 15, 1915 |
| John Wolf | July 15, 1915 |
| John McKuk | July 16, 1915 |
| Samuel W. Peel | July 16, 1915 |

The case of Flora Grass was an original hearing conducted by me on July 1, 1915, and the papers forwarded to the Indian Office the same date. Heirship reports were made by me in all others, except those of Andrew Barker in which supplemental testimony was submitted and the three Wolf cases, James, Jane and John, in which the testimony was insufficient, and the papers forwarded to the Indian Office without reports.

Very truly yours,

EAUpton
Examiner of Inheritance & SDA.

EAU js

---

[The following letter typed as given]

Topeka  Kansas
July 17-1915

Superintendant
  Sac & Fox Ind Agency
          Sir:

Mr. Peter W. Curley – real name Wisca – or Wisa – pronounced Wee-Saw- wanted me to inform one Warner L. Wilmet about some land he sold or supposed he sold belonging to his mother Ma-swa- (I believe that the name & himself – he did not know that he had sold his mothers land – I dont understand clearly but want to know if the deeds were signed by him or not

I am his wife and he told me the deeds would have to be signed by both of us to be good to the owner of land-

I know Pete never good full value for the land – I will write to the department of the Interior – probably if I can hear nothing from you about it  I believe there was 80 acres or over that was sold – which was his mothers – which should not have been sold – and if sold the title is not clear – Now truly I am not certain but I think that is the way – and I would like to get at the facts some way – I have no description of land I was so hurried & busy I did not get it.  Mr. Warner L Wilmet will likely know something about it.

I convenient let me know what you can find out about it

Mrs. Peter W. Curley
Room 203
807 Kansas Avenue
Topeka  Kansas.

**********

Land.

Sac and Fox Indian School,<br>Stroud, Okla. July 20, 1915.

Mrs. Peter W. Curley,
  807 Kansas Ave.,
    Topeka, Kansas.

Dear madam:

  I have your letter of the 17th inst., but am unable to give you any information about the topic about which you write.  We do not know Wisa here.  The address of Warner L. Wilmeth is not now Stroud, but Santee Agency, Nebraska and if you wish to communicate with him, you should address him at that place.

Very respectfully,

Supt. & S. D. A.

HJJ/AM

**TELEGRAM** ——— TELEGRAM 3

**DEPARTMENT OF THE INTERIOR** Sac & Fox, Okla.

Law,Heirship
69419-15
F W S

**OFFICE OF INDIAN AFFAIRS**

WASHINGTON

*Mail to*

June 22, 1915

Upton, Examiner of Inheritance,
Red Rock, Oklahoma.
Can you reach Sac And Fox July first hearing set that date?

6-AS-22

EBMeritt

Assistant   *Commissioner*

**CONFIRMATION OF TELEGRAM**

REFER IN REPLY TO THE FOLLOWING:
Law-Heirship
69419-15
70179-15
F W S

**DEPARTMENT OF THE INTERIOR,**

OFFICE OF INDIAN AFFAIRS,

WASHINGTON,

ADDRESS ONLY THE
COMMISSIONER OF INDIAN AFFAIRS

RECEIVED

JUL -1 1915  1915

SAC AND FOX INDIAN SCHOOL, OKLA.

Sac and Fox heirship
cases, Oklahoma.

Mr. Horace J. Johnson,

Supt. Sac and Fox School,

My dear Mr. Johnson:

Replying to your letter of June 17, 1915, you are advised that Examiner of Inheritance Upton will be at the Sac and Fox Agency by July 1, and can then take up the heirship case of Flora Foster and any other cases at your agency requiring attention.

You are further advised that it is the purpose of this Office to have the heirship hearings held by Examiners of Inheritance who will proceed from place to place as occasion demands. It will not, therefore, be necessary as a rule for Superintendents to devote any time whatever to this work; but on the contrary their time will be left free for the regular duties of the superintendency[sic]. Only in special instances where delay would be predjudicial[sic] to the interests of the heirs will a hearing by a Superintendent be authorized.

Very truly yours,

EB Meritt
6-HEB-25.                                    Assistant Commissioner.

---

T E L E G R A M

Oklahoma City, Okla.
June 30, 1915.

9:23 A. M.

Horace J. Johnson,
Stroud, Okla.

Will arrive Stroud One P. M. today.

Upton. Examiner

\*\*\*\*\*\*\*\*\*\*

[The above Telegram given again.]

---

REFER IN REPLY TO THE FOLLOWING:
Education-                                    ADDRESS ONLY THE
Industries.   **DEPARTMENT OF THE INTERIOR,**   COMMISSIONER OF INDIAN AFFAIRS
104863-1911.        **OFFICE OF INDIAN AFFAIRS,**
71657-1915.            **WASHINGTON,**         RECEIVED
L M C                                   JUL 22 1915

Mr. Horace J. Johnson

Supt. Sac and Fox School.

240

My dear Mr. Johnson:

This will refer to your letter of June 22nd, concerning funds alleged to be due Kah-ro-sah which were presumably paid to Wa-ka-zo in error.

The records of the Auditor's Office for the Interior Department have been examined and photographic copies made of certain affidavits alleging Wa-ka-zo to be the sole heir of Kah-ro-sah and his deceased wife, daughter and son.

The copies of the affidavits are inclosed herewith and you are requested to endeavor to locate T. J. Lazzell and Davis Hardin, whose affidavit states that they were acquainted with Wa-ka-zo, and know that the facts as stated in his affidavit are true.

If you are able to locate these parties, confer with them as to the facts as stated in their affidavits, also endeavor to locate Wa-ka-zo, and if you are able to do so ascertain whether or not he has funds which could be used in reimbursing Kah-ro-sah for the funds which have apparently been paid in error to Wa-ka-zo. Your prompt attention is desired.

Very truly yours,

7-S-19.
Copy to Keshena.
" " Shawnee.

EB Meritt
Assistant Commissioner.

**********

Education-
 Industries.
 104863-1911.
 71657-1915.

Sac and Fox Indian School,
Stroud, Okla. July 27, 1915.

O. J. Green, Supt.
 Shawnee Indian School,
 Shawnee, Oklahoma.

Sir:

Referring to former correspondence with reference to Wa-ka-zo who it appears drew certain funds belonging to Kah-ro-sah, a Mexican Pottawattomie[sic] Indian and for whom affidavits were executed by T. J. Lazzell and Davis Hardin before W. S. Pendleton, U. S. Commissioner for the third Judicial District of Oklahoma, on April 17, 1895. I have to ask if you know the whereabouts of the said

Lazzell and Hardin, or can ascertain them for me.  I have written Mr. Pendleton about the mater but thought it advisable to write you also.

Very respectfully,

Supt. & S. D. A.

HJJ/AM
Carvon[sic] for Indian Office.

---

REFER IN REPLY TO THE FOLLOWING:

Land-
  Sales.
38895-1911
J F M

Partition of allotment
  of William Clardy.

**DEPARTMENT OF THE INTERIOR,**
**OFFICE OF INDIAN AFFAIRS,**
WASHINGTON,

JUL 26 1911

ADDRESS ONLY THE
COMMISSIONER OF INDIAN AFFAIRS

July 31-4
Hold until answer
is received from
Outcelt & Hurst
    RHL

Mr. John A. Buntin,

    Superintendent Shawnee Indian School,

        Shawnee, Oklahoma.

Sir:

    Referring to the matter of the partition of the allotment of William Clardy, deceased, you are advised that on careful consideration thereof it is believed that there is no authority of law for the partition of a trust allotment in Oklahoma and the issuance of patents in fee to the heirs for their separate interests.

    If the heirs desire a patent in fee will be issued to them for the land jointly and they can then convey to each other their respective parts thereof in accordance with the decree of the District Court.

Respectfully,

CF Hauke<br>Second Assistant Commissioner.

7-AAC-3.

# DEPARTMENT OF THE INTERIOR

Education-
Industries.
104863-1911.
71657-1915.
L M C

## UNITED STATES INDIAN SERVICE

Sac and Fox Indian School,
Stroud, Okla. July 27, 1915

RECEIVED

JUL 31 1915

SAC AND FOX INDIAN SCHOOL, OKLA.

W. S. Pendleton,
Shawnee, Oklahoma.

Sir:

On April 17, 1895, while you were U. S. Commissioner for the third Judicial District of Oklahoma, T. J. Lazzell and Davis Hardin, appeared before you and made affidavit that they were acquainted with Wa-ka-zo, presumably a Citizen Pottawatomie Indian. It appears that there is some doubt about this Wa-ka-zo being the person whom he claimed to be and the Indian Office has instructed me to locate, if possible, T. J. Lazzell and Davis Hardin. Thinking that perhaps you might now these men personally, I am asking you for such information as you may have relative to their identity. Do you know if they are living and if so at what place?

Very respectfully,
Horace J Johnson
Supt. & S. D. A.

HJJ/AM
Carbon for Indian Office.

\*\*\*\*\*\*\*\*\*\*

Mr. Johnson: I knew both T.J.L. Lazzell and Davis Hardin. They are both dead. Davis Hardin once introduced an indian[sic] to me, as Wa-ka-zo. I had never heard of him before and never saw him afterwards. At the time above stated One A. Jones was buying indian lands, and was using both Lazzell and Hardin; that is, I have that impression. I also have the impression that Jones was present when Wa-ka-Zo[sic] was introduced to me by Hardin; at least I have Jones connected with Hardin and Wa-ka-z0[sic].

His Address is Shawnee, Okla.

Yours Truly,
W. S. Pendleton

\*\*\*\*\*\*\*\*\*\*

Sac & Fox – Shawnee Estates
1911-1919   Volume VI

Education-
 Industries.
 104863-1911.
 71657-1915.                    Sac and Fox Indian School,
    L M C                          Stroud, Okla., July 31, 1915.

Commissioner Indian Affairs,
      Washington, D. C.

Sir:
      Replying to the above noted communication, I have the honor to report that T. J.
Lazell[sic] and Davis Hardin are dead, consequently I cannot communicate with them.
I have not been able to locate Wakozo either but I have been informed that he is dead
also.

      I am today writing A Jones who witnessed the signature of Wakazo before the U.
S. commissioner[sic] to know if he knows anything about him.  If I obtain any further
information I will promptly advise the Office.

      Though the business in question seems to have been done through this office, the
interested indians[sic], if there are any living were segregated therefrom about the year
1900 and placed under the jurisdiction of the Shawnee Agency.

                              Very Respectfully,
                              Horace J Johnson
                              Supt. & S. D. A.

                    **********

## DEPARTMENT OF THE INTERIOR

Education-                **UNITED STATES INDIAN SERVICE**      **RECEIVED**
 Industries.                                            AUG 5 1915
 104863-1911.
 71657-1915.              Sac and Fox Indian School  SAC AND FOX INDIAN SCHOOL, OKLA.
    L M C                      Stroud, Okla. July 31, 1915

A Jones,
   Shawnee, Oklahoma.

Dear Sir:

      On April 17, 1895, as shown by the records, you witnessed the signature of
a Pottawatomie Indian named Wa-ka-zo before U. S. Commissioner Pendleton for the
3rd Judicial District of Oklahoma.

It is desired to locate this Indian if possible and I shall be obliged to you if you can give me any information as to his whereabouts at this time.

A Penalty envelop is enclosed for reply.  It needs no stamp.

Very Respectfully,
Horace J Johnson
Supt. & S. D. A.

Carbon for Commissioner.

Dear Sir.

Wa-Ka-Zo the Indian you mention above has been dead 15 or 16 years.

Yours truly
AB Jones

**********

Education-
  Industries.
  104863-1911.
  71657-1915.                    Sac and Fox Indian School,
                                 Stroud, Okla. Aug 5, 1915.

Commissioner of Indian Affairs,
            Washington, D. C.

Sir:

Referring to the above noted communication and to my letter of July 31, 1915, I have the honor to advise that I now have definite information that Wa-ka-zo, who is mentioned in Office letter is dead.  He died some fifteen or sixteen years ago.

I am therefore unable to communicate with Wa-ka-zo.

Any further information that I can give the Office with reference to this matter will be furnished upon receipt or request therefor.

Very respectfully,


Supt. & S. D. A.

HJJ/AM

**********

245

**DEPARTMENT OF THE INTERIOR** RECEIVED

Kaw-saut, or          **UNITED STATES INDIAN SERVICE**          AUG 12 1915

Kah-ro-sah.                                         SAC AND FOX INDIAN SCHOOL, OKLA.

Shawnee Indian School,

Shawnee, Oklahoma, August 7, 1915.

Supt. Horace J. Johnson
    Sac & Fox Agency,
       Stroud, Oklahoma.

Dear Sir:

       Referring to your letter of July 27th, in regard to Wa-ka-zo, who it appears drew certain funds belonging to Kah-ro-sah, a Mexican Pottawatomie Indian, and for whom affidavits were executed by T. J. Lazzell and Davis Hardin, etc., I have to advise that I have inquired around from different people, and am not able to ascertain the whereabouts of T. J. Lazzell and Davis Hardin, however, when some of the older Pottawatomies are in the office, I will inquire and if I find out where these two men are, and will advise you promptly, if you hae not already received this information from Mr. W. S. Pendleton.

Very respectfully,

John Jones
JJ/cx                                    Clerk in Charge.

**********

REFER IN REPLY TO THE FOLLOWING:                                 ADDRESS ONLY THE

E-Ind.                                                COMMISSIONER OF INDIAN AFFAIRS

104863-11        **DEPARTMENT OF THE INTERIOR,**       RECEIVED

M P R              **OFFICE OF INDIAN AFFAIRS,**

**WASHINGTON,**                      AUG 23 1915

                                        SAC AND FOX INDIAN SCHOOL, OKLA.
                          AUG 19 1915

Mr. Horace J. Johnson,

    Supt. Sac and Fox School, Okla.

My dear Mr. Johnson:

       The receipt is acknowledged of your letter of August 5, 1915, stating that you have now definite information relative Wa-ka-zo, mentioned in previous correspondence, and that you have ascertained that he is dead, having died some fifteen or sixteen years ago.

246

Please advise the Office immediately whether Wa-ka-zo left an estate, and if so, whether the same has been disposed of.  Kindly make a full report on this matter and forward the same to this Office at your very earliest convenience.

Very truly yours
EB Meritt
Assistant Commissioner.

8-MR-14

**********

( C O P Y )

Received Sep 8
1915

**DEPARTMENT OF THE INTERIOR**

E-Ind            **UNITED STATES INDIAN SERVICE**            Sac and Fox Indian
104863-11                                                   School, Okla.
M P R

Sac and Fox Indian School,
Stroud, Oklahoma, Aug 23, 1915.

A. B. Jones,
    Shawnee, Okla.

Sir:-

Sometime ago you advised me that Wa-ka-zo died 15 or 16 years ago. If you know please advise me where he dies[sic], where, if at all, he was allotted, and what, if any, estate was left by him.

A penalty envelope which requires no stamp is enclosed for a reply.

Very Respectfully,

Horace J. Johnson,

Supt. & S. D. A.

HJJ/SP
Enve. encl:

Dear Sir-  The Wa-ka-zo that I refer to was alloted[sic] the W/2 of SE/4 and E/2 of SW/4 of Sec. 8-T. 10- R 3 E.   this county. which has been sole I think he died W of this town about 5 mi.  If he left any estate I dont[sic] know of it.

Yours truly

A B Jones

**********

Ed-Ind.
104863-11
M P R

Sac and Fox Indian School,

In the matter of

Stroud, Oklahoma, September 9, 1915.

Wa-ka-zo.

Sup't. O. J. Green,

Shawnee, Oklahoma.

Dear Sir:

I am advised by A. B. Jones of Shawnee, Oklahoma, that Wa-ka-zo, a Pottawatomie Indian, I believe, was allotted the W/2 of the SE/4 and the E/2 of the SW/4 of Sec. 8, T. 19 N., R. 3 E, I. M., in Pottawatomie County, Oklahoma. This territory is now under your jurisdiction though the land above described has, I think, been sold.

Please advise me if your record shows of any other name that Wa-ka-zo may have had; also advise me as to whom the land above described was sold, when, and how much money was received for it. Also advise me if you have any estate under your agency belonging to this man or his heirs.

The above information is desired to answer inquiries from Indian Office. You will perhaps remember that we have had some correspondence about this matter in the past especially if you consulted Keo-tuck and Po-qua concerning it. I hand you herewith all correspondence in the matter so that you may be able to understand it as completely as do I. With your reply please return this correspondence.

Very respectfully,

HJJ/JWC

Superintendent.

Correspondence
encl:

Carbon copy to
Commissioner of
Indian Affairs/[sic]

\*\*\*\*\*\*\*\*\*\*

Ed-Ind.
104863-11
M P R

Sac and Fox Indian School,

Wa-ka-zo
matter.

Stroud, Oklahoma, September 241915.

Commissioner of Indian Affairs,
Washington, D. C.

Sir:

Referring to the above noted communication, I have the honor to enclose herewith a letter received by me from Superintendent Green with reference to Wa-ka-zo matter; also a note received by me from A. B. Jones of Shawnee, Oklahoma.

In view of the fact that heretofore in this matter I have been charged by the Office with being grossly negligent in handling public business in connection with the Wa-ka-zo, and the fact that over a month has elapsed since the Office letter above noted was written. I desire to ask the attention of the Office to the fact that neither Wa-ka-zo nor his heirs belonged under this jurisdiction and it has been necessary for me to get the information by mail. On August 23rd, the same date on which the Office letter above noted was received I wrote Mr. Jones of Shawnee, Oklahoma, asking him to give me information concerning Wa-ka-zo. The enclosed note from Mr. Jones was received in this office September 8th 1915, and on September 9th 1915 having ascertained that the Wa-ka-zo allotment was under the jurisdiction of the Shawnee Agency, I wrote Superintendent Green asking for information concerning it which information the Office will not by the dating stamp on Superintendent Green's letter was not received in this office until September 23rd. Consequently, the delay this time can not be charged to me.

If there is any further information desired that I can obtain concerning this Wa-ka-zo matter I shall be pleased to have you sign the receipt on the duplicate of this letter and return it to this office. to make an effort to obtain it.

Very respectfully,

HJJ/C
2 letters
encl:

Superintendent.

\*\*\*\*\*\*\*\*\*\*

249

(C O P Y)

Received SEP 23 1915
SAC & FOX Indian
School, Okla.

E-Ind
104863-11
M P R

DEPARTMENT OF THE INTERIOR
UNITED STATES INDIAN SERVICE

In the matter of
Wa-ka-zo, deceased.

Shawnee Indian School,

Shawnee, Oklahoma.

Sept. 20, 1915.

Mr. Horace J. Johnson,

Supt. Sac & Fox Agency,

Stroud, Oklahoma.

Dear Mr. Johnson:

This is to refer to your letter of Sept. 9, in the matter of the estate of Wa-ka-zo, deceased Citizen Pottawatomie Allottee No. 568, who dies[sic] 15 or 16 years ago.

This man was allotted the following lands:

NW/4 SE/4 of Sec. 8 T.  10  N.,  R.  3 East, 40 acres
SW/4  "   "   "   "       "      "    , 40 acres
NE/4 SW/4 "   "   "       "      "    , 40 acres
SE/4 SW/4 "   "   "       "      "    , 40 acres

The NW/4 of SE/4 and the NE/4 of SW/4 of the above above[sic] described land was sole to G. M. Asher, for $1000.00, deed approved by the Department on June 10, 1898, reference of Indian Office (Land – 26959-1898) in letter of June 15, 1898.

The SW/4 of SE/4 and the SE/4 of SW/4 of the above described land, according to the records, was transferred by the heirs of Wa-ka-zo, deceased, to G. M. Asher, for $400.00, deed covering this transaction approved by the Department on January 22, 1900, reference Indian Office letter of January 13, 1909, Land, 1489-1909, J M W. As to who such heirs were who transferred this part of the Wa-ka-zo allotment is not known to this office, for the reason that there is no affidavit of heirship by a business committee on file in this office covering this estate. The record of the Indian Office should show who signed the deed covering this last 80 acres as heirs of Wa-ka-zo, deceased, and who gave the affidavit of heirship based upon which the Department approved the said deed. It may be stated here, that the first 80 acres was sold by Wa-ka-zo, himself and his wife, M-sha-to-qua. She does not appear on

250

our allotment or any of the annuity rolls. No record appears to have been kept of the affidavit of heirship in the case.

The records show that there is no estate belonging to Wa-ka-zo or his heirs remains under the jurisdiction of this office.

We will have this matter in mind, and when some of the old Kickapoos or Pottawatomies call at this office, we will endeavor to ascertain, who the heirs are, if any living, and if they have any property etc., and further advise you.

Very respectfully,

O.J. Green
Superintendent.

JJ        P. S. Your file in the case is herewith returned.

**********

[Copy of original]

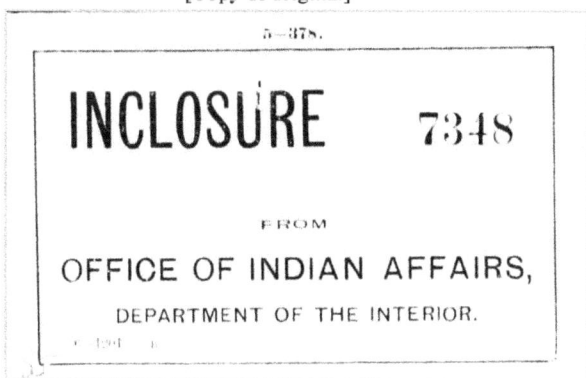

5—37s.

# INCLOSURE    7348

FROM

## OFFICE OF INDIAN AFFAIRS,

DEPARTMENT OF THE INTERIOR.

**********

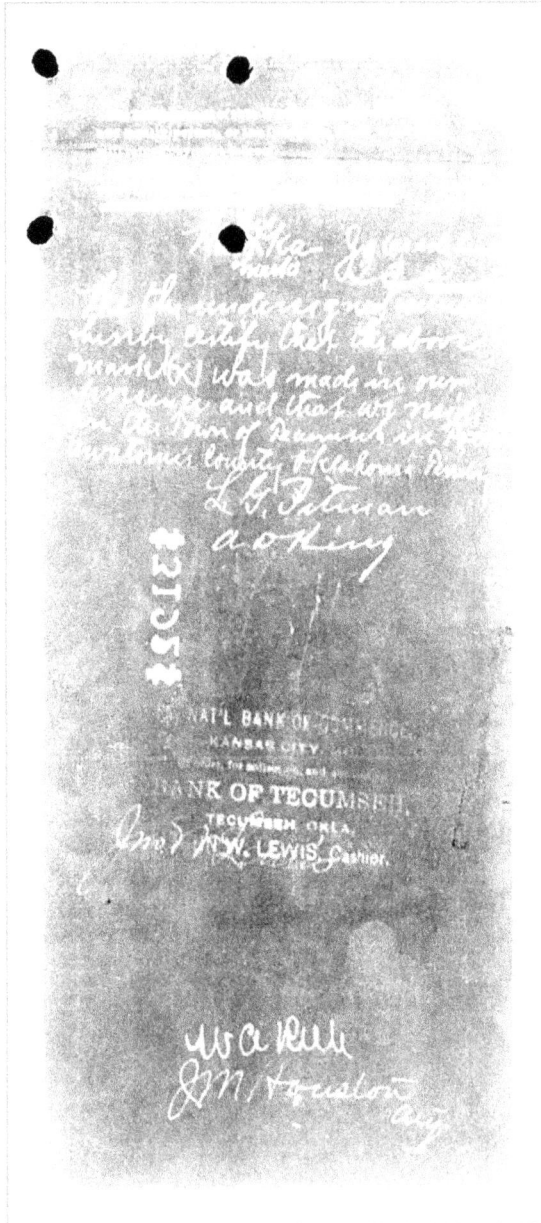

[Transcription of image on page 252]

The endorsement of this Warrant [illegible…] and legally perfect, or the Officer to whom it is drawn will re[illegible] payment thereof.

[This entry completely illegible]

his
Wa-ka-zo   (as sole heir)
X
mark

We the undersigned witnesses hereby certify that the above mark (X) was made in our presence and that we reside in the Town of Tecumseh in Pottawatomie County Oklahoma Territory

F. G. Pitman
A.D. King

NAT'L BANK OF COMMERCE
KANSAS CITY

BANK OF TECUMSEH
TECUMSEH  OKLA.

Jno [illegible] Lewis  Cashier

W A Rule
JM Houston
Aty.

\*\*\*\*\*\*\*\*\*

[Copy of original]

[Transcription of above image]

| | UNITED STATES |
|---|---|
| SETTLEMENT WARRANT | TREASURY DEPARTMENT |
| | $3192$ |

Washington, D.C.  May 25,  18[??]

Pay to    Wa-ka-zo    (as sole heir)

Three thousand, one hundred ninety-two    22/100  Dollars    $3,192.22

[Illegible]

P.O. Address  c/o U.S. Indian Agent, Sac and Fox Agency, Oklahoma

\*\*\*\*\*\*\*\*\*\*

254

[Copy of original]

Territory of Oklahoma
Third Judicial District.     ss          19352

Personally appeared before me,
W.S.Pendelton, U.S.Commissioner for Third Judicial District of
Oklahoma Territory,Wa-Ka-Zo, who being duly sworn upon oath says
that he is over twenty-one years of age,that he is a member of the
Citizen Pottowatomie Indians   and is the identical Indian
rolled under No. 341 Gardner Roll, that he is the half brother
and only living heir of Kah-ro-sah,M-Kko-qua-a, Wa-Sha-qua, the
siblings, Wah-we-gah-Kunk, deceased, No. 1,2,3,4,& 5? to
No. 810 to Bill,H.R.1741 in first session 54th Congress, appropriated by Indian Appropriation Act for fiscal year 1898 for the
Pottowatomies in the sum of Seventeen Thousand Nine hundred
Ninety-five and  45  hundredths ($17,995.45)  Dollars, and is
entitled to the shares due the above named deceased relatives in
the above appropriation and also the per capita share due them of
the Nine Thousand and sixteen and 14 hundredths ($9016.14) Dollars,
the amount due the Mexican Pottowatomies as shown by the books of
the Treasurer of the United States, and he hereby makes application for the same, and requests that the check be sent him in care
of the United States Indian Agent at Sac & fox Agency, Oklahoma
Territory.

                                        Wa-Ka-Zo

In presence of

A. Jones

M. C. Jones                  _____

Subscribed and sworn to before me this 17 day of April.A.D.
                                        M. S. Pendelton

[Transcription of image on page 255]

Territory of Oklahoma

SS          **19352**

Third Judicial District.

Personally appeared before me, W. S. Pendleton, U. S. Commissioner for Third Judicial District of Oklahoma Territory, Wa-Ka-Zo, who being duly sworn upon oath says that he is over twenty-one years of age, that he is a member of the Citizen Pottowatomie[sic] [sic] Indians and is the identical Indian enrolled under No. 341 Gardner Roll, that he is the half brother and only living heir of Kah-ro-sah, M-Kko-qua-[?]a, Wa-Sho-qua, Go-sho-was, Wa-wo-[??]-ah-Kunk, deceased, No. 1, 2, 3, 4, & 31 in report No. 210 to Bill, H.R. 1741 in first session 48th Congress appropriated by Indian Appropriation Act for fiscal year 1891 for Mexican Pottowatomies[sic][sic] in the sum of Seventeen Thousand Nine Hundred and Ninety-five and 46 hundredths ($17995.46) Dollars.  That he is entitled to the shares due the above named deceased relatives, of the above appropriation and also the per capita share due him of the Nine Thousand and Sixteen and 14 hundredths ($9016.14) Dollars, the amount due the Mexican Pottowatomies[sic] as shown by the Books of the Treasurer of the United States, and he hereby makes application for the same, and requests that the check be sent him in care of the United States Indian Agent at Sac & Fox Agency, Oklahoma Territory.

his
.......Wa-Ka~~X~~zo..................
mark

In presence of

....A. Jones.................

Witnesses to mark

....W. C. Jones............

Subscribed and sworn to before me this  17  day of April A.D. 1895.

W. S. Pendleton

U. S. Commissioner.

\*\*\*\*\*\*\*\*\*\*

[Transcription of image on page 257]

[Illegible]

    SS

[Illegible]  District.

     Personally appeared before me, [illegible] for the above Territory and Judicial District T. J. Lazzell and Davis Hardin [illegible...] parties, who being duly sworn upon [illegible...] they are well acquainted with the applicant [illegible] and know that he is over twenty-one years of age and [illegible...] as stated in his affidavit are true to the best of their knowledge & belief, and that they [illegible] directly or indirectly in the prosecution

       T. J. Lazzell

       Davis Hardin

--------------------------------

--------------------------------

  Subscribed and sworn to before me this  17  day of April A.D. 1895

       W.S. Pendleton

        U.S. Commissioner.
        3rd Jud. Dist of Oklahoma

    Sac & Fox Agency, Okla. Ter.

        1895.

  I certify on Honor that  Wa-Ka-zo  is the identical person he represents himself to be and to the best of my knowledge the facts as stated in his affidavit are true.

       Edward L. Thomas

     **********

[Copy of original]

[Copy of original]

[Transcription of image on page 259]

|                      |          |      |
|----------------------|----------|------|
|                      | 3,192.22 | 5315 |
| INDIAN DIVISION.     | 1,829.31 | 5316 |
| Form No. 41[??]      | 753.10   | 5317 |
|                      | 753.10   | 5318 |

No. 3176.

APPROPRIATION:

Fulfilling Treaties with Pottawatomies,

| | |
|---|---|
| Proceeds of lands. | 429.99 |
| Payments to Mexican Pottawatomies | 808.29 |
| Pottawatomie Citizens | 5289.45 |
| | $6527.73 |

Treasury Department

Office of the

AUDITOR FOR THE INTERIOR DEPARTMENT.

May 29, 1895

I Certify That I have examined and settled an account between the United States and Sundry Persons (named below) on account of the above names appropriations, and find that there is due the said Sundry Persons (named below) the sum of Six thousand five hundred twenty seven and 73/100 --------------Dollars, [Illegible...] of their shares as heirs [illegible...] deceased Mexican Pottawatomie Indians of the money due said deceased Indians under Act of August 19, 1890, viz:

Wa-Ka-zo, as sole heir of Kah-ro-sah,                5315
          M-Kko-qua-wa, Wa-sho-qua,
          Go-sha-was, and Wah-we-ah-kunk,
          deceased,
          4 shares of $609.78 each  2,439.12
          1    "    "            753.10
                  Total due    $3,192.22

\*\*\*\*\*\*\*\*\*\*

260

[Copy of original]

Wuh-Kto-qua, (as sole heir of
Mazhe-nah-nim'nuk-shkuk, 5316
Kas-qua, and Wain-he-qua,
deceased,
2 shares @ $609.77 each) $1829.31

Pu-a-dwa-dah, (as sole heir of
Muk-hise, deceased,) $753.10 537

Tah-naw-myuk-shuk, (as sole
heir of Mhuk-do-sko, 3318
deceased ) $753.10

Any claimants, in separate, drafts,
amounts set opposite their
names. Care of US Indian Agent,
Sac and Fox Agency
Oklahoma.

Samuel P Blackwell
Auditor for the Interior Department.

By _____                    Deputy.

THE SECRETARY OF THE TREASURY

[Transcription of image on page 261]

[??]-Shuh-Kto-qua, (as sole heir of       5316
          Mazhe-nah-nim-nuk-shkuk,
          Kas-qua, and Wain-he-qua,
          deceased,
          2 shares @$609.77 each) $1,829.31

Pe-a-dwa-dah, (as sole heir of       5317
          Muk-hise, deceased,)    $753.10

Nah-nem-muck-shuk, (as sole heir    3318[sic]
          of Mnuk-do-sko,
          deceased    )    $753.10

Paid claimants in separate drafts, [illegible] see opposite their [illegible] names, [Illegible] of U.S. Indian Agent,

    Sac and Fox Agency,

        Oklahoma.

                 Sam'l Blackwell
                 Auditor for the Interior Department

---

# Department of the Interior.

SUBJECT: Es-
tate of Eliza
Smith, nee Yahola,
deceased................
Ali.........…......LGK

        United States Indian Service.

        Local Field Representative

        Five Civilized Tribes.

        Holdenville, Okla., July 22, 1915.

Mr. O. J. Green,
Supt. Shawnee Agency,
Shawnee, Oklahoma.

Dear Mr. Green:

    I want to write to you to thank you again for your courtesy on the 15th instant, and through you to thank Mr. Jones also.

We were unable to get the Indians "with us" at the trial on the 16th, and in a way were unsuccessful in our contention in the case; however, Probate Attorney Walker gave notice of an appeal and the appeal will be perfected from the decision of the county court of Seminole County, ant I think ultimately we will win our contention.

Thanking you and Mr. Jones for your trouble and courtesy, I beg to remain

Very Sincerely,

A.L. Irvine
Supervising Field Clerk.

---

Heirship matters,
bonds, etc.

Shawnee Indian School,

Shawnee, Oklahoma, August 9, 1915.

Supt. John A. Buntin,
Tongue River Agency,
Lamedeer[sic], Montana.

Dear Mr. Buntin:

I hand you, herewith, correspondence from the Equitable Surety Company, of St. Louis, Mo., in which they are taking up the matter with you of certain premiums which were due 1914-15, in certain guardianship matters, which are self explanatory.

Very respectfully,

JJ/cx
Incl-correspondence.

Clerk in Charge.

---

REFER IN REPLY TO THE FOLLOWING:
Law-Heirship
E S M
Acts of Congress.

**DEPARTMENT OF THE INTERIOR,**
OFFICE OF INDIAN AFFAIRS,
WASHINGTON,
AUG 18 1915

ADDRESS ONLY THE
COMMISSIONER OF INDIAN AFFAIRS

Mr. Orville J. Green,

Sup't Shawnee Agency,

My dear Mr. Green:

In response to your letter of August 12, 1915, there are enclosed copies of the Act of June 25, 1910 (36 Stat. L., 855), and February 14, 1913 (37 Stat. L., 678).

Very truly yours,

EB Meritt
8-DAR-18                                          Assistant Commissioner.

---

## DEPARTMENT OF THE INTERIOR

Letters           UNITED STATES INDIAN SERVICE

Sac and Fox Indian School,
Stroud, Okla. Aug. 18, 1915.

Claud Chandler
U. S. Farmer,
Shawnee, Okla.

Sir:-

Referring to your letter of the 1st inst., I am enclosing herewith letters concerning testimony of Wa-pa-sa-mo-qua (Maggie Matthews) in the heirship hearing of May-mo-kee which you asked to have returned.

Very Respectfully,

Horace J Johnson
SP                                          Supt. & S. D. A.
Letters encl.

**********

## DEPARTMENT OF THE INTERIOR
UNITED STATES INDIAN SERVICE

Shawnee Indian School,

Shawnee, Oklahoma,  July 29, 1915.

Mr. Claud Chandler,
Shawnee, Okla., Rte. 3.
Dear friend:

I am inclosing, herewith a letter received today from Superintendent R. L. Russell, Sac & Fox Sanatorium, Toledo, Iowa, my old stamping ground.

Since I am not acquainted with George Foster, and because he is a Sac and Fox Indian, I am forwarding this letter to you requesting that you attend to the delivery of this notice of hearing for Superintendent Russell, and make proper report in this matter to him direct.

I shall appreciate your attention to this matter.

Very respectfully,

O.J. Green

OJG/cx                                       Superintendent.

Incl.

---

U.S. Indian Agency,
Shawnee, Oklahoma,
August 21st, 1915.

In accordance with the provisions of Indian Office authority 5-10-15,

A/c No. 1170 – PAUL M. HAAS . . . . . . . . . . . . . . . . . . . . . . . . . . . . .       $13.08

A/c No. 1169 – LUCENA (LUCILE) HAAS - - - - - - - - - - - - - $4.69
  "   No. 1168 – REUBEN HAAS - - - - - - - - - - - - - - - - - - -   8.05
  "   No. 1165 – ETHEL HAAS - - - - - - - - - - - - - - - - - - - -   .17
  "   No. 1166 – JOSEPH HAAS - - - - - - - - - - - - - - - - - - - -   .17     13.08

(Duplicate)

   H. R. Nichols    Cashier,

The First National Bank,
Tecumseh, Oklahoma.

* * * * * * * * * * * *

The balance of Authority 5-10-15 was paid out direct to
the heirs of Paul M. Haas. And the amount which had
accumulated on this decedent's accounts in both the
First National and Shawnee National Bank, amounting
to 87¢, was added to the above or paid direct to the heirs,
having been divided in five equal parts, as one of the six
heirs – Bernadine Haas, died in June, 1915.

. . . . . . . . . . . . . . . . .

\*\*\*\*\*\*\*\*\*\*

U.S. Indian Agency,
Shawnee, Oklahoma,
August 21st, 1915.

In accordance with the provisions of Indian Office circular No. 624, and the findings of the Department of the Interior in the matter of the estate of

WI QI PEA SE KI KI, as quoted below –

A/c No. 1265, WI QI PEA SE KI KI - - - - - - - - - - - - - - - - - - - - - - -     $5.41

has this day been transferred to the heir as follows:

A/c No. 1171 – PAH MAH COM SE - - - - - - - - - - - - - - - - - - - - - - - $5.41
(Duplicate)

        H. R. Nichols        Cashier,

The First National Bank,

Tecumseh, Oklahoma.

\* \* \* \* \* \*

COPY OF FINDINGS.

Law-Heirship
31520-13
E G T

Estate of Lo ah wah pea se (or Dapego)

Wah pah pe sca ca (Wi qi pea se ki ki) died in 1911, when his 6/36 inherited interest from his mother went to his surviving sister, Pah mah coomse – \*\*\*\*\*\*
The 5/36 interest inherited from his deceased brothers went to the father, (Charley Bob)\*\*\*\*\*\*.

                (Signed) E.B. MEritt[sic],
                Assistant Commissioner.

The amount due the father, Charley Bob,
was paid direct from the account during
the 1st quarter, 1916.

This minor had no estate except money received from the sale of his mother's land, and that which was inherited from his deceased brothers came from the same source.

\*\*\*\*\*\*\*\*\*\*

266

U.S. Indian Agency,
Shawnee, Oklahoma,
August 21st, 1915.

In accordance with the provisions of Indian Office circular No. 624, and the findings of the Department of the Interior in the matter of the estate of

MAH NO NE MAH, as quoted below -

A/c No. 1291, MAH NO NE MAH - - - - - - - - - - - - - - - - - - - - - - -     $89.80

has this day been transferred to the heirs as follows:

A/c #1550, MACK JOHNSON - - - - - - - - - - - - - - - - - - - - - - - - -.72
A/c #1557, MAGGIE JOHNSON (Pea che tha quah) - - - - - - - - - <u>89.08</u>   89.80
(Duplicate)

<u>H. R. Nichols</u>    Cashier,

The First National Bank,

Tecumseh, Oklahoma.

* * * * * * *

<u>COPY OF FINDINGS.</u>

Law-Heirship
103112-1914
E G T

The proceedings in the matter of the heirship to the estate of Mah no ne man[sic] ****** are hereby approved ****** and I find and adjudge that ****** the heirs to the estate of the decedent and their respective shares were as follows:

Nah she pe eth ******       1/2
Maggie Johnson ******     2/6
Maw ke puck e thee or Mack Johnson  **   1/6

***********

(Signed)  Bo Sweeney,
Assistant Secretary.

* * * * *

The amount due Nah she pe eth and that due Mack Johnson
was paid direct under Office authority 3-22-15, amounting to
$131.47 & $43.82. The interest which accumulated later,
amounting to $ 4.29 for the former was paid direct; Mack's share deposited
herewith.

**********

Sac & Fox – Shawnee Estates
1911-1919   Volume VI

U.S. Indian Agency,
Shawnee, Oklahoma,
August 21st, 1915.

In accordance with the provisions of Indian Office circular No. 624, and the findings of the Department of the Interior in the matter of the estate of

PAH KO NE, as quoted below -
(That part belonging to allottee #213)
A/c No. 1304, PAH KO NE - - - - - - - - - - - - - - - - - - - - - - - - - - - - -   $66.74

has this day been transferred to the heirs as follows:

A/c #1602, THY KA TOKE - - - - - - - - - - - - - - - - - - - - - - - - - - - - -   $66.74
(Duplicate)

H. R. Nichols     Cashier,

The First National Bank,

Tecumseh, Oklahoma.
* * * * * * *

COPY OF FINDINGS.

Law-Heirship
118197-12
 22834-13
 88847-14
1040780-14
E G T

The proceedings in the matter of the heirship to the estate of Pah ko ne, ****** are hereby approved ****** and I find and adjudge that ****** the heirs to the estate of the decedent and their respective shares were as follows:

Pe qua, husband - - - - - - - -   1/3
Ke ah qua moke, daughter - -   1/3
Thy ka toke, son - - - - - - - -   1/3]

* * * * * * * *

(Signed)  Bo Sweeney,
Assistant Secretary.

(The shares due Pe qua and Ke ah qua moke were paid direct
under Office authority 3-22-15, amounting to $132.89; and   : As explained, when
their share of the interest accumulated later, $4.34, was        : authority was
paid under Section 38.)                                                         : requested on this
(account, the funds belong to allottee 213 & 281

268

\*\*\*\*\*\*\*\*\*\*

U.S. Indian Agency,
Shawnee, Oklahoma,
August 21st, 1915.

In accordance with the provisions of Indian Office circular No. 624, and the findings of the Department of the Interior in the matter of the estate of

DA PE GO, or Lo ah wah pea se, as quoted below -

A/c No. 1609, DA PE GO - - - - - - - - - - - - - - - - - - - - - - - - - - - - -     $6.15

has this day been transferred to the heirs as follows:

A/c No. 1171, Pah mah com se - - - - - - - - - - - - - - - - - - - - - - - - - -     6.15

(Duplicate)   \* \* \* \* \* \*

          H. R. Nichols       Cashier,

The First National Bank,

Tecumseh, Oklahoma.

\* \* \* \* \* \* \*

COPY OF FINDINGS.

Law-Heirship
31520-13
E G T

The proceedings in the matter of the heirship to the estate of Lo wah pea se (or Dapego),  \*\*\*\*\*\* are hereby approved \*\*\*\*\*\* and I find and adjudge that \*\*\*\* the heirs to the estate of the decedent and their respective shares were as follows:

          Charley Robb, husband - - - - - - - - - - - - - 19/36 interest
          Pah mah com se, daughter - - - - - - - - - - - 17/36

(Signed)  Lewis C. Laylin,
Assistant Secretary.

(This account at the beginning of the 1st quarter, 1916, had a balance of $13.02, 19/36 of this sum was paid direct to Charley Robb )Bob)[sic] during this quarter, and the balance transferred to the minor heir as above.)

\*\*\*\*\*\*\*\*\*\*

269

U.S. Indian Agency,
Shawnee, Oklahoma,
August 21st, 1915.

In accordance with the provisions of Indian Office circular No. 624, and the findings of the Department of the Interior in the matter of the estate of

WILLIAM CHEROKEE, as quoted below -

A/c No. 1652, WILLIAM CHEROKEE- - - - - - - - - - - - - - - - - - - - - - - -   $16.83

has this day been transferred to the heir as follows:

A/c No. 1336, LUCY PECAN - - - - - - - - - - - - - - - - - - - - - - - - - - - -   16.83
(Duplicate)

_H. R. Nichols_____ Cashier,

The First National Bank,

Tecumseh, Oklahoma.

* * * * * * *

COPY OF FINDINGS.

Law-Heirship
96347-12
132664-14
E G T

The heirs of this decedent were found by the Department on December 19,1912 as follows:

Lucy Pecan, wife of allottee      1/3
Ruth Cherokee, daughter - - -    2/3
*******

IT IS RECOMMENDED that the finding be permitted to stand.

Respectfully,
(Signed) E.B. Meritt,
Assistant Commissioner.

Approved:  Apr 13 1915 (Signed) Bo Sweeney,
Assistant Secretary.

The amount due Ruth Cherokee was paid direct from the account during the 4th quarter, 1915 and the 1st quarter, 1916.

**********

U.S. Indian Agency,
Shawnee, Oklahoma,
August 21st, 1915.

In accordance with the provisions of Indian Office circular No. 624, and the findings of the Department of the Interior in the matter of the estate of

AMOS DEERE, as quoted below -

A/c No. 55 – AMOS DEERE- - - - - -- - - - - - - - - - - - - - - - - - - - - - -     $14.74

has this day been transferred to the heir as follows:

A/c No. 155 – ALBERT DEERE - - - - - - - - - - - - - - - - - - $4.91
  "  No. 334 – STELLA CURTIN - - - - - - - - - - - - - - - - -  4.91
  "  No. 333 – JOHN SHAWNEEGO - - - - - - - - - - - - - -  <u>4.92</u>      14.74

<u>[Illegible] Jones</u>      Cashier,

The Shawnee National Bank,

Shawnee, Oklahoma.

\* \* \* \* \* \* \*

<u>COPY OF FINDINGS.</u>

Law-Heirship
135513-14
E G T.

The proceedings as modified in the matter of the heirship to the estate of AMOS DEERE \*\*\*\*\*\* are hereby approved \*\*\*\*\* and I find and adjudge that \*\*\*\* the heirs to the real and personal estate of the decedent and their respective shares were as follows:

Albert Deere - - - - - - - - - - - - - - - -  1/3
Stella Curtin, nee Shawneego - - - - - -  1/3
John Shawneego - - - - - - - - - - - - - -  1/3

\*\*\*\*\*\*\*\*\*\*\*\*\*\*\*\*\*\*

(Signed)  Bo Sweeney,
Assistant Secretary.

Mayetta, Kansas,

July __12__, 1915.

Received of O.J. GREEN, Supt. & Spcl. Disbg. Agent, Shawnee, Oklahoma

__$87.98__

Transfer of funds of Kaw saut -     (Ck.No. 1063)

From First National Bank, Tecumseh, Oklahoma, Deposit No. 1196 -   $87.98


(Sign__ed)___A.R. Snyder____
Supt. & Spcl. Disbg. Agent.

---

Germantown, Kansas.

September __13__1915.


Received of O.J. GREEN, Superintendent, Shawnee, Oklahoma.

$1371.78 to be placed to the credit of Ta ta pe twa, or Tah tah tha peah.

____Edw Minor____
Superintendent.

---

## DEPARTMENT OF THE INTERIOR
### UNITED STATES INDIAN SERVICE

RECEIVED

Haynesville, La., SEP 8 1915

Sept. 6  1915  SAC AND FOX INDIAN SCHOOL, OKLA.

Mr. Horace J. Johnson,

Stroud, Okla;

Dear Mr. Johnson:

Your letter of August 24th addressed to me at Washington and forwarded to me here was received today and in reply will say that if you will forward the papers in the case of Bessie Davis to me at Shawnee, Okla. I will appreciate the favor.  I doubt, however, if the Office will vacate its finding, even though I think it in error.

I am also in receipt of carbon copy of your letter to the Commissioner relative to Robert Roubidoux's request to furnish further evidence in the case of May Murray, the same having been forwarded to me.

I have also received, from the Office, instruction to hold a supplemental hearing in the case of John McKuk to ascertain if Nancy Davenport Witonosee (or Nancy Morgan Witonosee) and Mo na che qua is the same person. I will take this matter up with you and the Office when I return to Shawnee. The Office has also written me that the Supt. of the Osage School has, at my request, forwarded testimony in the case of So-sah, a Potawatomi Indian, and states that there is no record there of an Indian by that name and requests me to inform the Office for what case the evidence is intended. I recall the case and my request of Supt. J. Geo. Wright, but can not now recall the English name of this allottee. I forwarded the papers in the case to the Office and requested that the matter be taken up with, I think the Supt. of the Potawatomi Agency in Kansas. If you will furnish me the other name of So-sah I will be glad.

I have been here three weeks and will return to Shawnee about Saturday or Sunday next. Have had a good rest, though I wish I had another month. I found Mrs. Upton and babies doing nicely. We now have two boys, the last one being born July 15.

Is Slaughter around the agency? I don't suppose he has told you, that he assaulted me in the Office at the Otoe Agency and that I told him he could either resign or allow me to wire the Office and ask for his discharge. He resigned immediately. I don't know what he is up to there, but I understand he is staying around your Agency.

Trusting that things are moving smoothly with you and with best regards to you and Mrs. J., I am,

Very truly yours,

EA Upton

HARRY COLVIN
GEOLOGICAL ENGINEER
AND CONSULTING
GEOLOGIST
LONG DISTANCE PHONE 693

Maud  Okla

Sept 10 – 15

Mr. O. J. Green

  Shawnee Indian Agcy

  Shawnee  Okla

Dear Sir your letter of Sept 7th received asking for the

P.O. address of some of the heir of William McLane deceased the heirs you named in

your letter were living at the Post Office address given below Nov 12 – 1914

Mrs. May Hammer (nee Storm) – 1618 Sumit St Kansas City Kans

  "   Zoa Whitmere (nee Storm) 1407 Van Buren St Topeka      "

  "   Eliza Lynn (nee Hartman) Berryton  Kans

  Nettie Hartman  506 Lawrence St Topeka Kansas

  Dora Stewart (nee Hartman) 506 Lawrence St Topeka Kansas

  Henrietta Beeler (nee Hartman) 506 Lawrence St Topeka    "

  Lynn Hartman            do       do       do      "

  Thomas Hartman         do       do       do      "

  Eliza Sage (nee Smith)  - Dover – Kans

  Zoa Denton (nee Smith) St Marys Kans

  Martha Mullins (nee Smith)  Rt 2  Maud Okla

  This is the best that I can do at the present time

Yours Truly

Mrs Eliza Colvin (nee Smith)
Rt 2 Maud Okla

---

[The letter below typed as given]

Johnson Supt.                             Whiting,

Second[sic] and fox agency                   Kansas.

Dear Sir                                  Oct 6 – 1915

In the matter of the heirship of Me-cho-kah-me-ke-ah she beening

member of Second & fox tribe of Indian of Oklahoma I am a son of Joe Oliver or

Meh-sko-cha-ka-ah of Second & fox tribe of Indian he was married up here at the state of Kansas Brown County when he was young men and my mother she was young at that time her and Me-sko-cho-ka-ah. they entered into an agreement by wich they agreed to live together as husband and wife that immediately after and in pursuance to said agreement they did live together as husband and wife for three years in Brown County, Kansas. that I was born as a result of said marriage in year of 1877. I may beening inherried some estate of my relations of the second & fox tribe of Oklahoma.

your very
Respectfully


Tom Oliver or Kah-[?]e-ah


info  W<sup>m</sup> Whitewater
Whiting
Kansas.


\*\*\*\*\*\*\*\*\*\*


Sac and Fox Indian School
Stroud, Okla., Nov. 22, 1915.

Tom Oliver
   Whiting, Kansas

Sir:

    I have your letter of October 6, 1915, and have to advise that I do not know Me-cho-kah-me-ke-ah; neither do I know Meh-sko-cha-ka-ah. If you can give me the English names of these people perhaps I can tell whether or not there are any such persons living here, and whether or not you have any interest in their estates providing they are deceased Sac and Fox Indians who have estates under this jurisdiction.

Very respectfully,

HJJ/ND                                       Supt. & S. D. A.

Heirship cases
of James, Jane,
and John Wolf.

Sac and Fox Indian School,
Stroud, Oklahoma, October 9th 1915.

Sup't. A. R. Snyder,

Mayetta, Kansas.

Dear Sir:

I have your letter of October first 1915, with reference to heirship cases of James, Jane, and John Wolf.

As I do not have the papers covering this hearing, and as I am not acquainted with any of the people living away from this agency whom it is thought may have an interest in these estates, I can not give you the desired information.

Regretting that this is the case, I am,

Very respectfully,

HJJ/C                                                Superintendent.

**********

RECEIVED **DEPARTMENT OF THE INTERIOR**

OCT 4 1915

SAC AND FOX INDIAN SCHOOL, OKLA. UNITED STATES INDIAN SERVICE

Potawatomi Agency, Mayetta, Kansas,

October 1, 1915.

Supt. H. J. Johnson,

Stroud, Okla.

Sir:

All of the papers in the Heirship cases of James, Jane and John Wolf have been forwarded to this office by the Indian Office with the request that I hold a supplemental hearing in order that additional testimony be taken from persons interested in these estates who are now living on this reservation.

Upon receipt of the papers I made inquiry among a number of the Indians who should have been in a position to give me the information desired but as yet I have been unable to find anyone who would be able to give testimony that would be of any value in any of the aforesaid cases. Can you tell me of anyone in the part of Kansas who might be interested in any of these cases, or who could give the information desired by the Office?

Thanking you for an early reply, I am,

Very respectfully,

AR Snyder

FJS-A-T                                              Supt. & Sp'l Disb. Agent.

---

Proof of heir-
ship upon Cos-
ke-pea-naka, or
Sam Dirt, dec'd.,                    Sac and Fox Indian School,
absentee Sahwnee[sic]              Stroud, Oklahoma, October 9th 1915.
Indian.

Mr. B. J. Burke,

307-10 Bliss Bldg.,

Tulsa, Oklahoma.

Dear Sir:

I have your letter of the 6th instant with reference to proof of heirship in the matter of Cos-ko-pea-naka, or Sam Dirt, deceased, absentee Shawnee Indian.

In reply you are advised that absentee Shawnee Indians are now under the jurisdiction of Shawnee Agency, and you inquiry should be made to O. J. Green, Superintendent of Shawnee Agency at Shawnee, Oklahoma.

Very respectfully,

HJJ/C                                               Superintendent.

**********

LOANS                        REAL ESTATE                    OIL AND GAS LEASES
                            **B. J. BURKE**
                          307-10 Bliss Bldg.
                            TULSA, OKLA.,        October 6th, 1915.

U. S. Indian Agent-Sac & Fox Agency,
Stroud, Oklahoma.

Dear Sir:-

I would like to get a Proof of Heirship upon Cos-ke-pea-naka, or Sam Dirt, deceased, absentee Shawnee Indian.

On Nov. 1, 1899, Dan Dirt, and Jennie Dirt, his wife, and Caesar Tiner deeded the allotment of Sam Dirt, located in the NW/4 of 13-9-4, as his sole and only heirs. This deed wad made before Lee Patrick, then U. S. Indian Agent, and approved in Washington January 29th, 1900.

If you have this Proof of Heirship, kindly send me a copy of it, or let me know, if possible, where I can get it.

Whatever expense is attached to this, if you will send me a statement, I will remit at once.

Very truly yours,

BJB:R

B J Burke

---

List of dec.
Indians and
their heirs.

Sac and Fox Indian School,
Stroud, Okla., Oct. 18, 1915.

Claud Chandler,
   U. S. Farmer,
      Shawnee, Okla.

Sir:-

Enclosed herewith please find a list of deceased Sac and Fox and Iowa Indians and their heirs which may be of some help to you in your work.

Very respectfully,

LGG.                                        Supt. & S. D. A.,

Encl:
List of dec. Indians
   and their heirs.

\*\*\*\*\*\*\*\*\*\*

List of dec.
Indians &
their heirs.

Sac and Fox Indian School,
Stroud, Okla., Oct. 18, 1915.

Arza B. Collins,
U. S. Farmer,
Cushing, Okla.

Sir:-

Enclosed herewith please find a list of deceased Sac and Fox and Iowa Indians and their heirs which may be of some help to you in your work.

Very respectfully,

LGG.                                                   Supt. & S. D. A.,

Encl:
List of dec. Indians
and their heirs.

\*\*\*\*\*\*\*\*\*\*
[Copy of original page]

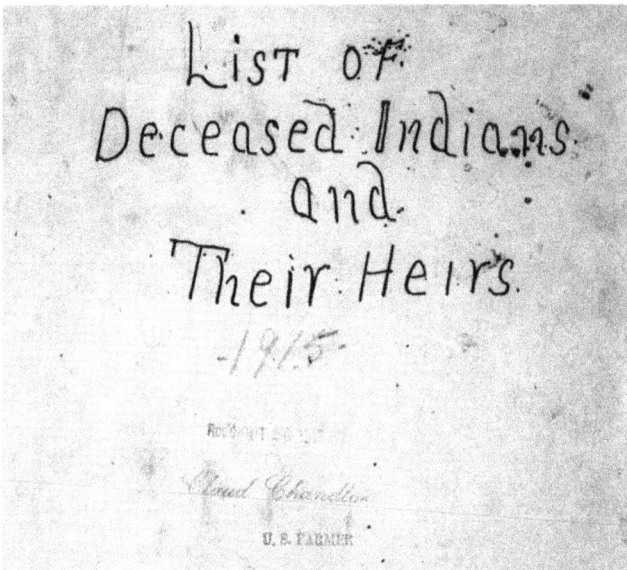

List of
Deceased Indians
and
Their Heirs.
-1915-

Cloud Chandler
U. S. FARMER

279

LIST OF DECEASED INDIANS AND THEIR HEIRS:

| Allottee. | Heirs. |
|---|---|
| Anigre. (Iowa)-------------------------- | Tom Hartico--------------------1/2 |
| | Mary Ford Bassett, nee Small------------1/2 |
| Benson, Laura Ellis,-------------------- | Harry Benson------------------------------1/2 |
| | Sarah Ellis,--------------------------------1/2 |
| Brown, Julia,--------------------------- | George T. Brown,-------------------------1/3 |
| | Noble H. Brown,-------------------------2/15 |
| | William T. Brown,-----------------------2/15 |
| | Elsie F. Brown,--------------------------2/15 |
| | Lorena J. Brown,------------------------2/15 |
| | Pearl Brown,------------------------------2/15 |
| Barker, Levi,---------------------------- | Andrew Barker,---------------------------All. |
| Bigwalker, Jennie,---------------------- | Sarah Bigwalker,--------------------------1/7 |
| | Dollie McClellan,------------------------6/35 |
| | Lelia Bigwalker,-------------------------6/35 |
| | Esther Bigwalker,------------------------6/35 |
| | Mamie F. Jennings,----------------------6/35 |
| | Osmong[sic] Franklin,--------------------6/35 |
| Black, Mary,--------------------------- | Amos Black,------------------------------1/4 |
| | Amos Black, Jr.,--------------------------3/8 |
| | Bertha Black,-----------------------------3/8 |
| Burgess, Maggie (Mohee)------------- | William Burgess,--------------------------1/3 |
| | Frank Burgess,----------------------------2/9 |
| | Roy Burgess,------------------------------2/9 |
| | Mark Burgess,-----------------------------2/9 |
| Bear, Jack,----------------------------- | Sarah Bear,--------------------------------2/8 |
| | William Bear,-----------------------------2/8 |
| | Mable Wakole,----------------------------2/8 |
| | George Oliver Morton,--------------------1/8 |
| | Mamie F. Jennings,----------------------1/8 |
| Butler, Benjamin----------------------- | Edward Butler,----------------------------1/3 |
| | George Butler,----------------------------1/3 |
| | Jane Foster, nee Butler,-------------------1/3 |
| Benson, Harry,------------------------- | Clara Ellis,--------------------------------1/2 |
| | Edith Brown,-----------------------------1/2 |

Black, Amos,---------------------------- Julia Sullivan Black,-----------------------1/3
Amos Black, Jr.,----------------------------1/3
Bertha Black,----------------------------1/3

Thomas Jefferson Buffalohorn,-------- Grace Lee,----------------------------------1/2
Mamie Buffalohorn,----------------------1/2

Buffalohorn, Clara,---------------------- Grace Lee,----------------------------------1/2
Mamie Buffalohorn,----------------------1/2

Brown, Josephine,----------------------- John Brown,------------------------------33/90
Thomas Brown,--------------------------19/90
Harry Brown,----------------------------19/90
Mary E. Brown,--------------------------19/90

Bear, James,----------------------------- Edward Butler,----------------------------1/3
George Butler,----------------------------1/3
Jane Foster, nee Butler,-------------------1/3

Bigwalker, Florence,-------------------- Inez Bass,---------------------------------1/3
David Pennock,--------------------------2/3

Coon, Nancy,---------------------------- Paul Gokey,------------------------------All.

Carter, Louise,-------------------------- Frank Carter,----------------------------1/3
Bertha Carter,-------------------------------2/3

Carter, Sadie,--------------------------- Milton Carter,----------------------------All.

Carter, Lewis,--------------------------- Milton Carter,----------------------------All.

Curtin, Nancy,-------------------------- Alex Jefferson,----------------------------All.

Conger, Silas,--------------------------- Andrew Conger,----------------------------1/2
George O. Morton,----------------------1/2

Crane, Lizzie,--------------------------- Sarah Ellis,----------------------------------10/30
Alice Morris Grant,----------------------- 2/30
Thomas Morris,-------------------------- 2/30
Grover Morris,-------------------------- 2/30
Susan Morris,-------------------------- 2/30
Edward L. Morris (Crane)---------------- 2/30
John Crane,-------------------------------- 5/30
Harry Crane,------------------------------ 5/30

Sac & Fox – Shawnee Estates
1911-1919   Volume VI

Conger, Jasper,-------------------------- Andrew Conger,-------------------------1/2
George Oliver Morton,------------------1/2

Conger, William,------------------------ Andrew Conger,-------------------------1/2
George Oliver Morton,------------------1/2

Conger, Hattie,------------------------- Andrew Conger,-------------------------1/2
George Oliver Morton,------------------1/2

Conger, Jay, -------------------------- Andrew Conger,-------------------------1/2
George Oliver Morton,------------------1/2

Crane, Charles,------------------------- John Crane,-------------------------------235/540
Harry Crane,-----------------------------234/540
Theresa Logan,------------------------- 70/540

Carter, Frank,-------------------------- Laura Manatowa, Carter,------------------1/2
Bertha Carter,-----------------------------1/2

Davis, Marie,-------------------------- Mary Hurr,----------------------------------11/27
Robert Davis,------------------------------ 8/27
Orlando Johnson,------------------------- 8/27

Duncan, David,------------------------- Dickson Mokohoko,----------------------1/2
Allen G. Thurman,------------------------1/2

Davis, Frank,-------------------------- Frank B. Davis,----------------------------1/2
Harry Davis,--------------------------------1/2

Duncan, Lottie,------------------------- Dickson Mokohoko,-------------------210/540
Allen G. Thurman,---------------------210/540
Sarah Ellis,------------------------------ 40/540
Alice Grant, nee Morris,-------------- 8/540
Thomas Morris,------------------------ 8/540
Grover Morris,------------------------- 8/540
Susan Appletree, Morris,-------------- 8/540
Edward L. Morris (Crane)------------ 8/540
John Crane,--------------------------------- 20/540
Harry Crane,------------------------------ 20/540

Duncan, May,--------------------------- Allen G. Thurman,------------------------1/2
Dickson Mokohoko,----------------------1/2

Davis, Rachel,-------------------------- Andrew Conger,-------------------------1/2
George Oliver Morton,------------------1/2

Embler, Joseph, (Iowa)---------------- Sophie Embler,---------------------------All.

282

Falls, Annie,---------------------------- Frank Smith,------------------------------All.

Franklin, Benjamin,-------------------- Leona Franklin,-----------------------------1/8
Osmond Franklin,---------------------------1/8
Randall       "       -------------------------1/8
Christine      "   now Boyd,---------------1/8
Harding Franklin,--------------------------1/8
George R.    "       --------------------------1/8
Alex          "       --------------------------1/8
Fryor Franklin Brown,--------------------1/8

Grant, Susie,---------------------------- Saginaw Grant,-----------------------------1/2
Jim Scott,-----------------------------------1/2

Gibbs, Hiram,-------------------------- Logan Kakaque,------------------------ 90/1620
Linda Brown (Roger)------------------306/1620
Manda Starr,---------------------------306/1620
Alice Hunter,--------------------------306/1620
Gilbert Gibbs,-------------------------306/1620
Amos Black,--------------------------- 84/1620
Amos Black, Jr.,-----------------------111/1620
Bertha Black,--------------------------111/1620

Givens, Gertrude,----------------------- John Brown,--------------------------360/1080
Lydia Grant,--------------------------180/1080
Eveline Givens,-----------------------180/1080
Isaac Givens,-------------------- --------180/1080
Jim Scott,----------------------------- 64/1080
Allen G. Thurman,-------------------- 29/1080
Roy V. Thurman,--------------------- 29/1080
Theresa Smith, Thurman,------------ 29/1080
Jennie Thurman,---------------------- 29/1080

Grayson, Watt,------------------------- Albert Moore,-------------------------------2/8
Ruth Moore,---------------------------------2/8
Sarah Thompson,---------------------------2/8
Ellen Mason,---------------------------------1/8
Hattie Mason,-------------------------------1/8

Gokey, Lizzie (Graeyes)--------------- Paul Gokey,----------------------------------1/4
Leona Gokey,-------------------------------1/4
Agnes Gokey,-------------------------------1/4
Ethline Carter,------------------------------1/4

Guthrie, Mollie,------------------------ Fryor Franklin Brown,-------------------1/3
Leona Chandler, (Graeyes)---------------1/3
Shelah Guthrie Fritz,---------------------1/3

Grass, Flora,---------------------------- William G. Foster,------------------------1/5
Green Foster,--------------------------------1/5
Roy Foster,---------------------------------1/5
Silas Grass,---------------------------------1/5
Edna Foster,--------------------------------1/5

Grass, George,------------------------- Silas Grass,----------------------------------1/2
Andrew Conger,----------------------------1/6
Florence Grass,----------------------------1/3

Hunter, Robert,------------------------- Henry or Harry Hunter,-------------------1/5
Harrison Hunter,--------------------------1/5
Daniel S. Hunter,-------------------------1/5
Emma Hunter,-----------------------------1/5
Gertrude Hunter,-------------------------1/5

Hollowell, Benjamin,------------------- Lizzie Hollowell (Deroin)----------------1/3
Emma Kent,-------------------------------2/3

Hollowell, Irene,----------------------- Lizzie Hollowell (Deroin)----------------1/3
Emma Kent,-------------------------------2/3

Julia Hodge,---------------------------- Inez Bass,---------------------------------1/2
Florence Grass,---------------------------1/2

Hawk, Silas,---------------------------- Ida Mansur Butler,-----------------------All.

Harris, Francis,------------------------ Mary Harris,------------------------------1/2
Moses Harris,-----------------------------1/2

Hodge Mary,-------------------------- Florence Grass,--------------------------All.

Hull, William,------------------------- Ben Hull Mansur,----------------------- All.

Hull, John,--------------------------- Ben Hull Mansur,-----------------------All.

Hull, Lucy,--------------------------- Ben Hull Mansur,-----------------------All.

Harris, Joseph,----------------------- Harris, Liza (Martin)--------------------1/3
Mary Harris, Peacore,-------------------1/3
Moses Harris,----------------------------1/3

Hollowell, Nannie,------------------- Lizzie Hollowell Deroin,-----------------15/36
Richard Roubidoux,---------------------- 3/36
Mitchell Deroin,------------------------- 2/36
Joseph Deroin,-------------------------- 2/36
William Deroin,------------------------- 2/36

Emma Kent,------------------------------12/36

Hawk, Richard,------------------------  Stella Grant, Hawk,----------------------- 4/9
Ida Butler, Hawk,-------------------------- 4/9
George W. Paddock,---------------------- 1/9

Harris, Irene (Jefferson)---------------  William H. Jefferson, ----------------------All.

Hall, Harry,----------------------------  Rachel Pate,--------------------------------- 6/12
Sarah Bigwalker,----------------------------1/12
Mamie Jennings,----------------------------1/12
Dollie McClellan,---------------------------1/12
Lelia Bigwalker,----------------------------1/12
Osmond Franklin,--------------------------1/12
Esther Bigwalker,--------------------------1/12

Houston, Judith,-----------------------  Samuel Houston,---------------------------1/2
Madeline Carter (Houston)---------------1/2

Hog-gra-ah-chey, ---(Iowa)-----------  Sophie Embler,------------------------------1/2
Mary Ford Bassett, Small,----------------- 1/4
Tom Hartico,------------------------------ 1/4

Ingalls, William,----------------------  Mattie Ingalls,------------------------------1/3
Sadie Ingalls,-------------------------------1/3
Henry Ingalls,-------------------------------1/3

Johnson, Samuel,-----------------------  Emily Johnson,-----------------------------All.

"    Harry,-------------------------  Orlando Johnson,--------------------------All.

"    Mercie,----------------------  "      "    --------------------------All.

"    Jane,-------------------------  "      "    --------------------------All.

Jefferson, Carrie,-----------------------  George Littlebear,--------------------------1/2
Florien Littlebear,--------------------------1/2

Jones, Henry C. Jr.,--------------------  Helen Jones,--------------------------------All.

Kakaque, Deborah,--------------------  Sadie Rhodes,------------------------------All.

Kakaque, Dosh,-----------------------  Logan Kakaque,----------------------------1/6
Linda Brown,--------------------------------1/6
Amanda Starr,-------------------------------1/6
Alice Hunter,--------------------------------1/6
Amos Black,---------------------------------1/18

|  | Amos Black Jr.,--------------------------1/18 |
|  | Bertha Black,----------------------------1/18 |
|  | Gilbert Gibbs---------------------------- 1/6 |

| Keokuk, Laura,------------------------- | Robert Peyton Keokuk,--------------------1/2 |
|  | Fannie Foote, nee Keokuk,---------------1/2 |

| Keokuk, Phoebe,----------------------- | Marie A. Fear,-----------------------------1/3 |
|  | Alice Lee,----------------------------------1/3 |
|  | Mary A. Keokuk,--------------------------1/6 |
|  | Frank Keokuk,-----------------------------1/24 |
|  | John Earle Keokuk,-----------------------1/24 |
|  | Fannie Foote, nee Keokuk,---------------1/24 |
|  | Robert Peyton Keokuk,--------------------1/24 |

| Keokuk, Charles,----------------------- | Frank Keokuk,-----------------------------1/4 |
|  | John Earle Keokuk,------------------------1/4 |
|  | Robert Peyton Keokuk,--------------------1/4 |
|  | Fannie Foote, nee Keokuk,----------------1/4 |

| Kakaque, Walter,----------------------- | Logan Kakaque,----------------------------1/2 |
|  | Sadie Rhodes,------------------------------1/2 |

| Kebolte, Eliza White,------------------ | Charles Kebolte,---------------------------1/2 |
|  | Sam Ellis,-----------------------------------1/2 |

| Logan, Hattie,------------------------- | Clarence Logan,----------------------------1/2 |
|  | Theresa Logan,----------------------------1/6 |
|  | John Crane,--------------------------------1/6 |
|  | Harry Crane,-------------------------------1/6 |

| Long, Thomas,------------------------- | Bertha Long Hodsdon,--------------------All. |

| Long, Agnes,-------------------------- | Bertha Long Hodsdon,--------------------All. |

| Logan, John A.------------------------- | Clarence Logan----------------------------1/2 |
|  | Theresa Logan,----------------------------1/6 |
|  | John Crane,--------------------------------1/6 |
|  | Harry Crane,-------------------------------1/6 |

| Lunt, Lina B.------------------------- | Susie Whitewater,-------------------------1/2 |
|  | Nettie Whitewater,------------------------1/2 |

| Logan, Mary E.----------------------- | Theresa Logan,----------------------------1/3 |
|  | John Crane,--------------------------------1/3 |
|  | Harry Crane,-------------------------------1/3 |

Lightfoot, Charles,---------------------- Jack Lincoln,-------------------------------1/2
                                         Edward Small,------------------------------1/2

Maw-tah-pwa,-------------------------- Hugh Wakole,-------------------------------All.

Miller, Ruth,---------------------------- Ida Miller (Spooner) -----------------------5/6
                                         Paul Gokey,--------------------------------1/6

Morris, Caroline,----------------------- Thomas Shaw Morris,---------------------All.

Madison, Harvey,----------------------- Bettie Groinhorn,---------------------------1/3
                                         Mary Hurr,----------------------------------1/3
                                         Me-ough-kaw,-------------------------------1/3

Mesawat, Julai[sic] ---------------------- Linda LaBelle, Mesawat,-------------------All.

Murray, Charles C.--------------------- Emily Roubidoux,---------------------------1/3
                                         Kirwin Murray,-----------------------------1/9
                                         Franklin Murray,----------------------------1/9
                                         Pearl Murray,-------------------------------1/9
                                         Vestina Murray,-----------------------------1/9
                                         Kate Murray,--------------------------------1/9
                                         Velinda Murray,-----------------------------1/9

Mason, Grace,-------------------------- Ellen Mason,--------------------------------1/2
                                         Hattie Mason,-------------------------------1/2

Mack, Edgar,--------------------------- Sarah Mack,---------------------------------1/3
                                         Elbert Mack,--------------------------------1/3
                                         Charley Mack,-------------------------------1/3

Morton, Melissa,----------------------- Mary F. Jennings,---------------------------All.

Maw-mel-lo-haw,---------------------- Sarah Ellis,-------------------------------150/384
                                         Mattie Ingalls,--------------------------- 36/384
                                         Anna McKosato,------------------------- 36/384
                                         Stella Ellis,--------------------------------36/384
                                         Jackson Ellis, --------------------------- 36/384
                                         Clara Benson,----------------------------- 45/384
                                         Jesse Kakaque,--------------------------- 16/384
                                         Maud Kakaque,------------------------- 20/384
                                         Edith Brown,----------------------------- 9/384

Manatowa, George,--------------------- Laura Carter (Manatowa)-------------- 1/3
                                         Bertha Hodsdon (Long)---------------- 2/9
                                         Lorena Manatowa,---------------------- 2/9
                                         Elmer Manatowa,----------------------- 2/9

| | | |
|---|---|---|
| Morton, Oliver P.------------------------ | George Oliver Morton,------------------ | 1/3 |
| | Mamie F. Jennings (Morton)----------- | 1/3 |
| | George Littlebear,------------------------ | 1/6 |
| | Florien Littlebear,------------------------ | 1/6 |
| Morton, Clifford H.--------------------- | George Oliver Morton,----------------- | 1/2 |
| | Mamie F. Jennings,--------------------- | 1/2 |
| Moore, Samuel L.----------------------- | Ellen Mason,---------------------------- | 1/2 |
| | Hattie Mason,--------------------------- | 1/2 |
| Mohee, Charley,------------------------- | Osmond Franklin,----------------------- | 1/2 |
| | Frank Burgess,-------------------------- | 1/6 |
| | Roy Burgess,---------------------------- | 1/6 |
| | Mark Burgess,--------------------------- | 1/6 |
| Mokohoko, Flora,----------------------- | Dickson Mokohoko,-------------------- | 1/2 |
| | Louisa Mack,---------------------------- | 1/2 |
| Neal, Victor,---------------------------- | Lilly Neal,------------------------------- | 1/2 |
| | Pearl Neal,------------------------------ | 1/2 |
| Nahashe, John ------------------------- | William Nahashe,----------------------- | 1/2 |
| | Emma Nahashe,------------------------- | 1/2 |
| Nahashe, Susan,------------------------ | William Nahashe,----------------------- | 1/2 |
| | Emma Nahashe,------------------------- | 1/2 |
| Neal, Pearl,----------------------------- | Lilly Neal,------------------------------- | All |
| Nahomosewe, William,---------------- | Frank Smith,---------------------------- | 1/4 |
| | Edward Rice,---------------------------- | 3/4 |
| Pattequa, Mamie,---------------------- | William Pattequa,----------------------- | All. |
| Pattequa, Bertha,---------------------- | William Pattequa,-----------------------All. |  |
| Plumb, Mary,-------------------------- | Minnie Plumb Barada,------------------All. |  |
| Paddock, Unice (nee Hawk)………. | George W. Paddock,----------------------1/3 |  |
| | Stella Grant, (Hawk),--------------------1/3 |  |
| | Ida Butler (Mansur),---------------------1/3 |  |
| Pickering, Julia,----------------------- | John C. Falk,----------------------------2/8 |  |
| | Margaret Bassett,------------------------2/8 |  |
| | Nellie or Nora Pickering,---------------3/8 |  |

Isaac Pickering,-------------------------1/8

Pennock, Hester,----------------------   Inez Bass,----------------------------------1/6
David Pennock,---------------------------5/6

Pennock, William,---------------------   Inez Bass,----------------------------------1/6
David Pennock,---------------------------5/6

Randall, Paul,-------------------------   Tom Penashe,----------------------------All.

Roubidoux, Mary,---------------------   Robert Roubidoux,----------------------14/36
Sevinah Roubidoux,---------------------11/36
Sophie Roubidoux,---------------------11/36

Rice, Lizzie,----------------------------   Frank Smith,--------------------------------1/4
Edward Rice,--------------------------------3/4

Rogers, Linda,------------------------   Samuel L. Brown-----------------------8/16
Manda Scott, nee Starr,----------------2/16
Alice Gibbs, (Hunter),------------------2/16
Gilbert Gibbs.-------------------------------2/16
Amos Black, Jr.,-------------------------1/16
Bertha Black,----------------------------1/16

Rice, Edith (Appletree),-------------   Edward Rice,----------------------------------3/9
Susie Rice,------------------------------- 2/9
Carrie Rice,-------------------------------2/9
Lucien Rice,-------------------------------2/9

Red Rock, Abby,----------------------   Na-wa-ke-ke,----------------------------All.

Sullivan, Neoma,---------------------   Pe-ah-ma-ske,----------------------------1/3
Albert Ketch-show-no,------------------2/3

Shaquequot, Cora,--------------------   Pa-phia-na,--------------------------------3/10
Ne-pau-sa-qua,---------------------------3/10
Ma-ke-so-pe-at,--------------------------3/10
Pone-wya-tah,---------------------------1/10

Smith, Webster,-----------------------   Frank Smith,-------------------------------1/5
Benjamin Smith,--------------------------1/5
Charley Smith,----------------------------1/5
Harry Benson,-----------------------------1/5
Rachel Franklin, nee Smith,--------------1/5

Shaquequot, Henry,------------------   Grace Lee,----------------------------------1/2
Kate Shaquequot,------------------------1/2

Sha-th-cher,---------------------------- Sam Ellis,---------------------------------All.

Smith, Cora (Bass),-------------------- Charley Smith,---------------------------3/6
Inez Bass,--------------------------------1/6
Lee Bass,---------------------------------1/6
Ione C. Bass,----------------------------1/6

Seaborn, Lena (McCoonse),----------- William M. Seaborn,--------------------1/2
Isabel Kenyon, nee  Barney,------------1/2

Sullivan, Bion,-------------------------- Albert Ketch-show-no,-------------------All.

Squirrel, Mary,------------------------- Jack Small Lincoln,---------------------1/2
Elwood Small,---------------------------1/2

Tohee, Lee Patrick,-------------------- David Tohee,----------------------------All.

Thurman, Mary,------------------------ Jim Scott,--------------------------------All.

Townsend,----------------------------- Annie Perry (Roubideau[sic]), ----------1/2
Sam Ellis,--------------------------------1/2

Thurman, Lucy,----------------------- Jim Scott,--------------------------------64/180
Allen G. Thurman,----------------------29/180
Roy V. Thurman,------------------------29/180
Theresa Thurman Smith,----------------29/180
Jennie Thurman,-------------------------29/180

Thorp, Charlotte,---------------------- James Thorp,----------------------------1/4
Mary Wilson, nee Thorp,----------------1/4
Adaline Rhodd, nee Thorp,--------------1/4
Edward Thorp,---------------------------1/4

Thorp, Hiram P.,---------------------- Julia Thorp Mixon,----------------------5/15
Minnie Rider, nee Thorp,----------------1/15
Frank Thorp,-----------------------------1/15
Fannie Grayson,-------------------------1/15
George Thorp,----------------------------1/15
James Thorp,-----------------------------1/15
Mary Wilson, nee Thorp,----------------1/15
William Lasley Thorp,-------------------1/15
Adaline Rhodd, nee Thorp,--------------1/15
Edward Thorp,---------------------------1/15
Roscoe Thorp,---------------------------1/15

Vetters, Joe,--------------------------- Nesojame Vetters,-----------------------3/9
Annie Perry Tohee,----------------------3/9

|                                        |                                        |         |
| -------------------------------------- | -------------------------------------- | ------- |
|                                        | Mary Murdock McGlaslin,---------------  | 1/9     |
|                                        | Fred Vetters,--------------------------| 1/9     |
|                                        | Lucy Ruth Vetters,--------------------- | 1/9     |
| Ward, Artemus,-----------------------  | Nora Barker,----------------------------| All.    |
| Washington, Mary,--------------------  | Juanita Washington,--------------------- | All.    |
| Washington, George,------------------  | Juanita Washington,--------------------- | All.    |
| Washington, Juanita,------------------ | Sadie Rhodes,---------------------------| All.    |
| Wilson, Samuel,----------------------  | Mary McGlaslin,----------------------------| 1/3 |
|                                        | Fred Vetters,----------------------------| 1/3    |
|                                        | Lucy Vetters,---------------------------- | 1/3    |
| Walker, Lidia,------------------------ | Leo Walker,----------------------------| 1/5     |
|                                        | Benjamin Walker,----------------------------| 1/5 |
|                                        | Guy Walker,----------------------------| 1/5    |
|                                        | Elmer Walker,---------------------------| 1/5   |
|                                        | Ira Walker,----------------------------| 1/5     |
| Wakole, Rufus,----------- ----------   | Anna McKosato, nee Ellis,------------------| 1/3 |
|                                        | Grover Wakole,------------------------------| 2/3 |
| Whitecloud, Jefferson,------------------ | Susan Whitecloud,----------------------108/324 |
|                                        | Dora E. Hudson (Jones),---------------- 36/324 |
|                                        | Julia Kihega,---------------------------- 36/324 |
|                                        | Emma Fawfaw,------------------------- 36/324 |
|                                        | Phoebe Black,-------------------------- 36/324 |
|                                        | Robert Roubidoux,-------------------- 14/324 |
|                                        | Sevinah Roubidoux,------------------- 11/324 |
|                                        | Sophia Roubidoux,-------------------- 11/324 |
|                                        | James Morris,------------------------- 12/324 |
|                                        | Charles Morris,----------------------- 4/324 |
|                                        | James Asa Morris,-------------------- 4/324 |
|                                        | George L. Morris,-------------------- 4/324 |
|                                        | Samuel R. Morris,-------------------- 4/324 |
|                                        | Herman Z. Morris,------------------- 4/324 |
|                                        | Florence Morris (Eliza F. DeRoin)- 4/324 |
| Whitecloud, Lizzie,-------------------- | Susan Whitecloud,----------------------108/324 |
|                                        | Dora E. Hudson,------------------------ 36/324 |
|                                        | Julia Kihega,---------------------------- 36/324 |
|                                        | Emma Fawfaw,------------------------- 36/324 |
|                                        | Phoebe Black,-------------------------- 36/324 |

James H. Morris,---------------------- 12/324
Charles H. Morris,-------------------- 4/324
Eliza F. DeRoin,---------------------- 4/324
James A. Morris,--------------------- 4/324
George L. Morris,-------------------- 4/324
Herman Morris,---------------------- 4/324
Samuel R. Morris,-------------------- 4/324
Robert Roubidoux,-------------------- 14/324
Sevinah Roubidoux,------------------ 11/324
Sophia Roubidoux,------------------- 11/324

Wah-taw-sah,-------------------------   Sarah Ellis,------------------------------ All.

Sampson, Jennie,---------------------   Emily Johnson,--------------------------- All.

Peel, Samuel W.,----------------------   Chief McKosato,--------------------------3/9
David Wakole,----------------------------- 3/9
Sarah Mack,------------------------------1/9
Elbert Mack,-----------------------------1/9
Charley Mack,----------------------------1/9

Pattequa, Charlotte,--------------------   Lydia Grant,---------------------------1260/5400
Eveline Givens,-----------------------1260/5400
Isaac Givens,-------------------------1260/5400
John Brown,-------------------------- 360/5400
Jim Scott,---------------------------- 448/5400
Allen G. Thurman,-------------------- 203/5400
Roy V. Thurman,--------------------- 203/5400
Theresa Smith, Thurman,------------- 203/5400
Jennie Thurman,--------------------- 203/5400

---

# DEPARTMENT OF THE INTERIOR
## UNITED STATES INDIAN SERVICE

Seneca School, Quapaw Agency,
Wyandotte, Oklahoma,
October 22, 1915.

Superintendent, O. J. Green,

Shawnee, Oklahoma.

Dear Sir:

The bearer, Mrs. Jane Jackson Pender, is an allottee and member of the Eastern Shawnee band of this Quapaw Agency, Oklahoma. Her mother, Laura

Jacquis (Jocko) left here some years ago, and was intermarried and it is believed was allotted under your jurisdiction. Mrs. Pender is endeavoring to obtain some definite information thereto.

Very respectfully,

Ira C. Deaver

W.                                        Superintendent.

\*\*\*\*\*\*\*\*\*\*

## DEPARTMENT OF THE INTERIOR

### UNITED STATES INDIAN SERVICE
Seneca School, Quapaw Agency,
Wyandotte, Oklahoma,
October 22, 1915.

Mr. F, A. Upton,
   Examiner Of Inheritance,
    Shawnee Agency,
     Shawnee, Oklahoma.

My dear Mr. Upton:-

This will introduce to you Mrs. Jane Pender, nee Jackson, an Eastern Shawnee allottee of this Agency.

She desires to have you to adjust the heirship case of her deceased mother who appears to have been an allottee of the Shawnee Agency.

Her mother's name appears to have been Laura who from what I have learned may have been allotted under the name of Flora Taylor. Her husband's name appears to have been John Taylor who survived her.

There has been considerable correspondence pertaining to this matter with the Superintendent of the Shawnee Agency and with Mr. Warner Wilmeth, Examiner of Inheritance.

Very respectfully,
Ira C Deaver
Superintendent.

# DEPARTMENT OF THE INTERIOR

## UNITED STATES INDIAN SERVICE
Sac and Fox Indian School
Stroud, Okla., Nov. 3, 1915.

Claud Chandler,
Shawnee, Oklahoma.

Sir:

Referring again to the Lena McCoonse partitionment proceedings, I am sending you herewith a petition for partition of this land that is not just exactly in accord with our former papers, although it is approximately so.

The diagram will indicate to you how the land may be divided so that each will have land of approximately the same value. Our former division gave Seaborn 37 acres, more or less, and Isabel Kenyon 43 acres, more or less. The new division will give one of the parties 43.75 acres, valued at $920.00, and the other 36.25 acres valued at $900.00

The application for partition has been fixed up leaving blank spaces for the names, William M. Seaborn and Isabel Kenyon. Of course the name that will go in the blank space will depend upon the selection of tracts.

If Mrs. Kenyon and Seaborn can agree on this method of division patents in fee can be issued to both. Application blanks for such patents are enclosed herewith, and you should have both Mrs. Kenyon and Mr. Seaborn fill out two copies each, having their signatures acknowledged before a notary public.

I should like to have this matter attended to as soon as possible.

I understood from your talk when you were here that Mrs. Kenyon is now ready to divide this estate, and if she is I think it would be well for her to sign the papers as we have prepared then. If she is not, or if the division suggested is not acceptable, please return all the papers with a report as to what division will be acceptable, if you can ascertain the same.

Very respectfully,
Horace J Johnson
Supt. & S. D. A.

HJJ/ND
Enclose Petition (3)
Application (4)

[The letter below typed as given]

11/15/15

NOV 15 1915

RECEIVED

SAC AND FOX INDIAN SCHOOL, OKLA.

Seminole Okla

Mr Horace J Johnson
   Dear frind I thought I would write & let you know whear we were so
when you get redey to pay the rent money & the [illegible] money Rosce
throp we have got him in school every day so when you get ready to pay
why send it to Seminole Okla
                    Yours Rep
                    Julia Mixon

## DEPARTMENT OF THE INTERIOR
### UNITED STATES INDIAN SERVICE.

Sac and Fox Indian School,

Stroud, Okla., Aug. 5, 19 15.

The heirs of ............ Hiram P. Thorp ............ deceased Sac and Fox

Allottee No. 239 , were determined by the Secretary of the Interior the

Interior, under the Act of June 25, 1910 (36 Stats. 855) .... May 22, ...., 19 15 .

and are entitled to inherit in this estate as follows:

| Name of Heir. | Interest in estate. |
| --- | --- |
| Julia Thorp, now Julia Mixon, wife, | 5/15 |
| Minnie Rider, nee Thorp, daughter, | 1/15 |
| Frank Thorp, son, | 1/15 |
| Fannie Grayson, daughter, | 1/15 |
| George Thorp, son, | 1/15 |
| James Thorp, son, | 1/15 |
| Mary Wilson, nee Thorp, daughter, | 1/15 |
| William Lasley Thorp, son, | 1/15 |
| Adaline Rhodd, nee Thorp, daughter, | 1/15 |
| Edward Thorp, son, | 1/15 |
| Roscoe Thorp, son. | 1/15 |

Sac & Fox – Shawnee Estates
1911-1919   Volume VI

Amount of funds credited to estate, $ _____

Respectfully,

Horace J Johnson

L.G.G.

**********

REFER IN REPLY TO THE FOLLOWING:

Ed.-Ind.

48940-12

63192-15

C H S

ADDRESS ONLY THE
COMMISSIONER OF INDIAN AFFAIRS

# DEPARTMENT OF THE INTERIOR,

### OFFICE OF INDIAN AFFAIRS,

#### WASHINGTON,

RECEIVED
JUL 6 1915
SAC AND FOX INDIAN SCHOOL, OKLA.

JUL -1 1915

Mr. Horace J. Johnson,

Superintendent Sac & Fox School.

My dear Mr. Johnson:

In compliance with your request of June 2, 1915, and for the reasons stated therein authority is hereby granted for you to pay directly to the adult heirs of Hiram P. Thorp, funds derived from his personal estate, as follows;

| | |
|---|---|
| Minnie Rider, | $46.00 |
| Frank Thorp, | 46.00 |
| Fannie Grayson, | 46.00 |
| George Thorp, | 46.00 |
| James Thorp, | 46.00 |
| Mary Wilson, | 46.00 |
| William Lasley Thorp, | 46.00 |
| Adaline Rhodd, | 46.00 |

Authority is also granted for you to pay to Julia Mixon, the mother of Roscoe Thorp, another heir to this estate, the sum of $46.00, this being his share thereof.

It is understood that the share belonging to Edward Thorp, the other heir, will be deposited in bank to his credit.

This authority is granted as above, because of your statement that the heirs are adults and the amount mentioned small, and the payees are said to be perfectly competent.

Very truly yours,

EB Meritt

Assistant Commissioner.

6-FG-29.

**********

Sac & Fox – Shawnee Estates
1911-1919   Volume VI

Law-Heirship
48940-12
33771-15                        Sac and Fox Indian School,
   F W S                        Stroud, Okla. June 2, 1915.

Commissioner of Indian Affairs,
            Washington, D. C.

Sir:

Referring to the above noted communication I have the honor to ask that I be granted authority to pay direct to the adult heirs of Hiram P. Thorp funds derived from his personal estate as follows:

| | |
|---|---|
| Minnie Rider, | $46.00 |
| Frank Thorp, | 46.00 |
| Fannie Grayson, | 46.00 |
| George Thorp, | 46.00 |
| James Thorp, | 46.00 |
| Mary Wilson, | 46.00 |
| William Lasley Thorp, | 46.00 |
| Adaline Rhodd, | 46.00 |

and to pay to Julia Mixon, the mother of Roscoe Thorp $46.00, the same being his share of the estate.

Julia Mixon is a white woman and though she has not kept Roscoe in school regularly, I believe she will use these funds properly if they are turned over to her.

The amounts above mentioned above are all small and I believe he heirs are perfectly competent to handle them properly.

The share belonging to Edward Thorp, the other heir, will be deposited in bank to his credit.

Very respectfully,


AM                            Supt. & S. D. A.

297

[The letter below typed as given]

**RECEIVED**

JUL 8 1915

Shawnee O. K. INDIAN SCHOOL, OKLA.

July 7-1915

Mr. Horce J. Johnston

Sir.

In regard to the rent due on my lease July 1st I will send it in in a few days as soon as I can get help to dig spuds as every body is trying to dig and hands are scarce.

Respt.

A. E. Littleton

\* \* \* \* \* \* \* \* \* \*

OKLAHOMA FARM LANDS
LOANS & CITY PROPERTIES
EXCHANGES & BUSINESS OPPORTUNITIES
SHAWNEE, OKLA.

**RECEIVED**

JUL 9 1915

SAC AND FOX INDIAN SCHOOL, OKLA.

July 7th 1915.

Mr. Horace Johnson,

Stroud, Okla.

Dear Sir:

Re Sac in Fox Allotte #239.

Relative to the heirship case, Hiram P. Thorpe, we are advised that the heirs have been determined in the above allotement, and we would be glad for you to indorm us as to the title of the Thomas H. Littleton land.

Thanking you to advise us as promptly as possible, we are,

Yours very truly,

LAMBARD-HART REALTY & INVESTMENT CO.

Per _____ US Hart _____

Sec'y & Treas.

\* \* \* \* \* \* \* \* \* \*

In the matter
of heirship
of the estate
of Hiram P. Thorp,
dec'd.

Sac and Fox Indian School,
Stroud, Oklahoma, July 10, 1915.

Lambard-Hart Realty Investment Co.,

Shawnee, Oklahoma.

Gentlemen:

Referring to your letter of July 7, 1915, concerning heirship of Hiram P. Thorp, I have to advise that your information seems to be advance information as no declaration in this case has as yet reached me.  When such declaration is received we will take proper steps at[sic] as early a date as practicable to have the matter of the title of Mr. Littleton taken care of.

Of course, you understand that Mr. Littleton has more land than he will probably be allowed to keep as the value thereof at the time when the court attempted to set it aside for him was considerably more than 1/3 of the value of the entire estate, and the widow is entitled to 1/3 of the estate as regards value and not as regards acreage.

Very respectfully,

Horace J Johnson
Superintendent.

HJJ/JWC.

**********

Check

Sac and Fox Indian School,
Stroud, Okla. July 22, 1915.

Mrs. Fannie Grayson,
Okmulgee, Okla.

Madam:-

299

I am enclosing herewith check number 5186 drawn on the First National Bank of Chandler, Oklahoma in your favor for $46.00 which is your share of the estate of Hiram Thorp.

Very Respectfully,

SP                                            Supt. & S. D. A.
Check encl.

**********

Sac and Fox Indian School,
Stroud, Okla. Aug. 5, 1915.

Commissioner of Indian Affairs,
        Washington, D. C.
Sir:

Referring to Office wire of the 3rd, I have the honor to confirm herewith my telegram of the 5th as follows:

"Thorp Heirship Declaration received.
What report is desired?  Office wire third."

Delay in forwarding this telegram was occasioned by the fact that my attention was not called to it until just now and then I found it among the papers on my desk. When the message came, I was not here and on the evening of the day when it was received, the clerk who received it was releived[sic] from duty. She placed all the uncompleted papers on my desk among which was this telegram and on my return it was found by me and answered at the very earliest possible date.

Very respectfully,

Supt. & S. D. A.

HJJ/AM

# Index

www.ingramcontent.com/pod-product-compliance
Lightning Source LLC
Chambersburg PA
CBHW032100040426

42336CB00040B/624